Becoming Egalitarian

Our Journey from Hierarchy toward Mutuality

Nicki Pappas

with contributions from Stephen Pappas

To each and every reader:

*May your commitment to curiosity be deep
and your healing ever deeper.*

Also by Nicki Pappas

As Familiar as Family: Leaving the Toxic Religion I Was Groomed For

Reflections from a Former Evangelical: Poems Reminiscent of My 2019 Worldview

Contents

Author's Note

Hɪ! Nɪᴄᴋɪ ʜᴇʀᴇ. Iɴ ᴛʜɪѕ ʙᴏᴏᴋ, I ᴀᴍ ᴊᴏɪɴᴇᴅ ʙʏ Sᴛᴇᴘʜᴇɴ Pᴀᴘᴘᴀѕ, my steady partner in the chaos since 2010. I am the primary voice in *Becoming Egalitarian*, but there are contributions from Stephen throughout, a nod to our egalitarian focus. We will be sharing our journey from male headship to a marriage of mutuality, from complementarianism to egalitarianism.

On her blog, the late Rachel Held Evans wrote a "Week of Mutuality" series in 2012. She explained that **"Christians who identify as complementarians believe that the Bible requires Christian women to submit to male leadership in the home, church (and, according to some), society."** So, complementarians will hold tightly to any verses that seem to plainly state this one-way submission without implementing verses that would require men to submit to women. She also wrote that another name for egalitarianism is mutuality and explained that **"Christians who identify as egalitarian usually believe that Christian women enjoy equal status and responsibility with men in the home, church, and society, and that teaching and leading God's people should be based on giftedness rather than gender."**[1]

This book is for you if you've internalized harmful messages about manhood and womanhood, inside and outside of conservative evangelical churches. It is for you if you are curious about what you've been taught about marriage within a complementarian framework and are willing to question what you've been taught. If you identify as complementarian and are beginning to question gender roles, I want to gently remind you it's okay to question and change. You are human, and it is human to investigate and change your mind as you expand your understanding. Don't stifle your curiosity, for your curiosity is a vital part of your humanity.

In the past, writing a book with Stephen would've been so others knew he approved of what I wrote, to demonstrate that I was submissive to him. Now, though, I asked him to write this with me in part to let him tell his own story. Did you know that some people think I led him astray? Those people sure do overestimate my influence (as well as underestimate his ability to think for himself). Granted, I'm sure if pressed, those people who attribute Stephen's supposed downfall to me would turn the blame to the ever-elusive religious scapegoat "Satan," echoing what one friend at our former church said to me when she accused me of doing "the work of the enemy." (The enemy being Satan, of course.) She said this to me when I pushed back on complementarianism during a gathering at her house. More to come on this much later in the book.

The goals when writing this book were for Stephen and me to capture our journey. This book includes my journey and Stephen's journey, because while the tracks may be connected, even intersecting from time to time, they're still separate tracks. Each of us is telling our own story in our own words. We also wanted to process more of our own stories and misbeliefs about marriage and gender/gender roles. Finally, we would also like to help others in similar situations to read a different perspective and empower and encourage them to ask questions and follow their curiosity.

This isn't a "how to" book or a "we have the answers and everyone should do what we did" book or even a "since becoming egalitarian all our problems have been solved" book. Instead, it's simply a book about our journey *toward* mutuality, not *to* mutuality. The distinction is important because "to" would indicate arrival, and the work of dismantling hierarchy is ongoing.

Quick note: The Enneagram has played a huge role in our lives and is referenced as part of our journey. The Enneagram consists of nine different personality types, denoted by the numbers one through nine. [2] The introspection that the Enneagram sparked for me and Stephen helped us understand so much more about ourselves. I resonate the most with the Enneagram 3, which Coach Milton Stewart calls "the achieving performer." Stephen resonates most with the Enneagram 9, "the easy-going mediator."[3]

One of the final points I'll make before we jump in is that our thoughts and experiences as captured in this book are just that — our own. We are not trying to represent all people who have identified as complementarian. With that said, there can be overlap between our experiences and the experiences of others, so you are encouraged to find the support you need to process the emotions that may arise in you as you read.

This book contains events from our lives and dialogue that we have reconstructed to the best of our recollections. When necessary, names and identifying characteristics of individuals and places have been changed to maintain anonymity. In addition, suicidal ideation, references to racism, homophobia, and transphobia, language that may be offensive to some readers, and abuse in various forms, including spiritual, sexual, physical, and psychological, are present in the experiences included in these pages. I also want to express the limitations of complementarianism, as this theology sets up a false binary of cisgender, heterosexual men and cisgender, heterosexual women, therefore excluding and erasing anyone outside of that false binary.

Thank you for holding space for our journey. Stephen and I are holding tender space for you and sending so much love.

-Nicki

Intro

My right breast was on fire. The number behind the decimal on the thermometer climbed by the minute. Redialing Stephen was no use. He was in a deacon meeting at church. That didn't keep me from trying again, though. After 10 attempts, I decided to call our pastor, Jake. No answer. It was a reminder that even when I was in pain, I shouldn't inconvenience the men in my life. They were busy doing Super Important Work for God's Kingdom. I existed to help them. Not the other way around.

Shivering on the bed with my two-month-old sleeping beside me, I felt cut off from everyone else. Even my husband, who should have been home with me and our newborn, had deserted me. Or so it seemed. Grabbing my phone again, I texted Nova, my midwife, because I speculated that a clogged milk duct was the culprit. She confirmed that the symptoms were reminiscent of rapidly developing mastitis. She responded with thorough instructions regarding how to treat the infection at home. Unfortunately, we didn't have the type of salt Nova recommended. Stephen picking some up on his way home was my only hope, but he still wasn't answering his phone.

Sobs shook my entire body. Nursing abandonment issues and an infant, I knew the ideal "biblical woman" would suck it up, suffer well for God's glory, and serve her family with a smile on her face in all circumstances. The teaching I'd absorbed about marriage told me that any support Stephen offered was an added bonus, not an included-in-the-covenant guarantee. If I could have paced the floor, I would have. Resuming the fetal position, I massaged my burning breast and waited for someone else — namely Stephen — to save me. I hated feeling like I was being "high maintenance." And because of the patriarchy, I categorized my situation as such simply because it would disturb Stephen, despite the fact that I was, at that moment, deeply disturbed.

Stephen had been asked to be the lead deacon of the first slate of deacons at our church, a high honor that affirmed his gifts. However, he was asked to do this even though the start up coincided with the birth of our second baby. Resentment in me was building. I couldn't keep living like this, like a secretary whose sole purpose was to serve the men in my home and church. But I did for two more years as cracks let light in until I could no longer ignore the moon and stars beckoning me into true flourishing.

* * * * *

In our marriage, Stephen and I weren't trying to make complementarianism "go away," a fear that a well-known complementarian leader has vocalized.[4] Where our flag was once firmly planted in the complementarian camp is now a healthier marriage. Egalitarianism provided a better framework for Stephen and I to dismantle hierarchy, both individually and collectively.

Why was Christian patriarchy the framework of the first eight and a half years of our marriage? How did we address, dismantle, and redress these misbeliefs? On the following pages are the stories that illustrate how two overly-committed complementarians are becoming egalitarian.

Buckle up. It's gonna be a bumpy ride.

Behind

Once upon a time in the deep South, there was a daddy who delighted in his daughter. She remembers that, at one point, her father *did* love her. He used to hold her high over his head and smile up at her. But for this young girl, there is not a happy ending. This same young girl is then neglected, malnourished, and severely abused. Violence replaces tenderness. Social services removes her from the environment. This forces her to grow up too fast. She bounces from home to home. Some are safer than others. Some are downright dangerous. All of this leaves her vulnerable. She makes herself small, hoping her invisibility provides some protection. She would do anything to leave the chaos behind.

A few counties over, a four-year-old boy self-sufficiently prepares his own lunch. He learns at the earliest age that he can only count on himself. This forces him to grow up too fast. The man who fathered him is a serial pedophile. Some people know this for a fact. Some merely suspect it but gaslight themselves into discounting the messages their bodies are sending them. No one knows for sure if the father's predatory behavior has been inflicted on the boy. The messages of masculinity internalized by this boy are connected to the military industrial complex. The men in generations before him served in numerous wars. Militancy is stitched into the family fabric, fabric that's splitting at the seams. Real men fight. Real men are militant. Real men dominate.

Elsewhere, another boy loses his father during some of his most formative years. This forces him to grow up too fast. He takes on responsibilities not meant for a child and carries the weight of caretaking. To ensure the people he loves have what they need, he sacrifices. Even if this means he must go without. He supplies what others lack. That's his job, and he's good at it. Though he doesn't mean to attach strings to his gifts, he pulls on the threads to get what he wants. An absence of boundaries translates to guilt trips that people don't want to go on but that they don't know how to opt out of. He does so much for them, after all, and they want to repay him in some way.

Across the country, a young girl helps her mother with child rearing and homemaking tasks. Her father is gone again. Not because he's out of the picture permanently. No, it's always temporary. He always comes back. But, that doesn't make the times of his departure any easier. This forces her to grow up too fast. She doesn't mind the extra duties, though. In fact, she enjoys them and hopes to do the same for her own children someday. A whole house full of people who rely on her and who she can make feel special. Her end goal is that others feel loved, and she conceals the repeated financial bind that she puts herself in by purchasing presents for her people. The ends justify the means every time, as she beholds the sheer joy on the face of the receiver.

Each of these complex, extraordinary characters hurled themselves over obstacles. And they didn't look back. But, sometimes, we have to look back to heal the here and now and to heal the future. These characters' stories didn't just impact them as the people directly experiencing them. No, there are ripple effects that continue reaching to the farthest ends of the muddy pond water. Generations bear that trauma in their bodies because we know that our personal origin stories are, of course, informed by the origin stories of those who came before us. How could they not be?

Before we were, many others were. Therefore, our origin stories begin before we were even a thought. Inevitably, the generations that came before us and their beliefs about gender, sexuality, race, power, and so much more shaped their interactions with us, thereby shaping our own beliefs. This is true both in an ancestral, familial sense as well as societally. Take the sadist James Marion Sims, for example. The hierarchical nature of patriarchy made it so that there were no repercussions when he rendered white women who experienced pain during intercourse unconscious so their husbands could rape them.[5] His disregard for women's autonomy and consent took an even more sinister turn when it came to his experimental operations on the enslaved.

In a white supremacist world informed by misogynoir,[6] Sims tortured enslaved teenage girls and women. He withheld anesthesia from teenage girls like Anarcha to experiment on them and perfect a method for curing vesicovaginal fistula. Their losses led to his personal financial gain.[7] And long before Sims existed, misbeliefs about women informed how male doctors interacted with us. What became known as hysteria was at one time called "wandering womb." Greek physicians were out there declaring, as medical fact, that a wayward uterus traveling around the body led to the extensive indicators of hysteria.[8] I think it's important to keep in mind how intertwined patriarchy and white supremacy are; we can't dismantle one without dismantling the other and everything else attached to them.

The trauma baked into all of our origin stories makes for some unhealthy humans if we don't learn how to process the pain and move it through our bodies. If we aren't emotionally healthy as individuals, we certainly won't be emotionally healthy in relationships with others. Whether you realize it or not, you've been influenced by patriarchy, by the belief that cisgender, heterosexual men are supposed to exercise authority over cisgender, heterosexual women (and the companion belief that anyone who exists outside of that false binary should be erased). All of us are born into a world where it's an indisputable fact that men have long committed acts of sexual violence as weapons of war. Even the everyday language we use makes the often violent nature of distorted masculinity seem normal.

When the sun peeks through during a drizzle, what do we say? *The devil is beating his wife.*
When a man is wearing a white, ribbed tank, what do we call it? *A wife beater.*
So, when a child witnesses a woman she loves cowering in fear of being beaten by a man, the little girl minimizes the violence. After all, violence against women has continually been minimized in the world around her. This forces her to grow up too fast. Boys and men that she should have been able to trust violate her, in her own family and outside of it. All of this leaves her vulnerable. She makes herself small, hoping her invisibility provides some protection. She would do anything to leave the chaos behind.

SECTION 1

"It was with a good end in mind — that of acquiring the knowledge of good and evil — that Eve allowed herself to be carried away and eat the forbidden fruit. But Adam was not moved by this desire for knowledge, but simply by greed: he ate it because he heard Eve say it tasted good."

-Moderata Fonte
in *The Worth of Women*

Chapter 1
Nicki's Origin Story

It's 5:00 a.m. The world outside my house is still. Inside, my mom is already bustling about. She's awake before the sun has risen to cook breakfast for my father. He works hard and must have a hot, hearty meal to jumpstart his day. While the oval hash brown patties bake, she scrambles eggs, flips sausage, and preps his lunch. After sending him and her kids off to work and school, she washes loads of laundry, laundry that she also hauls down the back porch stairs to dry on the clothesline. Rinse and repeat.

Then, she heads to work at the campground a mile down the road. Walking from cabin to cabin, she scrubs toilets, gathers linens, wipes baseboards, sweeps, and mops. Drenched in sweat and slightly hunched over because something in her back is pinched again, she switches out the laundry at the camp. For a solid seven hours or more, her entire workday is spent going cabin to cabin, down to the laundry room, cabin, laundry room. Rinse and repeat.

Back home, she has dinner on the table by 5:00 p.m. for us to eat together. After dinner, my dad pops open a can of beer and plops into his recliner to watch TV. He works hard and deserves the downtime. In the kitchen, my mom washes all the dishes in our burn-your-hands water. Rinse and repeat it all tomorrow.

* * * * *

I always knew from a young age that women were "supposed" to serve men and men were "supposed" to hold power over women. My dad didn't have a partnership with my mom, but I think he was fine with that. I think he wanted to exercise control, over my mom and me. Now, when I say my dad wanted to exercise control, what I'm not saying is that he is a bad person. What I am saying is that, from my point of view, it seemed this way. This interpretation would make sense given the patriarchal context in which the United States was deliberately designed.

To illustrate that my dad wanted to exercise control over us, I give you Exhibit A: hair. My dad likes long hair, so my mom kept her hair long. By extension, my hair needed to be long, which is creepy when you think about it. The reasoning goes like this: Because my dad prefers long hair on women, and that's what he finds attractive, I needed to keep my hair long. In the words of Alexis Rose, "Ew, David!" When my mom did chop her hair off, my dad was openly opposed and vocalized said opposition on numerous occasions.

Any time my hair was cut short (and by short, I mean at the top of my shoulders), my dad talked as if my femininity was diminished in some way as a result. When I got a pixie cut, he likened me to a lesbian, as if my short hair inevitably indicated attraction to other girls. Specifically, my dad compared me to Ellen DeGeneres, who he called "Ellen Degenerate" because what he lacks in originality, he makes up for by directly saying what he's thinking. This way, you know where he stands. He doesn't leave you second guessing.

Without bypassing necessary accountability for any harm Ellen has caused, when I think about how much vitriol she received from the white men in my life, I now understand that it was because she represented something they hated. Not just homosexuality but a woman who was unapologetically empowered in her sexuality, on her own terms. How dare a woman not exist for the pleasure of men or to be pleasured by them? And when I say to be pleasured by them, I don't mean for the woman's pleasure. I mean that they think she should be delighted that a man would deign to have sex with her.

Regarding my own sexuality, people were nervous when I did things that could be interpreted as being a lesbian. Like when I took my best friend Wendy to my junior prom as my date. She went to a different school and accompanied me to my prom because I'd wasted the entire year "dating" a pedophile who lived in Ohio. (Yes, that really happened.) But I didn't even entertain thoughts of dating a girl because I knew I was "supposed" to date boys. Plus, there were plenty of options when it came to boys I was attracted to.

Okay, back to illustrating that my dad wanted to exercise control over me. I give you Exhibit B: ears. More specifically, the amount of extra orifices I was allowed to have poked into them. The first set of holes wasn't an issue. At a local salon, the beautician made a red X on each ear when I was in middle school. I loved those first piercings. Then, I wanted more ear piercings when I was in high school. My dad emphatically said no. One of my favorite older cousins took me to a store in the mall where I got them pierced anyway by a disengaged employee I knew not to trust with that stud gun. I loved the rebellion inherent in those second piercings. I didn't love how they weren't symmetrical. (I still don't love how they aren't symmetrical.) Later, I wanted more ear piercings. And I didn't ask anyone for permission. I just went and got them. They are symmetrical with one another, but when I wear an earring in all six holes, I cringe at the one middle hole that isn't aligned with the others. But it's fine. Really. I'm totally over it. (whispers *It's actually not fine, but there's nothing I can do about it, so moving right along.*)

With few exceptions, though, I craved my dad's approval, so much so that I let him believe that the lyrics from a Toby Keith song were Nicki originals. That's right. I was writing some of the words from "Stays in Mexico" in a journal and then started singing. As the chorus filled the air, my dad was smiling. His face lit up as he said, "Hey, that's not bad." He proceeded to brainstorm some potential lyrical changes, some ideas for the instrumental track. I let him. He seemed proud of me, and I didn't want to disrupt that pride.

My dad was my hero. Granted, he'd set himself up to be my hero from the first time he met me. He stepped in to be a father when my biological father wanted nothing to do with me. My mom said that the man who adopted me as his own told his family, "I met a girl I love, and I'm going to marry her mom." I was expected to be forever grateful toward him for rescuing us. To be honest, I was grateful because I loved the man who rescued us. He also set himself up to be my favorite, to prefer him over my mom. He was the laid back, lenient parent in contrast to my mom's strictness, especially concerning boys.

Garnering my dad's approval was my motivation for just about everything. I lived and breathed for his happiness, validation, ego, and projected image. In doing so, I took on responsibility for regulating his emotions, a responsibility that wasn't mine to bear. Most of the time when he got home during the week, I was ready to walk on eggshells. Eventually, the tension in my body was too much, and I tried to avoid him by doing homework, studying, and reading in my room. It worked out because he was usually parked in front of the TV or computer playing some war game.

On the weekends, though, there was no avoiding him when he barged into my room, and then my little brother's room, to pull the covers off of us. Moving quickly, I jumped out of bed so he wouldn't douse me with a glass of cold water. Saturday mornings were no time for sleeping in. There were chores to be done. Joining the marching band provided an escape. I stayed in the marching band throughout high school for two main reasons. One, because I enjoyed it, and two, because I got a break from Saturday morning wake-up calls during competition season.

* * * * *

I aspired to be worthy of the attention of the boys and men around me, even in elementary school. Behind the playground equipment, classmates would gather to watch me kiss my boyfriend, Teddy. One day, a substitute teacher caught us. She laughed as she told my mom that afternoon. My body stiffened because I thought I was going to get in trouble. I didn't relax until I saw that my mom was laughing, too.

My obsession with boys and how they perceived me started before Teddy and extended far past him. Subsequently, I felt immense shame when they critiqued my appearance in any way. For example, I was in an elective class, woodshop or auto, and there were a lot of guys. Many of them would flirt with me, and I welcomed every innuendo. I'll never forget the day, though, when one of the guys pulled me onto his lap. As my wrist draped around his neck, he got a glimpse under my arms. I was wearing a shirt that exposed some of my armpits. My hair is dark, so naturally my armpit hair is dark, too. The follicles can be seen even if I've just shaved. He made a remark about how hot I was, even if he could see the hair under my armpits. I had never critiqued this classmate's body, yet he felt complete freedom to analyze what he perceived as a flaw in me. My cheeks turned red, and I received the message (once again) that my body existed for others, that my body wasn't mine.

But I loved the boys, so I excused their rude comments.

In loving the boys, I dated and kissed a lot of them, sometimes two at once, because I had a pattern of sabotaging the handful of healthy romantic relationships I had by cheating. The high school example of this that still ties my stomach in knots was when I was in a "long-distance" relationship with this guy that we'll call Isaac. He only lived an hour away, but when you're a teenager, that might as well be a faraway state. Long-distance was difficult for me, but I tried to solve the problems of my long-distance relationship with Isaac through another long-distance relationship. Naturally, this didn't work.

Though I was dating Isaac, I went out, and made out, with a guy from another high school. The following weekend, Isaac and I went on a double date with the newlyweds whose wedding brought us together. After what I had done, I knew I had to break up with him, so we went off alone. Clearly, I couldn't tell him the truth. I was invested in protecting my image, so I came up with vague excuses that in no way mended the heart I'd just shattered. I didn't tell anyone about cheating on Isaac, or any other time I cheated. People didn't know this side of me. The shame I felt was further fueled by the religious messaging that surrounded me every Sunday morning, Sunday evening, and Wednesday evening at church. The shame pushed me to retreat into myself and do all I could to lock away this aspect of myself, to keep this character defect hidden so that I wouldn't taint how others perceived me.

Yes, I cheated on some really great guys, and yes, I was cheated on plenty of times, too. All of this stoked my suspicion not only that guys weren't trustworthy but that I wasn't either. Not only could I not be trusted to be a good judge of someone's character (since I kept dating guys who would cheat on me), I also thought of myself as a "temptress." Because of the conditioning that takes place within the patriarchy, I assumed that all boys wanted sex and that sex was all they wanted (before I even really knew what sex was).

There was one trip I went on with the Future Farmers of America. I was the only girl, and many of the boys took turns violating me over the course of the few days we were together. On the bus ride back, one of the boys sat with me. We held hands the whole way home and never really talked again after that.

Being repeatedly sexually assaulted confirmed for me the misbelief that boys and men can't control themselves, and I knew I couldn't tell anyone because I likely wouldn't be believed. We aren't believed even though, "A review of research finds that the prevalence of false reporting is between 2 percent and 10 percent."[9] That means that 90 to 98 percent of sexual assault reports are substantiated. What that does not mean is that unsubstantiated reports definitely didn't happen, but just that they are unconfirmed based on the available evidence. (An important caveat to make here is that white women historically and currently wrongly accuse Black men of rape. Often, the lies have resulted in lynchings. As author Imani Perry explains, "Rape was a ritual of racial terror wielded against the spirits of Black women. Accusations of rape were a tool of racial terror threatening Black men."[10])

In my own life, I was definitely assaulted by boys and men, both inside and outside of my family. Though there may be insufficient evidence to back up my claims, it does not mean my claims are false. When the assaults happened, and for years after, I was silent. My silence was both expected and rewarded.

So, I thought that all boys and men wanted sex, and that they would get it one way or another. To feel even somewhat empowered that I was making the decision for myself as an active agent, instead of being acted upon without my consent, I got better at initiating sexual contact.

* * * * *

In addition to my sexuality, my emotions were constantly subject to scrutiny. It was, without a doubt, an insult for any of the boys or men in my life to be compared to a girl, whether because of how they hit (or missed) a ball or because of an "outburst" that included tears. The message was received loud and clear: your tears aren't welcome here.

Stifling my feelings, I knew I was still "too much" emotionally, that femininity was analogous with emotionality, and that emotionality was to be despised. Feelings were treated as weaknesses. This narrative was fed by the imagery I ingested via movies that starred men like John Wayne. Let's just say that John Wayne was such a staple in my family that there was a life-size cardboard cutout of him at my paternal grandparents' house. John Wayne made his way into several family photos as a result. All someone needed to do was slide him in. The misbelief that emotionality was a weakness permeated the air. It didn't keep me from being emotional, but rather from being able to move my emotions through my body in a healthy way.

As Kristin Kobes Du Mez explained in her packs-all-the-punches book *Jesus and John Wayne*, "John Wayne became an icon of rugged American manhood for generations of conservatives…In time, Wayne would also emerge as an icon of Christian masculinity. Evangelicals admired (and still admire) him for his toughness and his swagger…Finding comfort and courage in symbols of a mythical past, evangelicals looked to a rugged, heroic masculinity embodied by cowboys, soldiers, and warriors to point the way forward. For decades to come, militant masculinity (and a sweet, submissive femininity) would remain entrenched in the evangelical imagination, shaping conceptions of what was good and true."[11] I didn't hear about John Wayne from the pulpit, but we were a family of fervent white evangelicals who idolized and romanticized the so-called "law and order" that the actor John Wayne ushered in each time his looming presence dominated the screen. Other men reinforced this, such as

Rush Limbaugh during his radio talk show. Just hearing that man's voice in the car with my dad made my skin crawl.

References to war abounded onscreen and off, as there were several family members who fought in various wars, and there were so many movies, starring John Wayne and others, in this genre. I do find it interesting that "Wayne worked to recruit men to the war effort, ridiculing as 'soft' those who didn't enlist," when he himself "never actually served in the military. When the Second World War broke out, he'd been reluctant to put his budding film career on hold to enlist."[12] Regardless of his lack of active duty service, "Those inspired by Wayne's bravado came to see all of life as a war, and toughness as a virtue,"[13] and this was certainly true in my family, where paranoia reigned supreme. Life had to be war because someone was always out to get you. Looking out for yourself was a top priority and "protecting" white girls and women was a primary function of this toxic masculinity.

* * * * *

When it came to the Jesus part of Jesus and John Wayne, things were quite muddled. At the Southern Baptist Church I attended, there was an American flag on the stage. There were special services in honor of veterans and the military. In the Children's Choir, I learned "Onward Christian Soldiers" and that I was in the Lord's army. (And I knew that as a girl, it was frowned upon for me to even consider joining the U.S. Army.) At Vacation Bible School, I pledged allegiance to the American flag, Christian flag, and Bible. If the church doors were open, I was there.

Though I'd made a profession of faith as a young child and been baptized, I had a visceral conversion experience when I was a teenager. It was actually the pedophile I "dated" that I attributed my salvation to. One humid South Carolina evening, we were chatting on the phone about spiritual matters. He mentioned the necessity of praying each day to ensure salvation, but I disagreed. When he asked me why, I wasn't sure. Sitting with my legs crossed on the cold hardwood floor, I had my Bible open on my lap. While searching for answers, I stumbled upon Ephesians 2:8-9 in my King James Version. "For by grace are ye saved through faith; and that not of yourselves: it is the gift of God: Not of works, lest any man should boast," I quoted to him.

I explained that from the way I saw it, the ability to lose a gift wouldn't make it a gift. Since our works don't save us, I didn't think they could cause us to lose salvation. As I spoke, it dawned on me that the "good works" I was accumulating for myself through attending Sunday school, reading the Bible, and being involved in youth group wouldn't save me. Within that framework, I thought I had not truly accepted God's gift of salvation by faith. With the pedophile's guidance, I prayed to be saved. My outlook on life changed, and then everything else did, too.

There was a zeal that I felt about my salvation. I wanted to convert others that I thought were lost and strengthen the faith of people who were already Christians. This meant trying to lead family devotions that no one wanted to attend (and that my dad didn't attend as he kept playing his war game on the computer). As the oldest child, and as someone who possessed leadership qualities, I wanted to assist my family members in growing spiritually. (The irony is not lost on me of a brand-new convert secretly "dating" a pedophile thinking she has the answers that will heal the family.) Though family devotion time wasn't a success, I continued being vocal in my newfound passion.

On one annual Women in Ministry Sunday, where women utilize their gifts to edify the congregation, I even shared from the pulpit and felt what I've heard described as the call to be a pastor, even though I'd never had a woman as a pastor. My Sunday School teachers were women. However, the pastor was always, without exception, a man. The absence of women holding this position where they would formerly teach men communicated an implied message that those leadership roles were for men only. This influenced my thought that men were the pinnacle. More specifically, white men. And even more specifically, white, cisgender, heterosexual, Christian men. I believed these men were the modern day Moseses who would lead the world to the promised land. In thinking they were at the top, everyone else became less human.

It's interesting how I carried these beliefs while surrounded by strong, tenacious, resilient women who were changing the world around me. There was my mom. She'd endured decades of hardship, but somehow she kept going. Her laughter was one of my favorite sounds because it was like a middle finger to all the suffering. From before the sun rose until hours after it set, seven days a week, my mom cooked and cleaned, washed load after overflowing load of laundry, read to me and my brother, and so much more. She gave of her time and resources to so many people. She paved a path for me to become who I am becoming.

There was also my grandma. Grandma is my dad's mother, and she cultivated my love of music as she played the piano and took me to piano lessons. She has fulfilled almost every role in the church at some point, except preaching or leading the choir. Plus, even though most of her eight children had retired, Grandma was still driving herself to work after she turned 90. After she turned 90 years old, y'all. And she still hosts lunch at her house after church on Sundays, bakes sourdough loaves regularly, makes mini banana bread loaves upon request, and so much more.

I also had aunts who inspired me. Each of them in their own way. One of my aunts wanted me to be a model because it seemed like I was going to be tall. Well, I stopped growing at 5'6" (though I thought I was 5'7" until 2019 and was super bummed to lose that inch). Unable to fulfill that aunt's dream, I decided to embody another aunt's dream, a dream she brought to life when I job-shadowed her. Her enthusiasm was contagious (just like the germs that kids carry with them into classrooms). Like my aunt, I desired to make a difference in the world, gain recognition for being one of the best in the biz, and mentor aspiring teachers. With two other cousins studying education, I joined the line of educators who had gone before me and wanted to make my family proud.

At the root of my outward behaviors was the motivation to have people look at me and be impressed at how successful I was. Granted, the barometer of success changed depending on the situation, and that's where my "chameleon-like" qualities came in handy. I didn't know any of this until much later when I encountered the Enneagram. Now, remember, I identify as an Enneagram 3, "the achieving performer." Wanting to achieve the goals that would garner the praise of my family, I decided to study Early Childhood Education and was going to give teaching my all.

Turns out, the combination of misbeliefs I picked up in childhood about masculinity, the men I saw in leadership at church, and my tendency to merge to fit someone else's definition of success primed me to become a poster child for complementarianism. And, quite frankly, a lot of trauma and abuse went into making me a complementarian as I internalized the misbeliefs that my body was not my own and I was not autonomous. My first memoir, *As Familiar as Family*, goes more in depth about the sexual trauma I endured and its impact on me. For the purposes of this book, I will summarize by saying that I was groomed and conditioned — by society, my family, and a myriad of experiences — to think I needed a man to exercise authority over me. I held to the principles of complementarianism before I even knew what complementarianism was.

As I navigated trying to fit in with a whole new group of people after moving away from home, I found that the goalpost for what "success" looked like had shifted. This new reality had an impact on me in many different ways, most notably in my underlying motivations for buying all into complementarian ideology.

Chapter 2
Stephen's Origin Story

I grew up in the southern United States where the culture and conservative Christianity are intertwined. Men occupied a lot of leadership positions and women occupied a lot of the behind-the-scenes support roles. I am the fifth of six kids and the youngest son. My mom brought me home from the hospital on Christmas Day and somehow still managed to cook Christmas dinner. When my younger sister began school, my mom started working outside the home as a bus driver during the school year. In later years, she also worked at McDonald's in the summer to help support our large family. I don't remember my parents talking about gender roles, but my dad was the one who brought in the most income. This subconsciously influenced what I believed about roles because I saw him as the "provider."

My parents didn't fight or argue in front of me, at least not that I saw or heard. As I got older, I could pick up on the frustration my dad felt toward my mom about various things, especially when it came to unnecessary purchases. Their lack of arguing informed my ideas about what a healthy relationship looked like. If there was fighting and conflict in a relationship, I thought the relationship wasn't healthy and that there was something wrong. The model my parents set was the first experience I had with conflict, and that contributed to my conflict avoidance later down the road.

I don't remember much about my childhood, but whenever I sprawled out on the ground because I didn't get my way, a close family friend would say, "There's Stephen, slain in the Spirit again." There are many pictures of me asleep, and it's a running joke how I could sleep practically anywhere. In front of the fridge where the warm air was blowing out. On the toilet. Yes, on the toilet. Basically any and every where I could, and likely did, find a way to fall asleep. (As an adult, I've learned that falling asleep like I did was a form of narcotization. Sleep provided me with an escape from the chaos around me.) When I got a little older, I developed OCD as a way to gain a little more control over my life. Each night, I had to check every door and window throughout the house before I could go to sleep. When I say life was chaotic, I don't mean anything bad by that. There was just a lot going on with six different kids, schedules, and school assignments. For the most part, I sort of disappeared because I didn't need much. If I did need something, it was hard for me to make that need known.

* * * * *

From the time I was young in the non-denominational evangelical church I was part of, the roles I saw men and women filling shaped my perceptions. The men were the ones speaking, teaching, leading in song, and preaching. I don't recall ever seeing a woman welcome the congregation, take up an offering, or administer the Lord's Supper. I did see women play instruments or sing in the choir but not lead the choir. I didn't think about it back then, but now I can definitely see how even those things shaped me.

Outside of church, I was also shaped by the jobs I saw women filling, such as teachers. In elementary school, I didn't have any teachers who were men, except for P.E. That teacher and the assistant principal may have been the only men on the faculty at the school. The messaging there was that teaching children was a feminine job, unless you're in charge of the entire school or teaching athletics. As a boy, I didn't want to be perceived as "girly" because I equated that with weakness. My parents didn't teach me this, but I picked up on it from other kids at school. I thought it was "girly" and weak to cry and tried to avoid crying in front of others.

Around the time I was in kindergarten, I was playing Coach Pitch for baseball. At one game that sticks in my mind, I struck out or hit the ball and got out. Either way, from my point of view, I didn't succeed. I remember crying and feeling completely embarrassed, like I failed. I let my team down. I let my family down. Walking back to the field to play defense, I was pouting. An older teammate who knew I was upset put his arm around me in a gesture of comfort. Shrugging my shoulders, I pushed him off of me; his acknowledgment was only highlighting what I was feeling, and I didn't want to draw attention to it.

Not only did I stuff down my emotions, but I also could get aggressive. One time, I was playing with my neighbors outside when I was in third or fourth grade. There was pine straw on the street. A friend's younger sister tried to tag me. Slipping on the pine straw, I fell face down on the road. I was hurt, yes, but I also felt embarrassed and worried what people would think. Were they going to think I was less than her, less than a little girl? Were they going to think she brought me down? Yelling out, I called her an idiot.

In middle school, I was still on the smaller side. Another student that was much bigger than me lifted me over his head. Though this embarrassed me, by this time I'd disconnected from all my emotions, including (and maybe especially) anger. I also withdrew more into myself as I got older. In high school, my siblings and kids who lived on the same street as us were my closest friends. I didn't really have any friends at school, which was painfully obvious when I would eat lunch alone. Finding notes from my mom in my lunch box helped me feel seen and valued, which she always tried her best to do even with six kids.

* * * * *

Because of books I read in college like *Every Young Man's Battle*, I didn't trust myself to not give in to sexual sin. That book is about pornography, and the author, from what I remember, argues that men are wired to objectify women. Therefore, I internalized the misbeliefs that I was powerless against "temptation" and that I couldn't trust myself. Though I didn't look at pornography, I assigned a negative value to the presence of any sexual desire because it was characterized as lusting. Lusting isn't what God wants because "everyone who looks at a woman with lustful intent has already committed adultery with her in his heart" Matthew 5:28 (ESV). Also, "I made a covenant with my eyes not to look lustfully at a…woman" Job 31:1 (NIV). At men's retreats, this topic of lust was talked about often. A repeated message was that since we are powerless against sexual temptation, we can't fight it. Therefore, we must flee it, per 1 Timothy 2:22.

When it came to romantic relationships, I didn't date until college, and then I only had a couple of girlfriends. I dated one girl my sophomore year and then another beginning junior year through my first year out of college. Though I had sexual desires, I was told, repeatedly, that the desires in and of themselves were bad because I wasn't married. So, if I would kiss someone, at a certain point, there would be shame attached to the kiss. Or if I thought about somebody in a sexual way, I would experience shame because it wasn't what I was supposed to be doing, it wasn't what God wanted. The shame I felt wasn't about the ways I objectified or dehumanized women. It was more about failing to follow the command of God to not lust after a woman. So, even the reason for the shame wasn't rooted in not treating women with dignity but rather in ways I thought I was not living up to God's standard. As Nicki pointed out recently, I centered myself and my shame rather than the women and their humanity. Describing it at the time, though, I would have said I was centering God, God's glory and perfection, and how I fell short of that and, therefore, needed a Savior.

During this time, I was involved with the Baptist Collegiate Ministry (BCM) at Winthrop University. A woman was the campus minister. There were women on the leadership team and even presidents of that ministry. I didn't feel like there was a problem with any of that. I did think that men were supposed to be leaders, and that's who came as speakers to teach at BCM. We would have different themes each semester, and the visiting speakers would talk about different topics within those themes. Once I got connected to reformed theology through a youth pastor named Jake, I began to notice people making a much bigger deal out of gender roles. Jake would go on to play a huge role in my life, though I didn't know it at the time.

My first year out of college, I was interning with BCM. Jake was one of the visiting speakers who came that spring to speak. He talked about Philippians 1:21, "For me to live is Christ, and to die is gain" (ESV). That night, he talked about John Piper's book *Don't Waste Your Life* and the connection of that book to the verse from Philippians. The way Jake taught the Bible and preached was so different from any of the other speakers that we had. He spoke with authority and certainty; I was immediately drawn to him. He was teaching the Bible with such passion and teaching the cultural and linguistic context of the verse. Sitting there, I was thinking, "Oh my goodness, this is amazing," and it just really resonated with my heart. Something was awakened in me as I felt like he was putting into words what I wanted to live. That night was impactful as it changed the trajectory of my life.

After that, I read *Don't Waste Your Life*. For my high school graduation, my sister and brother-in-law had given me a copy of it, but I didn't read it until after hearing Jake talk about it. That summer, between semesters for BCM, I needed a job. That led to me searching for youth ministry options. One church needed a youth minister, so I went to talk with them. There was lodging provided, which would have been a big plus. Then, I heard that Jake was looking for an intern.

I thought interning with Jake would be a great opportunity for me to learn from someone who had been doing youth ministry for a while instead of trying to do something on my own. Though I'd been involved with youth ministry, it had only consisted of helping out here and there. So, I didn't feel equipped to take on the youth minister role at the first church I'd been interested in. Instead, if I were to intern with Jake, I'd be able to learn from what he was doing and hear his teaching on a more consistent basis.

In the summer of 2007, I began interning with Jake. That's when the teaching of complementarian theology became much more explicit, along with the teaching of "systematic" theology. "Systematic" theology was idolized in that environment, as it was all about what you believe and having "correct" doctrine. As a youth pastor, Jake taught through books of the Bible. This was different from other youth ministries where the teaching was topical. As a result of Jake's expositional teaching, a lot of the youth were well versed in theology. I didn't have the level of knowledge or the background that the youth there had. So, I even felt a little intimidated.

There was one student in tenth grade who was a genius in general. He also ate up the theology. Jake had given a task to the youth to memorize Romans 8 before going on a trip to a student life camp. That one student decided that if he was going to memorize Romans 8, he needed to go back to the beginning of Romans and also memorize the first seven chapters to put the eighth chapter into context. That was part of the rigorous climate that Jake created. At one point, after I'd been interning a while, that same student approached me.

"What's the chief end of man?" he asked.

The answer I should have given was, "To glorify God, and to enjoy him forever," from some catechism. But, I didn't know what to say. Though I felt intimidated at times in that youth group, spending time with Jake was good, not just because of everything I was learning from him, but also because I felt like I had a place of belonging. I was part of a youth ministry. Jake and I would go have lunch and hang out with the students at their school once a week.

Reflecting on our relationships with the youth, I think about how we had good relationships with them regardless of their gender, but we would never meet one-on-one with the girl youth. It was a general ministry rule that men youth leaders wouldn't meet with girl youth. Jake instructed me not to be alone with any of them. This rule was in place because, according to the way everything was presented, many men in ministry "lose" their ministry because of adultery or sexual sin that "just happened," as if they had no control over it. Therefore, they shouldn't be alone with a woman. This then informed interactions with teenage girls in the church youth group as well. Men in leadership positions in the church shouldn't be alone with a teenage girl, at a minimum, because of the way it looks. Additionally, they shouldn't trust themselves or be trusted to not be "tempted." Let that sink in.

The pillar of "total depravity" that was part of reformed theology taught me that I was so desperately wicked that I should never trust myself. According to this belief, I was capable of any and every terrible thing. I'd also done things that I deeply regretted and experienced shame for not holding boundaries in romantic relationships, which only increased the lack of trust in myself. There was one girl in the youth group who was a senior in high school. She seemed to like me, so I talked with Jake about it because I was concerned. One of the women leaders later approached Jake to ask what he thought about a relationship between me and that youth. Even though I was close to her age, I didn't think it would be a good idea. Jake agreed. She was still in high school, and I was a youth leader. I concluded it was best all around to avoid being alone with any of the girl youth.

This was the case even though we know that men youth leaders also sexually abuse boys. That doesn't prevent one-on-one meetings between boys and men. We simply ignore this reality because of our disdain for same sex attraction (even though this wouldn't be homosexuality but pedophilia, assault, and a misuse of power, the same as if the youth leader violated a student who wasn't a boy). In reformed circles where total depravity is touted, we don't want to think that male youth leaders would be capable of violating a boy. The leaders themselves wouldn't want anyone to think they were capable of that. So, why are they okay with parents thinking that they may be capable of abusing their daughter but still want the parents to trust them? What is it about girls that we're supposed to just accept the line of reasoning that says, "I can't be alone with her because she's a girl, and I have to protect my ministry"? If the leader hides behind not meeting one-on-one with girls because he wants to be above reproach and remove temptation, why should he be trusted to have leadership over any of the youth?

By allowing one-on-one meetings with the boys but not allowing one-on-one meetings with the girls, there's still a distinction made that even as girls, they bring some temptation to the dynamic that boys don't.

In making this distinction, girls are edged out instead of changing the system to where the youth leaders don't meet one-on-one with *any* student. In my opinion, there should always be at least two adults present, adults who have proven themselves trustworthy.

* * * * *

When I was interning with the youth, not only was I part of a community, but I also had a mentor in Jake. He was invested in me. I would eat dinner with him and his wife Caroline and their children. The big thing that drew me to Jake was the passion with which he taught the Bible. He seemed to have such deep insights that awakened my soul to give me a purpose for which to live, something greater than myself and that lasted beyond this life. Each week, I got to hear Jake's teaching. We would also prep for the youth group, pray for the students, and have deep conversations.

After a year, he left to plant Entrench Church. When he left, the church allowed me to be the interim youth minister. I'd built relationships with the students and families, so it was a good set up. The new position paid more money. I actually had the choice to either be the interim BCM director at Winthrop or interim youth minister at the church. Before meeting Jake, I likely would have taken the position at BCM. When talking through the decision with Jake, though, he emphasized the importance of the church versus parachurch organizations like BCM.

He explained that the local church should take precedence because the local church is "biblical." BCM leaders always made a point to say, "This is not your church. You need to be plugged into a local church." The distinction of BCM being "just" a parachurch ministry wasn't that big of a deal to me until talking about it with Jake. These conversations with Jake influenced me toward taking the interim youth minister position.

Rather than unbiasedly presenting the options and the possible advantages and disadvantages of each and telling me, "I trust you to make the decision that is right for yourself," Jake didn't hide his thoughts and feelings about what he thought was the right decision. As someone that was my mentor and a spiritual authority I trusted, I gave more weight to Jake's insights than my own. This led to me making the decision he wanted me to make. Obviously, I am responsible for the things I believe and do, but the environment was one where you had to believe a certain way. Otherwise, you weren't as serious of a Christian, or you weren't as holy and sanctified. That was the underlying message. Plus, I wanted to attend seminary, and the church was planning to help with some of the expenses so I could do that.

Additional layers that complicated the decision-making process were that I'm an Enneagram 9, "the easy-going mediator." It's easier for me internally to just go with the flow of what others want from me. This contributed to a fear in me of taking responsibility for the choice because it was such a big moment that would define my path forward. It was easier to defer to someone else, to defer to a pastor in this case, rather than risk not getting the approval of the other person. A part of me was thinking that if I made the decision Jake wanted me to make, then he would be pleased with me, and that would strengthen our relationship. And Jake was so certain of everything he said. The certainty provided the stability I crave as an Enneagram 9. The certainty provided a framework I could work from of what "truth" is. If what Jake was saying was the truth, then all the other interpretations outside of "systematic" theology were wrong.

An integral component of "systematic" theology was complementarianism. Those teaching complementarian theology, like Jake, said that this was the correct way to interpret scripture because the biblical texts were "plainly stating" a view that supported men leading. Based on many sermons and books that approached certain texts from a complementarian interpretation, I became entrenched in this theology and everything that branched from it.

Chapter 3
Our Origin Story

Free lunch and Bible study, Room 114. That's how Stephen and I met one afternoon in August 2007 when a sign caught my eye on campus my freshman year of college. I walked into a BCM meeting at the Lancaster branch of the University of South Carolina (USC-L). Stephen was the guy who put out the sign that enticed students, namely me, with the promise of free food. That was really all it took to reel me into the classroom that would serve as a hub for pizza, conversation, and spiritual instruction for the next hour.

BCM met every Monday, and I was excited to find a group of college students that I could study the Bible with. When Stephen taught, there was a quiet confidence paired with a tender humility. As I listened to him teach, I felt grateful to be in that room, learning from him. I felt a gentleness from him toward all of us. I enjoyed and looked forward to the weekly meeting, yes, for the free lunch, but more so for the feeling of belonging and community that followed.

Stephen was the first person I heard teach about complementarianism, though he didn't call it this. During one of the Bible study sessions, Stephen explained that husbands were supposed to love their wives and wives were supposed to submit to their husbands, using verses from Ephesians 5. When addressing the women in the room, Stephen told us that if a husband was truly loving us in a sacrificial manner as Christ loves his Bride, it isn't hard to submit to that type of love. Implicit in this message is that if wives submit to their husbands, husbands find it easier to love, protect, and provide for their wives. Though I didn't know it at the time, I now recognize this for the lie it is.

Author Emily Joy Allison wrote, "Purity culture is the spiritual corollary of rape culture created in Christian environments by theologies that teach complete sexual abstinence until legal, monogamous marriage between a cisgender, heterosexual man and a cisgender, heterosexual women for life — or else."[14] Because of the work of people like Emily Joy, I now understand that complementarianism cannot deliver on the promises it makes. In upholding hierarchy, complementarianism undeniably gives the framework for husbands to harm their wives, and there is no accountability, only excuses. By extension, purity culture cannot keep us safe. In the words of author Meghan Tschanz, "Women don't need protection if men stop hurting them."[15]

For eight months during my freshman year, I faithfully occupied a seat on the front row each Monday at BCM, frantically taking notes as I absorbed Stephen's teaching like a sponge. The frequency and depth of our conversations increased, and I enjoyed our talks. I didn't like him, per se, because I thought he was just the nice guy that led Bible study. I also thought he was too good for me, so I wouldn't risk putting myself out there to be rejected.

Aside from one embarrassing (for me) interaction with Stephen that I won't tell you about, the beginning of our friendship was fairly uneventful.

Okay, fine, I'll tell you the embarrassing story.

When I attended Converge, a BCM conference, in Myrtle Beach, I was with a couple of friends. We were the only ones from the USC-L BCM. Once we were in the lobby at the hotel, none of us knew what to do. Stephen told us hello, but then he joined the rest of the students he knew from Winthrop's BCM. I was complaining to my friends when Stephen walked up behind me just as I said, "Our leader sucks." I told you it was embarrassing for me. Later that night, Stephen overheard me talking with an intern about an ex-boyfriend. I was showing her the guy's MySpace and how he was wearing the sweater I'd bought him in the most recent picture he'd posted. We were speculating about what it could mean. Later, Stephen would tell me that in that moment, his only thought was that I was completely obsessed with boys. He wasn't wrong. It's surprising he ever decided to give me a chance.

* * * * *

I continued to attend BCM every Monday to learn from Stephen. Well, every Monday except for one when I went out to eat with Oliver from my debate class. After a few flirtatious interactions, he invited me to get lunch. I weighed the options of free food from Bible study or free food from Oliver. Oliver was cute and charming, so he won.

An hour after my lunch with Oliver, I was scrunched up in my favorite blue armchair with comfy padding in the library. I was studying before my next class when I saw Stephen through the shelves of books. He was headed for the bathroom. I whispered his name as loudly as I could. He smiled as he ambled over to me. He said they'd missed me at Bible study and tossed me a leftover Little Debbie Swiss Roll.

A couple of months later, as summer got into full swing, I was preparing to leave for a "mission trip." Stephen called to say he'd be praying for me and the team while we were gone. I appreciated his thoughtfulness but knew he would do the same for literally anyone else. There is a lot I regret about this trip, with white saviorism at the core. During that Argentina summer, I consumed all the sweet treats: café con leche, cakes filled with dulce de leche, and medialunas. There were also plenty of savory empanadas and several asado feasts. A completely new experience for me was sharing a bombilla, sitting, sipping mate made from yerba leaves. When I think back on those circles we made on the grass, where we were invited in and trusted enough to take part in this intimate gathering, I know that my time in Argentina was made infinitely better by and in the presence of beautiful people who didn't need a team of missionaries to host English clubs as a gateway to sharing "the gospel."

That's right. We led English clubs on various campuses and also at the hotel where we were staying. Big yikes about all of it. At the time though, I thought a summer in Buenos Aires was my ticket to acceptance in a community. It was on this trip that I received small group and one-on-one discipleship from a staff member. During one of our small group Bible studies on the book of Galatians, our leader taught us, a group of young women, that we were made "sons of God." We were told that the language of being sons shouldn't offend us because it was a high honor in the culture in which the Bible was written to be adopted as a son. Though I wasn't necessarily thrilled by the concept, I didn't push back on it either.

Through my private meetings with that staff member, I learned I could stop looking toward boys to feel worthy because I was already righteous before God, in Christ of course. There was no way to empower hurting people to know their worth without tying it back to Jesus. Let's just say, Oliver was not a keeper. Halfway through my trip, we broke up. I learned I didn't have to keep repeating the same patterns of dating guys that wouldn't treat me well and cheating on the guys that did. I wondered how I would ever stop the pattern of self-sabotaging my healthiest romances. This trip became a true turning point for me. It changed my thinking about my relationships and my future. At the age of 18, I was determined that moving forward I would only date men I could see my-self marrying.

Also on this trip, I met Jasmine. We immediately stuck together like glue. A few days after breaking up with Oliver, I wrote out bullet points of "biblical qualities" my future husband (FH) must possess to ensure I didn't date anyone like Oliver again. These were attributes I'd observed in Stephen, and Jasmine could vouch for him because she knew him and his whole family.

The qualities I listed included walking with the Lord, God is his first love, spiritual leader, encourager, humble, Christ-confident (whatever that means), faithful to the Lord and me, hard worker, slow to become angry, defender of the faith, optimistic, and realistic. So deep, I know. I mean, I still agree with some of those, but I don't think they're necessarily biblical and don't think you have to be a Christian to possess the qualities I still admire. After the non-negotiables, I threw in some extra qualities, like physically attractive. Some other extras of note were that he should make me laugh and play frisbee with me. I'm sad to say that him being a good listener, believing in me, and telling me I'm beautiful weren't part of the non-negotiables.

I also wrote a list of qualities I needed to possess because I didn't want my FH to be shortchanged. My list mirrored the FH requirements with the addition of putting others above myself and being respectful. I guess I didn't think I should require my FH to put others above him-self or to be respectful, but that's what the patriarchy does to girls. We're taught to consider everyone else above ourselves, to our own neglect, and to show men respect even if they haven't earned it.

At the end of the trip, my parents picked me up from the airport. Bubbling over with excitement, I relayed the events of the summer. When I notified them of the list I'd compiled of biblical qualities my FH must possess, because I was not going to settle, they were not enthused. They complained about me trying to find a perfect man that doesn't exist. I tried to explain that I wasn't expecting a perfect man, just a man who was striving to exemplify these characteristics. The scowls remained on their faces.

* * * * *

Over the next month after getting back from Argentina, Jasmine and I regularly texted and called each other. After meeting her room-mates, we all decided it would work out for me to move in with them.

My next step was interviewing for a job at Chick-fil-A, and I was hired. It would be a few weeks before I moved in with Jasmine, so I temporarily moved in with my cousin Lily and her husband. I also decided to check in on Stephen. Since he had called me prior to my departure, I wanted to catch him up on my trip and hear about his summer. While on the phone, I mentioned moving in with Jasmine. He asked where. When I told him, "Manchester Apartments, behind the movie theater," he revealed he was also living there. I was ecstatic to have another friend in the city.

The first time I drove to Rock Hill by myself, I was scared and took every back road to ensure I didn't get on any major highways. It worked for a while, until one day, I accidentally got on the interstate. So many cars. Going so fast. But after that, I drove on the interstate again. And then again. Each time, I was less anxious. I thought about my mom not driving outside of the bubble that she's comfortable driving in. Expanding my horizons, I felt accomplished when I drove on the interstate (and I still do). A feeling of empowerment stretched the restrictions I'd inherited from my mom; it was exhilarating. To feel free enough to drive wherever I want to go — wow! I think Miriam Delaney Heard said it best in an interview on my podcast, *Broadening the Narrative*: "A woman who can drive her car anywhere in the continental U.S. of A…that's freedom."[16]

* * * * *

On September 1, 2008, Jasmine and I unpacked boxes in the largest bedroom of a posh apartment. That night, we grilled out. Stephen drove by in his black, hand-me-down Honda Civic. We all waved to get his attention. He came over. The two of us chatted. I took a picture of us, our very first picture together. Stephen and I were completely washed out, but our whole faces were smiling as he wrapped his arm around me to take our selfie. The rest, as they say, is history.

Before Stephen and I began dating, we got to know each other more in the form of informal hangouts at my apartment. There was my 19th birthday a couple of weeks after moving in when my roommate Jasmine made the cutest cupcakes inside of ice cream cones. I had no idea that was even possible, but she made them, and they were delicious. Stephen had already written a happy birthday message on my Facebook wall. My smile couldn't have been any wider as I read the generic greeting. In our recollection of the story, neither of us can remember if I texted to invite him over to eat the ice cream cone cupcakes or if he texted me about swinging by. Either way, he came over, and we had the best time during the dessert portion of my birthday evening.

Things ramped up when Stephen's sister, one of Jasmine's best friends, came to stay with us for a weekend. I made cookies one night, and we managed to eat them all before Stephen arrived. Before heading to bed, I baked another batch. Stephen's sister told him, "I think Nicki likes you," citing the extra cookie baking as evidence.

Stephen responded, "She would do that for anyone. She's just nice."

His sister's rebuttal was, "Yeah, well, she also put on makeup before you came over the other night."

Maybe I did like him after all. Following that exchange, any time I texted Stephen about coming over, he always happily obliged. There was the time took the lid off a soda bottle. (I promise it was on really tight.) Then, there was the time he started tossing pieces of (wrapped) candy at me in a teasing way when we were sitting around the table. I felt playful with him, and I liked that we brought this fun side out of one other. The flirting was everything.

Stephen and I started spending more time together and devising more excuses to see each other. Like when he came into the Chick-fil-A where I worked to order a milkshake. He was on his way home from the church where he was the interim youth pastor. Even though there was a more direct route home that didn't include passing Chick-fil-A, he did because he knew I was working a double. And one of my favorite stomach-flip-flopping-when-seeing-my-crush moments was when I pulled into the apartment complex and caught a glimpse of Stephen. He had been across the street taking a walk around the park and was headed back to his apartment. I stopped to talk with him and told him to climb in because I'd give him a ride the rest of the way. We then talked in my truck for at least an hour. I rode those endorphins for weeks afterwards.

We texted throughout the week, and I would light up each time I saw his name on my phone screen. He was still leading BCM on Mondays, and I was leading Campus Crusade for Christ (Cru) on Thursdays. My work schedule interfered with attending BCM, but Stephen would save extra drinks, unopened bags of chips, and snacks for me to use on Thursdays. This was because I paid for lunch out of my own pocket for Cru. I think Stephen felt badly because I'd unsuccessfully tried to get churches to sponsor lunches for Cru. Each person I spoke to said they were already providing meals for BCM, so they couldn't help me.

As the months sped by, Stephen and I grew closer. I really cared about him but put thoughts about dating him on the back burner. This is because of one night when Stephen had been hanging out with me and my roommates. At one point, Stephen and I started having a side conversation in the living room while everyone else was watching a movie in the nook where the TV was set up. After he left, I was floating. As Jasmine and I lay in our beds talking that night, I fell right off that cloud when she told me she liked Stephen. I didn't want to risk my friendship, as I had during an earlier high school romance. (Side note: whenever I get angry at the lack of communication and the terrible timing in a rom-com, I remind myself of the actual footage like this from my real life.)

Believing that Jasmine was a better person than me, I thought she deserved to be with Stephen. I decided I would be happy for them if they got together. Stuffing down my desires, I continued to be into Stephen but dedicated myself to celibacy so I could "focus on my relationship with the Lord."

* * * * *

Stephen invited the students from the USC-L BCM to the fall retreat for Winthrop's BCM in November. Jasmine and I rode with Stephen. It was on this trip that I met Jake and his wife Caroline. Jake was Stephen's mentor and a pastor who was "planting" a new church in the city where I was living. He was hired for the retreat to lead the large group sessions. During the trip, I felt like an outsider. I didn't know anyone except Jasmine and Stephen. The entire weekend, I went back and forth convincing myself Stephen was totally into me one moment and then completely not the next. He cleared my tray when I was done eating, which made me sit up a little taller, only to slump as I watched him clear every other person's tray, too.

It was confirmation to me that he was just a nice guy who did nice things for literally everyone; there was nothing special about me. The second night of the retreat, I told Jasmine the truth I'd been repressing. I liked Stephen. Her response was basically, "Duh." We talked through it, and she assured me that things were going to be fine between us. The next day, Stephen drove us back to our apartment. A couple of hours later, he texted to ask if I had some time to talk.

My heart fluttered on November 8th when we sat across from one another at the Joe Muggs inside Books-A-Million. We took turns flicking a football Stephen constructed from a paper napkin. He told me the words I'd been longing to hear followed by words I was not stoked to hear. He rambled on and on, "You have a beautiful heart, love people well, serve with joy, and there are so many other qualities I admire in you, not that you aren't beautiful on the outside, too, because you are, and um, I really like you, but I don't know if you even like me, so all of this could be really awkward." This was music to my ears. I reciprocated all of his feelings, but then he reluctantly explained a hurdle.

Since he was on staff with BCM on the campus where I was a student, he was unable to "pursue" me. Further, because it was difficult for him to be around me and not be able to advance a relationship with me, he thought it would be best to stop texting and take some time apart. I didn't know what to say. If you know me, you know how rare that is. We took a walk and prayed. He drove me back to my apartment. I didn't see him or hear from him for about a week. It felt like a thousand days. In that time, worry crept in that Stephen didn't actually like me. The creeping became all-consuming. Finally, I broke down and called him.

The butterflies were in my throat when he answered his phone. We then talked for three hours about every topic we could think of that night. When I tentatively spewed out the reason for my call (the whole "do you even like me or are you just saying that so I don't feel bad" bit), Stephen assured me that he did like me. However, he didn't want me to feel like I had to wait until May, when I was no longer a student at USC-L, to date him. If someone else came along, he thought I should go for it. I promptly told him that would not be happening.

He told me that Caroline, Jake's wife, had asked him if he'd thought about me as a prospective girlfriend. She was delighted when he filled her in on how he'd declared his "like" for me at the conclusion of the fall retreat. Though we were already one step ahead of Jake and Caroline, it helped to know we had some people in our corner who were supportive of us dating.

A week later, my parents were coming to my apartment for dinner on my dad's birthday. I'd made chili cheese and fries, a meal I'd loved growing up. It's literally just chopped up hot dogs in chili spread over fries and topped with cheese. I wasn't much of a chef in those days (or in these days). Stephen was at a wedding, but he stopped by afterwards to meet my parents. Jake was persistent that Stephen should use that night to ask permission to date me. Stephen didn't think the timing was right. He kept the conversation light so we could just enjoy celebrating my dad's birthday.

The following Wednesday, Stephen drove me home for Thanksgiving and decided he would talk with my parents then. He intended to talk to *both* my parents. However, my mom prodded me out of the living room and toward the kitchen where we just listened from the next room. Stephen requested permission to date me. It caught my dad off guard because it was unprecedented, but he said yes. I assumed we would begin dating that night. I assumed wrong.

I want to interrupt this program to bring you a special segment about the whole idea of "permission." The very notion of me needing to have permission from my father to date someone, especially since I was over 18, enforces the patriarchy. What I desire and want out of a relationship, as well as my autonomy and agency over my life, were not valued. They weren't even considered in the conversation. These themes will resurface throughout the retelling of our dating, engagement, and marriage stories, but I wanted to hit them on the head while I held the hammer. Now, the regular broadcasting will resume.

Stephen and I still weren't dating yet when he invited me to attend a pre-launch service for Jake's church, Entrench. Stephen told me it would be a good way to meet more people in the area. Once Stephen and I found some seats inside, I was moved to full-body praise by Entrench's hipster worship team of talented and attractive people. The church was different from anything I'd experienced. I wanted to be a part of whatever God was going to do through Entrench.

As I prepared to date Stephen, I thought I was getting a chance at love done the "right way" after sabotaging healthy relationships. At dinner on December 5th, I told Stephen about the things I'd done that led to failed relationships. He also shared some of his own failures. We accepted each other despite our serious secrets.

After dinner, Stephen and I went for a walk at a park. The last topic he wanted to broach with me was about marriage. He explained that he didn't want to date just to date me. No, he wanted to date with the intention of moving toward marriage. If I didn't want that, because I was only 19, he completely understood. In hindsight, I wish I could tell younger me to date and have fun, that there's no rush, and that 19 is too young to be thinking about becoming a wife.

Instead, I agreed that moving toward marriage was what I wanted, too. Because of purity culture and the whole movement bolstered by the book *I Kissed Dating Goodbye*, I thought marriage was the next logical step. Stephen and I made our way to one of the covered shelters. Sitting on the edge of my seat at a chilly metal picnic table, Stephen asked me to be his girlfriend. It was official. Stephen was my boyfriend.

We pretty quickly discussed boundaries we wanted to put in place to "protect" each other and ourselves in our relationship. (When I say "pretty quickly," I mean the night we started dating.) I was hoping that the boundaries would be a way to guard my own heart to mitigate pain if things didn't work out between us (as if rules somehow sever us from emotions). In previous relationships, I'd fallen so far so fast, and I wanted to "protect my heart." I also knew that these types of boundaries for relationships were popular within the purity culture movement, so I wanted to demonstrate my dedication to upholding the system. It was like I was playing a part in an effort to be what Stephen would find more attractive.

The first dating boundary on our list was that we wouldn't kiss until our wedding day, if we married one another. My past relationships made it easy to agree to this one. Stephen and I also established a 12:00 curfew because "nothing good happens after midnight." Not being alone together went on there. Even with my roommates in the apartment, we were too "tempted" to kiss if they weren't in the same room with us. Not being alone with someone of the opposite sex was another very simplistic rule that set up a false gender binary. I was insecure, which meant no women friends for Stephen, at least not genuine, authentic friendships. Jake and Caroline endorsed this one, stating Stephen should avoid even talking to other women if I felt insecure about it. The last boundary was that we wouldn't say "I love you" to one another until we were engaged. I'd thrown around "I love you" before and wanted to say it within a more committed relationship the next time I said it.

We signed and dated our pact. Instead of asking, "How close can we get to the line?" we thought we were so holy asking the question, "How much can we glorify God?" Whew, relationships entrenched in purity culture, am I right?

THOUGHTS FROM STEPHEN

My second year leading BCM at USC-L, Nicki came into the first Bible study that semester. She jokes about how when I saw her, I was breathless as a bright light shone down and the "Hallelujah" chorus from Handel's *Messiah* played. That's not entirely accurate. Actually, it's not even a little accurate. I did think she was friendly and vivacious. We had a few conversations here and there but nothing of deep substance. I do remember the conversation that had me thinking Nicki was a little obsessed with boys.

It was the winter conference for BCM, the one where I walked up while she was saying, "Our leader sucks." (Insert awkward turtle here.) I had no idea why she was saying that, and felt offended, but just moved on. For the next half hour at the hotel lobby computers, Nicki talked about boys. She tried to rope me into the drama, but I declined the invitation to get involved.

Aside from that instance, I did enjoy being around her. She was full of energy, passionate about her relationship with God, and easy to talk to. At that point, I definitely wasn't romantically interested in her. I wouldn't have said we were friends either, not because I wasn't friends with girls, but just because we were only around each other on Mondays when I was on campus.

When I found out Nicki was going to Argentina on a mission trip with Cru, I gave her a call. I just wanted to let her know I'd be praying for her while she was gone. A couple months later, I was on a retreat with the youth from the church where I interned. Nicki gave me a call and left a voicemail about how she was back from Buenos Aires. After I settled back at home, I returned her call. We had a meaningful conversation, and I could sense a difference in her, a shift in how she talked about God. This interaction marked a turning point for us.

There was something about her energy that drew me in, and I was more and more impressed with every conversation we had and how "far" she'd come spiritually. She was no longer the girl who was consumed with talking about boys. She was more serious about her commitment to Christ, and I was starting to like her. But there was one major obstacle standing in the way. I knew we couldn't be together because of my position as the BCM leader at USC-L. I told my roommate Will about my feelings for Nicki but that I knew I couldn't act on them and needed to keep my distance from her. I asked him to hold me accountable for this. However, the next week, I entered the apartment late. He asked where I'd been. I told him I'd been hanging out at Nicki's apartment. I didn't tell him we were the last ones awake, alone together with the tension building between us, but I didn't need to. With the information he had, he shook his head. This was quite a source of contention with Will, one of my best friends at the time.

Finally, one November evening at Joe Muggs, I let Nicki know that I liked her. (This was after stalling as long as possible until they announced they'd be closing in 10 minutes.) Then, I told her I thought we should quit communicating throughout the week because we couldn't pursue a relationship at the time. Will was appeased and there for me until a week later when I came in from a three hour phone call with Nicki. He'd had enough and lost it with me. This led to a point of decision. I decided to take a chance and called the state BCM director to get his advice. After I explained the situation, the director said he trusted me and suggested I talk to Nicki's parents. He thought I should get their permission because of the age difference between us. This was not a problem because I had already resolved in my heart that the next person I dated, I would ask her parents' permission. I didn't want to be in another relationship with someone whose parents weren't supportive, as I'd experienced previously.

* * * * *

A couple weeks later, I met Nicki's parents for the first time at her apartment when she had them over for her dad's birthday. I was intimidated by her dad, to say the least, and I didn't think his birthday dinner was the appropriate moment to bring up wanting to date Nicki. I waited about a week until I took Nicki to her parents' house the Wednesday before Thanksgiving. Though I wanted to talk to both her parents, her mom, sensing why I was there, left the room and took Nicki with her.

Feeling nervous with sweaty armpits, I spoke with Nicki's dad about why I was there. I told him how much I liked her and that I wanted to ask his permission to date her. I shared that my goal was to move toward marriage and not to date willy-nilly. My intentions were to honor her and them in the way I dated her. He gave his blessing by saying something to the effect of, "Well, you seem like a decent guy." I guess the bar was pretty low. After that awkward conversation, I took Nicki to her grandmother's house because that's where she was staying for the night.

Before leaving, I put my hand up to give Nicki my trademark salutation (well, my trademark for saying goodbye to girls and women). That's right, instead of asking Nicki to be my girlfriend or giving her a hug, I gave her a high five. You may be wondering why I would do that. There are a couple of reasons. I acted cautiously to try to guard my heart from getting too far ahead. I didn't want to engage in what I was taught was a romantic gesture or lead Nicki on by nonverbally communicating something more serious before we were officially dating.

I also didn't trust myself to hug her and "open the door" to more. Yes, I thought a hug was that serious. Thanks to purity culture, I didn't want to get into a mindset of letting myself be receptive to a romantic relationship if it wasn't going to work out. As a guy, if I did hug a girl, it had to be a "Christian side hug," which even has a whole song written about it. Plus, with my previous girlfriends, I'd come on strong and was dedicated. After a tough breakup, I became defensive and put my guard up even more. I'm still working through how much of my detachment was me just trying to protect myself from being hurt again.

That night, I drove to my parents' house. They asked where I'd been, and I told them I'd dropped off a friend. During the course of our conversation, I asked them, "Is six years too much of an age difference to date someone?" They excitedly answered, "No!" They thought I was asking because of a woman who was six years older than me that they were trying to set me up with. Crushing their excitement, I told them it was because Nicki was six years younger than me. They cautioned me about dating someone so young. I'd taken my previous breakups hard, and my parents didn't want to see me hurt again if Nicki broke up with me.

In December, a week after Thanksgiving, I officially asked Nicki to be my girlfriend. From there, I told my friends about her. One friend laughed after I described her and commented, "Dude, you talk about her like she's 19."

"She is," was all I could muster as I avoided eye contact, feeling embarrassed about the age difference. When it was time for her to meet my friends, I was a little apprehensive, but they loved her. She jumped right in and got along with all of them. She even put on a performance for them in her cowgirl boots and three pairs of mismatched earrings. Admittedly, I was a bit embarrassed by her performance, but we were all too busy laughing for it to distract me from a good time.

A few weeks after Stephen and I began dating, he invited me to meet his family and celebrate his birthday with them. I felt right at home from the very beginning. Joy was the undercurrent of each interaction between people who I could tell genuinely enjoyed being together. Then, to ring in the new year, Stephen and I took a trip to Atlanta so I could meet his brother and sister-in-law who weren't there when I met the rest of his family. When they went to bed on New Year's Eve, Stephen and I stayed awake. That night, we broke our first date pact and kissed. We weren't as disciplined as we wanted everyone to think we were.

Then, it was time for Stephen to meet my extended family. He braved Sunday lunch at Grandma's after church about one month in. Grandma didn't seem to think this relationship would stick. One of the first sentences out of her mouth to Stephen was, "Nicki changes guys like she changes underwear." I rolled my eyes from the next room and became determined then and there to prove her wrong. While this may have been true in the past, Stephen was different. He believed the best about me, so I believed the best about me. I wasn't going to fall back into my old patterns. Not this time. I couldn't risk losing him.

Stephen was such a thoughtful person. He would write me letters, sometimes just because and sometimes when he was going to be out of town for some reason. There was one time when I went out of the country for a week on a mission trip. He wrote me one letter to open for each day I was going to be gone. Stephen was also funny. He came up with nicknames for each of us. He wanted to be called Henry and Vern. He called me Vernette and Minnie, as a play off my first name: Minyon. I laughed with him pretty much all the time, except when he was late to pick me up for one of our earlier dates. Punctuality matters to me.

With my busy school and work schedule, Stephen and I got creative about spending time together. On Mondays, I was awake bright and early at 5:00 to get to Chick-fil-A for opening at 5:45. I worked until 4:00 in the afternoon. Then, I had an evening class from 5:00-8:00 at USC-L. Before leaving Chick-fil-A, I'd get a small coffee, add ice cream, a little sugar, and flavored creamer. Stephen and I would get about 15 minutes together before my class. One of my favorite memories is when he tried my coffee. After the first sip, he grimaced. I was surprised when he reached out for a second sip, but he didn't want any more after that. "It has a *terrible* taste but great aftertaste that tricks you into coming back for more," Stephen remarked. With all his germ-consciousness, he must have had it really bad for me to share a drink. Not only did he share a drink with me, but on our first Valentine's Day, I was sick. He still came over, and we watched *Enchanted.*

With Stephen, I stood with arms high and heart abandoned to embrace Hillsong United, reformed theology, and complementarianism. I kept cheering for Clemson, though, in direct opposition to his love for the Carolina Gamecocks. Before we started dating, there was a playful lightheartedness between us. We were fun, flirty, and thriving; however, there was an expectation that dating lead to marriage lest the dating be a waste of time. As a result, you don't want to be too playful with someone and open your heart to them if that's not who you're going to marry. This could be akin to emotional cheating on your future spouse (such illogical logic). All this gradually and naturally stifled the playfulness in our relationship and replaced it with such a serious vibe.

The general feeling was that Stephen and I needed to get married. And quickly. Jake didn't support a lengthy engagement, and his opinion was held in high regard by us both. When it came to my family, Jake's oft-repeated advice was for me to leave and cleave. It was easy advice to implement. I was just waiting on Stephen to propose.

Chapter 4
What Would Our Marriage Be Like?

Stephen and I were happy, most of the time, but our relationship was far from easy-breezy. A repeated source of conflict for us was other women. From my vantage point, it seemed like Stephen was often openly flirting with other girls in front of me. For example, there was that time at Chick-fil-A when my roommate (and co-worker) Jasmine walked by with the mop bucket to go clean the bathroom. Stephen and I were eating at a booth. As Jasmine went past us pushing the cleaning supplies, Stephen pretended to trip her. They shared a big laugh about it. I, however, didn't even smile. To make matters worse, I couldn't escape detrimental teachings about women.

During a breakout session at my second BCM conference, seeds of doubt were further sown about my ability to trust myself and other women. The pastor preached that we could not fight sexual temptation. According to him, we were incapable of it and needed to look only at David, a man after God's own heart, to realize that. The pastor derided Bathsheba for bathing on a rooftop (but not the king who sent for her and used his powerful position to rape her).

The way that pastor portrayed Bathsheba confirmed the stereotype of the Jezebel who would seduce a man to his ruin, even though it was an inaccurate portrayal. The uneasiness in me resolved as I reminded myself that the pastor was ordained and gifted by God to correctly interpret the passages and teach us well. After all, he had started a church that had grown quickly, so he must've had God's blessing. In addition, I reminded myself that I'd been that temptress before, and I'd been unfaithful by cheating on guys in relationships.

Also on that trip, one of the students from USC-L was at a table between sessions snacking with me, Stephen, and some other students. Stephen began throwing candy at her, which is something he'd done to me before we were dating. All I could think was, "Hey, that was *our* thing." Storming off, I went to my hotel room. Stephen tried calling, but I refused to answer. He then came to my room, but I wouldn't let him in. It's sad that back then I couldn't appreciate his playful personality when it was directed toward other women.

Another source of conflict for us was that I felt like our relationship was uneven. I was convinced I was more into him than he was into me. When Stephen had gone to Boston for a mission trip with BCM, one of the managers at Chick-fil-A acted inappropriately toward me. The manager asked me, "Where's Sebastiano?" Sebastiano is the name he used for Stephen.

When I explained that Stephen was out of town, the manager replied, "When's Sebastiano going to marry you?"

Shrugging, I said, "I don't know."

"Well, he better hurry up and marry you because if he doesn't, I will. I'm gonna run a Chick-fil-A of my own, so you'll get all the free chicken you want as my wife."

I told Stephen about this during lunch the day after he got back. Instead of being concerned that the manager was trying to make a move on me, Stephen nonchalantly replied, "If you want to break up and be with him, I understand. It would be sad, but I'd be okay. We'd both be okay because we'd still have Jesus."

That was not what I was hoping to hear. Another fight ensued.

"If we fight this much and we're not married, what would our marriage be like?" Stephen wondered aloud. I thought he was about to break up with me. To help us navigate this conflict, we went to talk with Jake and Caroline. Jake told Stephen that I needed to feel like he wanted to be with me. He agreed with Stephen that even though we would "be okay" without each other, the better message for me to hear would be that he *didn't want* to be without me. Jake also reminded me that Stephen had put up a wall after being hurt in prior relationships and asked, "Can you be with him even if he's never able to love you like you want?"

I said, "Yes, because I love him," even though we weren't telling each other I love you, per the boundaries we'd established. Maybe it's my unhealthy attachment style, but his slowness to commit to me didn't stop me from going all in on him. However, I was constantly worried that I would mess things up between us.

* * * * *

Beginning when Stephen and I were dating and continuing through our engagement, we met together weekly for book studies and Bible studies. We both proudly identified as complementarians, though for the most part it was in name only. I still wanted Stephen to lead me, though, as soon as we started dating. For starters, I was conditioned to think I needed a man to lead me. Plus, the complementarian theology I was being taught at Entrench Church specifically stated that men were supposed to be leaders. Further, I wanted to show Stephen how skilled I would be at submitting. Yikes! During our first book study conversation, I asked Stephen to take the reins and plan our weekly sessions. I was trying to make him not be so "passive," though he's just a more passive guy, and there's absolutely nothing wrong with that. At the time, though, I thought there was everything wrong with that.

Though I wanted Stephen to lead me, I had ideas about the direction in which he should be leading. The environment around me revered missionaries, so I wanted to marry a missionary and be a missionary family together. Again, I didn't realize how much white-saviorism was baked into this desire. I was nervous that I would be perceived as trying to lead us, which was Stephen's responsibility, but I figured that the seemingly altruistic end justified the means. I took it so far as to go down to the front to commit to being a missionary during that second BCM conference. Stephen was concerned that our desires didn't align since he didn't feel "called" to be a missionary. We decided to pray about it, and praying is something we did together constantly.

In the summer of 2009, Stephen baptized me. I credited him with so much of my spiritual growth up to that point. When I'd asked if he could be the one to baptize me, Jake said yes. My baptism wasn't fueled by a fear of hell as it had been when I was a child. Rather, it was a public recommitment to live like the new creation I was in Christ. There's a video of me sharing my testimony on Facebook, but I started cringing and couldn't press play. I'm sure I wouldn't agree with most of what I said and can't bring myself to watch it. I'd invited my parents to my baptism, but they didn't come. When I felt like my parents weren't there for me, Stephen and the people of Entrench were.

* * * * *

Meeting Stephen is what led me to attend Entrench, where I encountered *a lot* more complementarian instruction. Entrench is affiliated with the Acts 29 church planting network and the Southern

Baptist Convention. Stephen deeply trusted the pastor, Jake, and Jake's wife, Caroline. We quickly became close knit.

In addition to Stephen's relationship with Jake and Caroline, I trusted them both simply because Jake was a pastor. I'd been conditioned to trust pastors by nature of them inhabiting that role in our society, as if "pastor" is synonymous with trustworthy. I'd not had any bad experiences with the pastors I grew up learning from. Also, I trusted them because they made time for us, seemed to enjoy counseling us through the tough times, and were there to celebrate the good times. They were, for all intents and purposes, replacing my family, and I soon began to value their opinions over anyone else's. In some ways, as my grandma insisted the church was a cult, I reacted by burrowing even deeper into the church. There was a part of me that wanted to show my family that I had a support system that knew the worst about me and accepted me without making me feel like a burden.

When Jake launched Entrench, I eagerly started attending, serving, and getting connected. I felt like the knowledge I was gaining was filling in spiritual gaps. The first step for me to become fully entrenched under Jake's leadership was to consume the white male pastors he quoted, both dead and alive. Complementarianism is a non-negotiable cornerstone for Jake and his "he-ologians." I don't think I'd even heard the word "complementarian" until Jake preached about it. At Entrench, the verses that seem to plainly state this one-way submission were held tightly.

Oddly enough, I was leading Cru at USC-L when I started attending Entrench. Just like when I tried to organize family devotions as a passionate new convert, I was still a vocal leader. I loved hosting times of prayer, creating space for people to share their testimonies, and teaching theology to a room of college students (even though women teaching men is not simply frowned upon but considered sinful in the complementarian camp). Within a year, I harbored disdain for women pastors and judged the churches they pastored (and I was more self-conscious when I prayed aloud, even if it was just with Stephen).

Entrench was so different from the church I grew up going to. There was the hipster worship team I mentioned, but there was also prayer for other local churches and a focus on "unreached people groups." A major additional difference was there was no flag to pledge allegiance to on the stage and no special services in honor of the United States in any capacity.

After I finished my first two years of college at USC-L, I

moved an hour south to Columbia to attend classes at the USC main campus. My social anxiety was through the roof when I realized how big USC was while locating each building the day before classes started. Struggling to find where I belonged at school, Stephen suggested I check out the BCM at USC. There was one night at BCM when my misbelief in the mischaracterization of women as temptresses was further confirmed. The pastor preached from Proverbs 7. He taught that the young man in the passage was simply lacking sense when he crossed the street near the house of a woman. The woman begged the young man to come into her home for some lovemaking while her husband was gone. The young man couldn't control himself and followed her, joining the countless victims the woman led astray before him.

The takeaway was to not even get near temptation. I knew that was a warning for the men to avoid any woman deemed dangerous, which was most of us. The few who were considered safe for men were quiet, dressed modestly, and tirelessly served their churches and parachurch ministries with a smile on their faces. Men still shouldn't be alone with those women, of course, and if they were alone and something happened, it would still be the woman's fault. In that patriarchal Christian context, women were an easy scapegoat to blame for the "ruin" of any "misguided" young man. The men in these scenarios were portrayed as victims of women's wily ways.

While living in Columbia, I still drove an hour and a half back to Rock Hill each weekend and stayed with some friends so I could attend Sunday services at Entrench. Going to Entrench is what let me know that so much of what happened to me in childhood wasn't normal. At Entrench, I was encouraged to be vulnerable with my church family. The only thing that would gain me more acceptance in the community would be changing my marital status, which I was trying to do at the age of 19.

$$* * * * *$$

At Entrench, marriage was the norm, and the younger you got married the better it seemed. Stephen and I had been discussing marriage throughout our relationship. Jake insisted that marrying young and having a short engagement was the only way to live a pure life without being consumed with lust for one another. (A quick timeout to add that if "burning with lust" is the driving force behind a marriage, that's just not a good enough reason to tie the knot. Further, if a Christian man is primarily interested in marrying because he thinks that will quell what he believes is an unholy desire, and then he thinks he is entitled to sex whenever he wants it, he needs to seek professional help and is not ready to be married. Time in.) Stephen and I had been dating for seven months in July when I began to grow impatient and wonder if he didn't want to get married. Our friends in the church were getting married and people, including Jake and Caroline, continually questioned us about when we'd be getting engaged.

I thought marrying Stephen was the answer to all my woes. If he proposed, it would show he was seriously committed to me and not going anywhere, a stability I longed for — to know I couldn't be left alone, abandoned, discarded.

Stephen candidly told me one night that he *did* want to marry me, but he felt a lot of pressure coming from others, including me. He also wanted to attend seminary in the fall of 2009 and was trying to figure out a plan. We prayed. We anticipated and discussed many scenarios. We also sought counsel from Jake and Caroline, as was our way through any challenging situation. Stephen knew that if he was going to enroll in seminary, he had to finalize his area of study, financial aid, and class selection. He also knew that if he decided to go to seminary, hundreds of miles would separate us.

To my amazement, Stephen decided to stay with the intention of marrying in the near future. There were two main problems, though. His internship concluded, so he was without a job. Also, his lease had ended, so he was without a place to live. He needed a job to secure a place to live, and he needed a place to live to apply for a job. Within two weeks, he had a part-time maintenance job at a church. He house-sat and couch-surfed for about a month. Then, with the help of a friend, he was able to find an apartment he could afford. A few weeks later, he spoke with Peter, a business owner at Entrench who was hiring for a full-time bookkeeper position at his company. He was aware of Stephen's math degree and integrity, so he offered him the job.

When September rolled around, Stephen and I had been dating nine months. Without my knowledge, he drove an hour from Rock Hill to Liberty Hill. The objective of his trip was to ask for permission from my dad to marry me. My dad responded, "Well not anytime soon, I hope."

Stephen said, "We were thinking December, but we could wait until the end of the school year."

Throwing out December first made May sound better. Instead

of just giving a straightforward answer, my father mandated that Stephen speak with my grandma.

Following the conversation with Grandma, Stephen and I went back to my dad. From there, an obstacle course was erected that included multiple conversations with other family members for various reasons. When I completed my dad's checklist, Stephen coordinated what would be the perfect proposal. He obtained his great-grandmother's one carat diamond engagement ring with a gold band from his mom and had it put in a sterling silver setting. Five days before his planned proposal date, he wrote a song with the words he thought best encapsulated how he wanted to love me, his future bride, and point me to Christ, because he thought that was the role he was called to occupy in my life. The day before he proposed, he recorded the song, guitar and all, at Jake and Caroline's house. Then, he burned it on a CD. He wanted to record the song instead of performing it live so that when he proposed in the song, he could kneel in front of me with the ring. So romantic.

It was Friday, October 2, 2009, and Stephen had a friend distract me so he could cook dinner and prepare his apartment. Unlocking the door, my senses were overloaded by the mingling of lasagna, garlic bread, and Italian salad dressing. Looking around, I also noticed several lit candles that added cinnamon, vanilla, and pumpkin spice to the mix. It was at that moment Stephen informed me that instead of dining out at Olive Garden, he had flexed his culinary muscles to bring Olive Garden to the comfort of his second-story apartment. He led me to the plaid checkered couch from my old place. Grabbing his computer, he told me about a song he'd heard that made him think of me. When the song started, I told him it sounded like him singing. Stephen didn't confirm or deny. He just replied, "Really?"

The singer of this enthralling melody referenced Proverbs 31, Song of Songs, and Ephesians 5 as he sang about a beautiful woman. Toward the end of the song, I heard, "Nicki, I love you. Will you marry me?" A few measures of instrumental music allowed time for me to answer the question, but I didn't. Still confused, my mind was racing as I questioned how the person singing knew my name. Then, I looked down to see Stephen kneeling in front of me with a ring in his hand. Through a smile, I cried a little as I nodded before finally saying, "Yes! A thousand times, yes!" like Jane Bennet in the 2005 version of *Pride and Prejudice*. Stephen tenderly slipped the ring on my finger.

Stephen had me come to the table where he pulled a chair out for me as he bowed. "I would be honored to serve you tonight." That's when I noticed his attire: a white dress shirt with black pants. He gave me a red rose, symbolic of love, to commemorate saying, "I love you" for the very first time. Between bites of the Italian cuisine Stephen had prepared, I stared at my ring and pinched myself to make sure it wasn't all a dream. Our celebration was interrupted when I informed my parents of our engagement. Apparently, the manner in which I completed the to-do list from my father wasn't satisfactory. He made his disapproval known.

My mom apologized and said, "You know how your Daddy is. I'm happy for you."

Nothing my mom said could mend what had been broken. In the immediate aftermath, Stephen and I went to celebrate with Jake and Caroline. Then, the countdown to our wedding was on.

$$* * * * *$$

During our premarital counseling with Jake, Stephen and I heard over and over again that marriage is primarily about our holiness, not our happiness. That phrase was the tagline of one of the books we were assigned to read. The books we had to read emphasized that Stephen and I would be entering a covenant in marriage, not a contract. In a covenant, we were expected to honor the vows we made and not divorce, no matter what. This is such a dangerous ideology to instruct people in without leaving room for nuance or caveats.

We also had to listen to a podcast episode from one of the white male pastors Jake revered. The episode was about birth control. The pastor argued that Christians should not use any type of birth control that acts as an abortifacient. When Stephen and I discussed the episode with Jake and Caroline, we asked what we could do to protect ourselves from conceiving too early in our marriage. The counting method was endorsed as an acceptable solution, so what did we implement? If you guessed the counting method, you're really good at this.

Another topic we discussed was effective communication, an area I was not particularly skilled in. To illustrate how unskilled I was in the communications department, let me tell you about how I almost self-sabotaged my engagement a month and a half before the wedding. Self-sabotaging relationships was my practiced pattern in prior relationships. In the middle of a minor dispute, that neither Stephen nor I can remember, I defiantly declared that Stephen and I should cancel the wedding and break up. Stephen knew me well enough to understand I was trying to protect myself by running. He assured me in his signature steadiness that he loved me and would not be calling off our nuptials. We plowed ahead.

Stephen was my safest place. A byproduct of having him in my life meant my body could relax. I could shed some of the self-protective coping mechanisms I'd developed and perfected. I wouldn't always need that self-protectiveness. As Pastor Emmy Kegler explains, "Coping mechanisms that served me well, even saved me, five years ago may suffocate me now."[17] On my wedding day, though, I absolutely needed my self-protective coping mechanism. Stephen's steadiness calmed the turbulent sea of emotions in me.

It was rare for me not to operate as programmed by the patriarchy. My most obvious resistance to my father's power over me was simply making the decision to go through with my wedding. We were standing in front of the doors that hadn't yet been opened for my grand entrance. He said, "There's still time to make a run for it," and he was completely serious. He didn't want to "give me away." Also, big yikes about that language. I'm not an object to be given away. I would have walked myself to the altar if he couldn't get his act together.

Taking my place at the front of the church, I held Stephen's hands as Jake tenderly smiled at us. "Welcome to your wedding," he offered. Chuckles scattered through the crowd. "Today is about you. Mostly. Primarily, it's about God's glory." To ensure the day was about God's glory, we'd asked Jake to really hammer home the complementarian gender roles Stephen and I needed to fulfill as husband and wife. He happily did as he taught from Ephesians 5 about wives submitting to their husbands and husbands loving their wives. We recited our vows, which we'd written ourselves. Don't worry, we reiterated our devotion to complementarian theology, for God's glory. Sarcasm aside, my most treasured memory from that day was pouring our unity sand as an updated version of the song Stephen wrote floated through the sanctuary.

The reason I loved the unity sand portion of the ceremony so much was because we were affirming two things. One, the thick layer of sand on the bottom symbolized Jesus, confirming that Jesus was the stable foundation we were building our marriage upon. As we poured our individual colors, mini mountains alternating blue and brown stacked one on top of the other. My blue sand could not be easily separated from Stephen's brown sand. It was a visual illustration of two becoming one. Enmeshment was fostered by the "two become one" rhetoric that was often emphasized by Jake in our counseling sessions, in his sermons, and on our wedding day. Of course I didn't know the dangers of enmeshment at the time. And for someone who feared abandonment, the promise that two would become one and nothing could ever separate them brought a feeling of security to me.

* * * * *

When Stephen and I returned to our (now shared) apartment following our honeymoon, we settled into married life. We got to really put into practice the patriarchy we'd had preached to us (and that we'd been preaching to anyone who would listen). We were no longer going to be complementarian in name only. As the representative of the Bride of Christ, I was determined to be the glowing image of submissive perfection. The "secular" patriarchy of my childhood shook hands with the "spiritual" patriarchy I encountered at Entrench. They weren't meeting for the first time because the two sides of the same patriarchal coin knew each other well.

Before marrying me, Stephen made himself microwave quesadillas. After marrying me, I made his quesadillas and used the toaster oven instead. JK. But, I did take over dinner duty, and I stressed myself to have it on the table as soon as he got home from work every night, just as I'd seen my mom do. Dinner on the table by 5:00 p.m. before my dad got home had always been the expectation. Following in my mom's footsteps, I made Stephen's plate and put it at his spot by 5:15, the time when he should arrive home if he left work by a little after 5:00. Rarely was he home by 5:15, so his dinner was often cold, and by the time he got home, I was pretty heated. But I swallowed my resentment and played the part of the perfect partner. Well, not partner per se, at least not in the "we're in this together and actually equal" way. He was the head, after all, and I was the helper.

Stephen's role in our marriage was framed as "servant leadership," which is part of the "soft/benevolent patriarchy" rebranding that happened because of the bad reputation the language of "male headship" had gotten. According to the sermons Jake preached at Entrench, and the sermons we listened to from other pastors who had Jake's stamp of approval, Stephen's life was to be one of sacrifice and service to me and me to him. However, his sacrifice and service were representative of Christ's love for the Church, and my sacrifice and service were representative of the respect the Bride of Christ, the Church, has for her husband Jesus.

At Entrench, at least once a year, usually in a series but sometimes as stand-alone sermons, Jake taught about marriage. He stated each time that healthy marriages make a healthy church. Back in the beginning, I wasn't even asking where my single friends fit in with this mantra. Jake's hour-long orations on the gift of marriage resulted in this immense pressure for me to think about how to be a better wife by becoming better at submitting.

When preaching about marriage, Jake framed true submission for wives as joyful and willing, a gentle spirit, and respect for your husband's authority. Careful to not be accused of teaching idolatry, Jake made sure to state that submission did not mean that a wife's husband took the place of Jesus or that she needed to give up independent thoughts. While I appreciated this sentiment, to truly accomplish what I was being told was another story. If God called me to respect Stephen as the authority in all matters, ultimately my opinions were insignificant. Privately, I was explicitly told that the final decision was in his hands, and I must joyfully and willingly submit to his headship even if he made a foolish decision. Stephen is compassionate, patient, wise, frugal, and faithful. In many ways, it wasn't difficult to submit to him, but when it was, *I* was the problem.

Over time, my insecurities around other women increased. I was suspicious of myself and my motives as well as of other women and their motives. Like a dutiful pupil under the tutelage of Jake and those he appointed, I learned to scoff at feminism, judge women according to the standards I was inheriting, and lean on Stephen, Jake, and older women to guide me into truth. The complementarian teaching was just an introduction.

Stephen and I were all in on complementarianism and wanted others to be all in, too. It was working for us, after all, because Stephen was easy to submit to, and we hadn't faced any real adversity yet. Everything was picture perfect, or as close it could be. The foundation of our marriage was unshakeable.

Until disaster struck.

* * * * *

It was Thursday, September 16, 2010, the day before my 21st birthday. Leaving Winthrop's West Center after an intense session on the treadmill, I was still wearing my workout clothes as I neared Deerfield Run apartments. Sirens blared from the fire engine turning in ahead of me. Smoke billowed from a building in our complex. I sent up a silent prayer that everyone had gotten out safely. Things quickly got personal when I realized the blaze was coming from our building and, more specifically, our exact apartment. I screeched into a parking spot. I couldn't see if Stephen was at home. Fumbling for my phone, I called him.

No answer.

Pounding eardrums. Clammy hands. Escalated breathing. Tight chest. In the middle of a panic attack, I pressed the next name that flashed in my mind. Margaret. She's married to Peter, Stephen's boss at the time. "Is Stephen there? I tried calling him and couldn't get a hold of him," my distraught hysteria translated as laughter to Margaret.

She responded, "What? I can't make out what you're saying."

After a few deep breaths, followed by the most measured reply I could muster, she understood the assignment. She contacted Peter, who sent Stephen home. While waiting, I collapsed against the car. Someone passed me a bottle of water. Garbled speech surrounded me. Time was waxing and waning. Nothing made sense. As Stephen rounded the corner, I ran to him and sobbed into his only remaining shirt. Peter was right behind him, on the phone with Jake. Some friends from Entrench joined Peter to circle up around us. Peter cupped Stephen's shoulder and said, "Y'all are coming home with me. We're going to take care of you. Everything's gonna be alright."

It was Stephen's turn to fold into me and speckle *my* only remaining shirt with tears.

At Peter and Margaret's house, Stephen declared the sovereignty of God as our hope. God's sovereignty was a new concept to me. It felt cruel to invoke the sovereignty of God to suggest that all the suffering I experienced, the suffering we were currently experiencing, was not only known by God but ordained by God. Stephen was the most devoted poster child to this doctrine as he praised God during this trial and tribulation where we were being "tested by fire." Jake elevated Stephen for his steadfastness. There was no room for my lament. The theology didn't allow it.

The next day, Stephen and I went to the site and dug through the rubble. Jake accompanied us and moved charred beams and debris as we searched for anything salvageable. Since the fire originated outside, the rooms along that wall were completely destroyed. The kitchen was further in, so we inspected it first. Popping the microwave open,

Stephen revealed the cake he'd baked for me the day before. In the guest room, there were curled remnants of the paper that Stephen had used to wrap my presents.

Happy birthday to me.

A few friends came over. Together we packed cardboard boxes with the items worth saving. One of the few books that wasn't incinerated was by a pastor we adored back then. It was a book about fighting for joy when you don't desire God. Jake held it up for us to see. We made sure to slide it into a box. We also grabbed what was left of our unity sand from the top of the hutch in the kitchen. The top was off, and some water from the hoses must have gotten inside because the sand was compacted. We took that packed-down sand as proof that our foundation on Jesus and our "oneness" with each other were made stronger. (A friend did get us a new container and sand, but we held onto the original as a testimony.)

Jake asked Stephen to lead worship on Sunday. We invited one of our neighbors to come to church with us after he'd asked us how we were so hopeful while rummaging through our burned belongings. This was our opportunity to "suffer well for God's glory" in front of him, to witness to him. He even went out to eat with us, Stephen's parents, and a few close friends after church. One of my favorite songs came on the radio while we were there, and yes, I did sing and dance at the restaurant. My little performance was added to the list of things that embarrassed Stephen.

Though Peter and Margaret insisted we could stay in their basement as long as we needed, I hated that "I'm a burden" feeling welling up inside of me. One of the managers at Chick-fil-A asked me how much we'd been paying in rent at our now burnt apartment. He then offered his vacant townhouse to us for $25 less a month. Stephen and I just had to take him up on his invitation. As soon as the townhouse was ready for us, we moved in and started all over again.

* * * * *

In our day-to-day over the next few months, it was becoming more difficult for me to conceal my resentment about dinner being cold on the table by the time Stephen got home from work. Finally, one night, I let it all out. Caught off guard, Stephen didn't understand why it was such a big deal. I told him that I wanted him to leave by 5:00 because he was paid to work 8-5. He replied, "I'm paid to work until I get the job done." As we dug deeper, I revealed how I wanted to know when he would be home because I didn't want him to get upset if I didn't have dinner ready. That's when we decided he would text me to let me know when he was wrapping things up at work and that he would help me when he got home. He didn't expect me to have dinner on the table waiting for him. I didn't need to try to do it all on my own. Wow, what a concept.

Even though I struggled with that building resentment, I also still had so much fun with Stephen. Like the time we went with our closest friends to watch a (Christian) comedian perform at a church. Or the time Stephen surprised me with tickets for a (Christian) music artist. He was also supportive of me in my teaching. He was present for "Meet the Teacher," passing out glasses of lemonade and brownies. On weekends, he helped me grade papers and plan lessons.

However, complementarianism required me to submit to *all* of Stephen, which included submitting to his self-preservation instincts when it came to finances. This created a cocktail of shame for any unnecessary purchase I made, so I tried not to make such purchases. Unnecessary was broadly defined. With plenty of money in the bank for joining friends after church for lunch, we rarely indulged in "out to eat" treats. We continually said no when people invited us out. Eventually, people stopped inviting us altogether. We deprived ourselves of nice things and judged as frivolous those who didn't live like us. We called it being frugal.

* * * * *

During our pre-marital counseling and in our small group, Stephen and I were part of so many conversations about the "passivity" of men. Men were, after all, created to take charge, not to be passive. Well, trust me, I wanted Stephen to be more assertive at times. At Entrench and in the sermons we consumed, more misbeliefs about being a woman were piled on. An Acts 29 celebrity pastor named Matt Chandler, and other men like him, derided the "Christian Church" becoming so feminine and emotional as they mocked worship song lyrics. (Years later, a friend from Entrench pointed out that it's funny how men like Chandler lament the "feminization" of the Church since the Church is considered the Bride and a bride is feminine within the context. At the time, though, a theology of "biblical manhood" was layered onto the misbeliefs I had from childhood about emotions.)

Before Chandler, this lamentation over the "feminization of the Christian Church" was shared by Jerry Falwell who said that Jesus was a "man with muscles."[18] And before Falwell, Billy Graham emphasized via "athletic and military metaphors" that "his faith did not conflict with his masculinity."[19] And before Graham, good ol' Teddy (Roosevelt, not my first boyfriend in elementary school) wanted to "restore American manhood."[20] There were plenty of other major and more minor contributors to these beliefs in the 1900s and early 2000s. (Read *Jesus and John Wayne* by Kristin Du Mez for an in-depth analysis of this history.)

Speaking of Matt Chandler, though, Stephen and I participated in a marriage course where we went through some of Chandler's curriculum. Chandler talked about being married to three different women, and he meant three versions of his wife. He didn't credit anyone with this, but I know it isn't an original thought and have since heard Esther Perel describe this as well.[21] Regardless of where the sentiment originated, that was the first inkling of "permission" to grow, change, and evolve, though I knew at the time that the expectation was to grow, change, and evolve as determined was acceptable by men like Chandler, Jake, and Stephen.

Changing who I was for Stephen's comfort and to make him look better was the path I chose to take. One of the biggest ways I shifted my personality was by being less outgoing because it embarrassed him. Gone were the days of singing loudly in restaurants and shouting out things like, "Look at that sexy beast." And I learned from the fire at our apartment that I had to suppress any "difficult" emotions and suffer well for God's glory as a way to witness to others. And finally, I knew Stephen didn't like my signature open mouth pose, something I'd done during our engagement photos and many times before that. I knew that pose embarrassed him, so I stopped doing it. I didn't want him to be embarrassed of me. I wanted him to be proud to be married to me, to be proud that I was his wife. Changing parts of who I was highlighted my codependency, insecurity, and lack of confidence.

Regardless of our dynamics, I thought our marriage would be fine and all fractures repaired if I simply submitted. This was the framework of the first eight and a half years of our marriage, and Stephen was great when I needed his protection. Like that time my younger brother tried to hit me. Stephen stopped my brother's arm and said, "You will not hit my wife." My brother responded, "She's my sister." Yes, there is a better reason to not hit me other than "She's my wife," such as "She's a person," but I'm glad Stephen stepped in.

To quote a tweet from Jo Luehmann, "I want men to defend me, to stand between me and other men being abusive, to stand in solidarity with me. I want men to tear down the patriarchy alongside me by not tolerating misogyny, racism, or any abuse toward me. I can defend myself, and I want to not have to."[22]

* * * * *

I remained a theologically vocal leader, confident in my insights, until the first marriage conference at Entrench. A dismissive interaction with a visiting seminary professor of Jake's broke something inside of me.

The marriage conference took place at the Winthrop BCM building. Stephen's parents were there, as was Stephen's ex-girlfriend and her husband. We all sat in rows of stiff chairs facing the front of the room. The seminary professor stood atop a stage, dispensing marriage advice based on his interpretation of the Bible. The professor began speaking about Adam and Eve. One of the pastor's wives spoke up to share her thoughts. She noted it was interesting that whenever the story of Adam and Eve is represented in pictures or children's books, Eve is shown with the Serpent and Adam isn't present in the picture. She pointed out that the text says, "And she gave [the fruit] to her husband *who was with her*" Genesis 3:6 (ESV). It was empowering for me to hear a woman point out a textual feature no one else had noticed.

When the professor asked a question a bit later, I excitedly answered. Though I can't remember what I said, I remember how I felt. I was proud of myself and sat up a little straighter when I received positive feedback from the professor. The next time I tried to answer a question, though, he wouldn't let me complete my thought, even though no one else was trying to respond. Instead, he let me know, "I'd love to hear from your husband because you've already answered a question." Apparently, he thought I'd already talked enough. He didn't want to hear from Stephen and then circle back to me. No, he wanted to hear from Stephen *instead* of me. A sure-fire way to shut someone up is to humiliate them in front of a group of people.

Going forward, I became nervous to speak in church settings. I would still speak up and share from time to time, but I was always worried about it. Praying with Stephen also began to feel too vulnerable. I felt hypocritical praying in front of someone who knew my deepest flaws. In bed at night, he wanted both of us to pray, but I asked if he could just do it. I couldn't get past the discomfort of expressing myself in this way with him.

Also, because of the seminary professor who silenced me, I internalized the belief that God hated me as a woman, or at least liked men more. If the seminary professor was a representative of God, and he wanted to hear from Stephen instead of me, then maybe God wanted to hear from Stephen instead of me, too. I didn't vocalize any of this, though. Stephen was worried about what it meant for me spiritually to not pray aloud with him, and what it meant for us, so he continually tried to pressure me into praying instead of respecting my boundary.

THOUGHTS FROM STEPHEN

Early in our relationship, Nicki and I encountered bumps because of my friendships with women. The books Nicki and I read and things we were taught were that men were only lust-craving beings, unable to control our sexual desires. This led to me feeling like I couldn't trust myself, and it led to Nicki feeling insecure about all other women. It was a cycle of distrust and insecurity which resulted in conflict and arguing. Even when I knew nothing romantic was going to happen when I hung out with my female friends, nothing I said assured or reassured Nicki of that.

Things didn't get any easier when I went away on Spring Break with BCM for a week to do a short-term mission project. While I was gone, one of the managers at Chick-fil-A told her that if I didn't hurry up and marry her, he would. The man was everything I wasn't. Buff, outdoorsy, wealthy. As Nicki told me about what he'd said to her, I responded that if she wanted to break up with me so she could be with him, that was fine. We'd be okay because we had Jesus. She was understandably wounded and thought I didn't even want to be with her. The truth is, I did want to be with her, but I was emotionally detached. That conversation led to another argument between us. This was seeming to become a pattern.

Remember how I never saw or heard my parents fight, argue, or even disagree? In a relationship, I interpreted a lack of conflict as a good thing and as the goal. My conflict avoidance relates to my Enneagram type. As a 9, "the easy-going mediator," I fear conflict and anything that would disrupt my internal peace and harmony. My personality wants stability and consistency. I don't want to exert a lot of energy working through conflict. So, when conflicts kept arising with Nicki, I would have doubts about us staying together. I didn't have the energy to keep arguing. Based on the assumption I held that a lack of disagreement was a sign of a healthy relationship, all the fights were hard for me. I voiced my concern to Nicki, "If we fight this much and we're not married, what would our marriage be like?"

I wasn't trying to break up with her but wanted to ask an honest question and navigate the possible answers that arose. How would we make it married if that's what it was like for us dating?

Over and over, I heard that marriage was hard, so if dating was hard, how would we get through something even more challenging? We heard sermons about how marriage brings out the worst in those involved because it reveals our sin and our selfishness. Instead of being encouraged to think about how to bring out the best in each other, we were already resigned to knowing that marriage would bring out the worst in each of us, that we would bring out the worst in each other. If life together being married was going to be so much harder than it already was, I didn't want that. I didn't want all that conflict and fighting.

By telling myself that marriage is not primarily for our happiness but for our holiness, I tried to remind myself that God uses marriage to reveal our sinfulness. Maybe Nicki was exactly who I needed to help reveal the things about myself that I needed to grow in. Conflict also relates to boundaries, and for so many years of my life, I lived without any. I thought that if I didn't have boundaries in place for people to cross, then I wouldn't ever have to face any conflict. No boundaries, no boundary-crossing. Problem solved. Another layer of why I didn't develop boundaries was because I didn't think I was important enough. My needs didn't matter.

* * * * *

Nicki shared the story about the night we got engaged. All I'll add about it was I knew that I no longer wanted to live without her as a part of my life. A conversation with Jake opened something up in me, gave me permission to let my guard down a little more. I loved her and was ready to start a new adventure together. There were still some challenges, though. I struggled with the ways Nicki fully engaged in life and lived the way she wanted to, without concern for what others thought of her. It also felt to me like she was vying for the limelight, but mature Christians were supposed to follow the teaching of Jesus and decrease so that Jesus could increase.

When we were dating and engaged, we were hardcore in the complementarian world and believed strongly that it was Nicki's role to submit, and it was my role to lead. In leading, I needed to guide us spiritually as the leader for our relationship. This idea was taught to me in lots of sermons and messaging from books and speakers at conferences. For years, I'd repeatedly heard that as a man, I'm supposed to be the leader. I'm supposed to be the strong one. I'm supposed to be the one who looks out for my future wife and protects her from attacks of evil and sin. If something goes wrong in our relationship, then I'm the one who is going to be held accountable for it. I'm the one who's going to have to answer to God for the way I led Nicki and for the things we did or didn't do.

All of this goes back to the way I was taught Genesis 3, the story of "the fall." The teaching I heard about "the fall" was that Eve is the one who sinned, in the sense that Eve ate the fruit and didn't obey God. But who did God call for? Who did God come to and hold responsible? He called out for Adam, "Where are you?" Then, Adam shirked the responsibility and blamed Eve.

It was preached by people like Matt Chandler that men's biggest problem is not lust. Men's biggest problem is passivity. It's this idea that Adam was passive with Eve in not leading and protecting her in the garden, so she was deceived and sinned. As a result, we have this fall that has happened and destroyed creation. It's all because Adam didn't fulfill his role in leading Eve like he was supposed to. Now, people will go to hell because of Adam's lack of leadership. If Adam's passivity led to the destruction of creation and results in people going to hell, what will *my* failed leadership lead to? Subconsciously, I worried about the consequences of my sin of passivity in leading Nicki.

In addition to leading Nicki, I thought I needed to prod others toward what I was convinced was holy, good, and pleasing to the Lord. Just as Jake influenced me to take the interim youth minister position over the BCM position at Winthrop, I replicated that same mentality once I had "power" as a leader. I interfered with the lives of others because I wanted to lead them to make the decisions that I thought were the right ones rather than trusting them to make the best decisions for themselves.

There are numerous instances of this that I regret, but I'll share one of them. A friend of mine from college was getting married. She'd been involved in BCM and was a Christian. She was marrying a nice man. The only thing I considered a problem was that he wasn't a Christian. Drafting an email to her, I wrote about how she shouldn't marry him because the two of them would be "unequally yoked." Assuring her that she should trust God and wait for a Christian man, I hit send.

Today, I would approach this situation with my friend differently. Instead of trying to convince her to not marry someone because they believed differently, I would be concerned with how their different beliefs work together to make them better people.

* * * * *

When it came to the pressure to provide, losing my job in the spring of 2012 fostered feelings of inadequacy. This feeling runs deep for me. From the time I was young, I have been physically smaller than others and put pressure on myself to succeed, whether in sports, school, or church. When I played little league sports, I had this fear of failing (striking out in baseball or missing a shot in basketball). When I was in first grade, I felt less valuable because I struggled with reading. When I participated in a Christian children's program, I wasn't as good at reciting Bible verses as the other kids in my group. I wanted to do well to get attention, make my parents proud, and prove to myself that I had value and worth.

Thinking that I needed to do well to get attention was often in opposition to the message my ego was telling me. My ego believed I needed to be self-effacing. I had grown up hearing that everything I did should point to God and not myself because I was a sinner who deserved hell. Further, if I died without trusting Jesus to save me, then God would send me to hell to be eternally punished in everlasting torment. I could do nothing to save myself but had to trust in Jesus and his life, death, and resurrection for my salvation and deliverance from such punishment.

Somewhere along the way, I started believing this limiting belief that I would fail. I felt inadequate when I graduated college and didn't know what I wanted to do, making it challenging to land a job in the "real world." I felt inadequate when our apartment burned because I hadn't done the responsible thing to secure renter's insurance.

Losing my job also fed my inadequacy narrative. I believed that I wasn't good enough. Being laid off made me feel like I was failing to perform my duty, failing Nicki. It triggered this buried fear that I would fail at life. The blow to my ego was tough when so much of my identity was wrapped up in being the breadwinner and making sure that I took care of Nicki. When she started making more money than me, I didn't really care, but I felt I should care. The climate within complementarianism, through direct and indirect teaching, made it clear that as the husband, I was supposed to bring in more income than my wife. There were conversations where I was told that it was okay for the husband to make less money than the wife as a short-term solution, but that it should not be a long-term plan.

Back then, it felt like the fate of everyone around me was on my shoulders. That's a lot to carry, and I wish I'd learned sooner that I could, and should, put it down. It isn't good for anyone, and it isn't healthy. I learned that the hard way when I woke Nicki up one night. My chest was tight. It was hard to breathe. She drove me to the ER. The doctor asked questions about stress. Yes, I was experiencing a lot of stress: at work, at home, at church. Turns out, all the stress led to a panic attack. Too bad I didn't learn the lesson then that there were certain burdens that weren't meant to be mine.

* * * * *

When it came to Nicki's insecurities, it was getting harder to keep reassuring her. How could Nicki think I wanted to be with anyone else? It all came to a head one night after a wedding we attended for some people from Entrench. Nicki was feeling insecure because an ex-girlfriend of mine was there with her husband. I talked to them, and Nicki didn't like that. Nicki didn't want me anywhere near her, much less engaging in conversation. This led to an argument we'd had numerous times before about my interactions with this ex-girlfriend and how Nicki felt. We left the wedding early.

When we got back to the apartment, we were still fighting. Nicki wanted to take a break. She was planning to go to Starbucks. I took the keys, which I should not have done, and she decided to just walk to the shop up the street. I calmed down a little, and then I remembered that we needed more coffee for the services at Entrench the next morning. Stomping down the stairs, I saw Nicki walking and my heart started pounding again. By the time I passed her, she was on the road outside of the complex. She thought I was stopping to pick her up and take her to Starbucks, but I glared at her and laid on the horn as I kept on driving.

I was upset that she'd left for a few reasons, though mainly because she wasn't staying to work through our disagreement. During our pre-marital counseling, Jake had talked with us about Ephesians 4:26, "Be angry and do not sin; do not let the sun go down on your anger" (ESV). Jake explained that this meant Nicki and I should quickly work through any disagreement so that resentment and bitterness didn't fester. When I took the keys, it's because I was trying to get her to stay so that we could address our frustrations together. Me taking the keys didn't stop her from leaving. Her willingness to walk away, instead of staying like I wanted her to, scared me.

I now know that I feel my anger in my chest, around my heart. When I saw her, that's why my heart started pounding hard again. Seeing her walking down the road without any regard for my supposed "authority" brought back the feelings of anger. In that moment, I felt betrayed by the failed promises of complementarianism and by what I perceived as her defiance and disobedience. This was the first time this side of her had shown itself. I was so emotionally unhealthy (not that my emotional unhealth is an excuse because it is not), and in that situation, that's how I responded, by letting the anger take over.

During this time in my life, I had been feeling out of control and uncertain in my role as a husband who was supposed to be a leader. Clearly, I had some repressed and unresolved anger I needed to address, but I didn't think that then. No, back then I thought that Nicki was the only one who needed to change whenever something like this happened, even though I did regret honking at her and driving angrily past her. I thought that she just needed to trust me, in this situation and every other situation. This was long before I was interrogating the disconnection from emotions that comes with white supremacy and patriarchy, especially in white evangelicalism.

Things between us would have been so different if I had taken a posture of curiosity and listened to why she was feeling the way she did. I wouldn't have viewed her feelings as a problem. I would have reflected on things I did that were leading her to feel that way and change where I needed to. But back then, I thought that if Nicki would just submit to me and trust me, then we could effectively live out our complementarian values all the days of our lives, until death do us part.

Something had to give if we were supposed to keep going.

Sadly, I personally know too many women from Entrench and conservative Christian circles that only stay married because they feel like they have to. They stay married based on the commitment/covenant, and their husbands are shocked to hear there's not more to it than that. Those husbands want it to be more than that, because even they understand what Emily Joy Allison explained when she said that it's more romantic that you choose the partner you're with every day rather than staying with that partner out of obligation.[23]

But, if marriage is primarily about your holiness and not your happiness, and if "God hates divorce," and if your marriage is supposed to be a picture of the "gospel" and Jesus never divorces the Bride — well, then, you stay. You stay even if you feel stuck, because that's what you're told brings God the most glory. Oh, and if you've been a stay-at-home mom (SAHM) with no income, it's scary to think about getting a divorce and having to figure out childcare, providing for your kids, and doing everything on your own (even if you have done basically everything on your own).

I bought a #StayingMarried shirt at the next marriage conference at Entrench. I have since redefined what success is for a marriage/partnership. Staying married isn't the barometer for success, and #StayingMarried isn't the flex I once thought it was. At some point in 2022, I saw a tweet about how complementarians want women to think marriage is so hard regardless of who you're married to; therefore, they constantly harp on the difficulty because they want women to stay stuck in abusive and unhealthy marriages.[24]

Despite ups and downs, Stephen and I were going to keep going when it came to both our marriage and a life of complementarianism. At the time, we had no idea that the questioning and unraveling of the entire foundation of our relationship (and our lives overall) was not too far down the path.

SECTION 2

IF ADAM PICKED THE APPLE

There would be a parade, a celebration, a holiday to commemorate the day he sought enlightenment. We would not speak of temptation by the devil, rather, we would laud Adam's curiosity, his desire for adventure and knowing. We would feast on apple-inspired fare, tortes, chutneys, pancakes, pies. There would be plays and songs reenacting his courage.

But it was Eve who grew bored, weary of her captivity in Eden. And a woman's desire for freedom is rarely cause for celebration.

-Danielle Coffyn
first published in *The North Meridian Review*

At the beginning of our relationship, I felt like I was indebted to Stephen as my protector and provider and could never repay him. Though I didn't like that feeling, I had been able to explain it away by reminding myself that he represented Christ in our marriage as the head, the one who sacrificed and served, and I needed to be grateful. As time went on, that was no longer working. We began to question complementarianism across various facets of our lives.

In the following chapters, we'll do a deep dive into some of the areas we've navigated within a complementarian relationship, from purity culture and parenting to finances and advocacy within the church.

Chapter 5
Modesty and Sex

Complementarianism dictated the way I dressed and my choices in regards to sex. This reveals the difference in power for Stephen to be able to tell me what I should or shouldn't wear. In addition, I was led to believe that Stephen's commitment to me hinged on: maintenance of my pre-marriage figure; adherence to damaging ideologies that reduced me to an object rather than a whole human with a body that changes as I age; and catering to him sexually at the expense of myself. These misbeliefs harmed us as individuals and as a couple.

The Tank Top

Nicki's Perspective

It was one of those muggy summer days. Stephen was on his way to pick me up for a dinner date. When he arrived, I bounced down to meet him. Sliding into the passenger seat, I was wearing a red tank top. It was one of my very favorites because of the vintage look. There were some funky brown beads around the cream circular emblem in the middle of the shirt. Seriously, I felt so cool and confident when I put it on.

Shifting uncomfortably in the driver seat, Stephen wouldn't make eye contact with me. Staring straight ahead, he asked if I could change my shirt. Apparently, all the extra exposed shoulder skin was a problem. With a flushed face, I blinked back tears as I said, "Yeah, of course." As I ran up the stairs, I was confused, thinking to myself, "It isn't even a spaghetti strap top." This dehumanizing interaction reduced me to my body. But to prove how good I would be at submitting, I didn't question Stephen or his request.

Knowing Stephen was waiting for me, I obsessed and second-guessed several shirt options. The one I settled on was so forgettable that I couldn't even tell you the color now. Pulling it over my head, I then freshened my face in the bathroom. Slowly taking one step at a time, I self-consciously approached Stephen's car. He thanked me once I buckled my seat belt. I waved it off like it wasn't a big deal. We went to dinner and didn't talk about the tank top for many years.

Following the humiliation of being asked to change, I paid more attention to the clothes I wore. I wore that tank top, and others, less and less. Not wanting to draw attention to my body, I continued fading bright and vibrant colors out of my wardrobe. Tank tops were replaced with t-shirts, short shorts with capris and jeans. That day in Stephen's car was the first time I was hyper-aware of the clothing I was wearing and how others might perceive me. But it wasn't the last. Every time, I felt hot buckets of shame being poured on me as I was blamed for causing a brother to stumble.

The Tank Top

Stephen's Perspective

There was one afternoon when I was picking Nicki up for a date. She came downstairs wearing a tank top. The tank top that I asked her to change to prevent the possibility of "temptation." She did. I didn't give the interaction a second thought. I didn't know it then, but she later told me how ashamed she felt when I did this. Sadly, asking women to change didn't start with Nicki. There was one time when I was leading worship with BCM and asked one of the students wearing spaghetti straps to put a cardigan on, not even because I was "lusting" after her but because I didn't want the possibility of a "temptation" for the other guys there.

Under the modesty standards put forward by patriarchy in general, and Christian patriarchy more specifically, it was not only permissible but commendable for me to dictate the clothing of the women around me. Let me state plainly that it is not my place, or the place of any man, to tell other people what to wear or what not to wear. I should not have done that to Nicki or that student. I'm a work in progress as I am seeking to repair the damage I did and to heal from the harm the system caused against me as well. My commitment is to continue disrupting the systems of oppression I've participated in and benefited from, beginning with examining how these still show up internally.

Through their television show *19 Kids and Counting*, the Duggar family brought into the mainstream the idea of men and boys not even looking at women or girls if they were showing "too much skin" or their clothes were "too tight." The parents would see an "immodestly dressed" woman or girl and instruct their sons to avert their eyes by staring at the ground.

When I go for walks now and am wearing just a sports bra, I can easily tell if a man has been influenced by this ideology. He refuses to acknowledge my presence and keeps his eyes straight ahead as we pass each other. I don't want to be ogled or objectified as I have been on many occasions. Men look me up and down, keep situating the trash can at the end of the driveway so they can talk to me, or stop their car to wave and won't drive away until I wave back. (Those are all things that have happened to me walking in my neighborhood. Stephen got me pepper spray, and I refreshed myself on some self-defense techniques.) I also, however, don't want to be ignored and made to feel invisible because I have breasts and my stomach is showing, as if my mere existence in this body is a temptation. Too few men operate in the middle space between the two extreme reactions.

The hierarchy built into complementarianism is a breeding ground for brothers to sexually abuse their younger siblings. In Heather Heath's book *Lovingly Abused*, she wrote about sitting in a circle with a group of girls connected to the Institute in Basic Life Principles (IBLP). The girls were discussing how their bodies had "tempted" the boys and men around them. Apparently, the only reason Heather was "spared" was because she didn't have a brother.[25]

* * * * *

You already know about how my dad exercised control over my hair and ear piercings. Well, I also consistently witnessed men in my family claiming authority over women's bodies. I had a cousin who told his girlfriend she couldn't leave the house without makeup on. I remember the day that I'd just clicked my seatbelt when she relayed this message to me. She was inspecting her face in the visor mirror. Without another word, she snapped it closed, put her white Nissan in drive, and sped off for our girl's day. All these types of behaviors from my dad and other men in my family were about juxtaposing their view of toxic masculinity with their enforced perception of acceptable femininity.

My dad was actually no stranger to compliments on his own physical appearance. On one family vacation to Tweetsie Railroad, we were watching one of the shows that takes place at the top of the hour. An employee was asking for volunteers to come up on stage to do "The Twist." She pointed to my dad and called out, "You, the Tom Cruise look-alike." He acted like he didn't want to as he climbed up there, but I think he liked the attention.

It was of utmost importance to be conventionally attractive as determined by the ever-evolving Eurocentric beauty standards. Numerous times, I heard the story about my beautiful blonde aunt who entered a beauty pageant as a favor for one of her brothers (or something like that). Lo and behold, she won and advanced to another round. She continued through the ranks until she was competing for Miss South Carolina. The way my grandma told me the story, when my aunt was asked, "Why do you want to be Miss South Carolina?" she replied, "I don't." And that was that for her pageant run.

Hoping to one day be beautiful enough to win a beauty pageant, I obsessed over my appearance and my weight. Throughout high school, I drank Slim Fast, all the while comparing myself to every girl who was skinnier than I was. When I rode in the church van beside a couple of my friends who wore size 0 jeans, I would slightly raise my legs off the seat so they would appear thinner. Most days at school, my lunch consisted of a chocolate chip cookie and Yoo-hoo. One reason I ate this sugary "lunch" was because I was embarrassed that I qualified for "free and reduced lunch." The other was because control was something I didn't have much of, so I began to control what I could, such as food intake. By restricting the amount of food I ate, I ensured I would stay within an approved weight range (and the patriarchy was, of course, the arbiter of approval).

Being thin enough allowed me to cash in the currency of desirability. The trade-off was that I wasn't allowed to be human. Instead, I had to remain a fantasy and some things about me had to remain a mystery. For example, there was a guy I worked with who refused to acknowledge that teenage girls poop. It was totally fine for him to do so, and to talk openly about it, but not for me or our female co-workers. In another instance with a guy I was dating, he was completely disgusted when he realized I was on my period. We were kissing when he rubbed my butt. At that moment, he felt my pad through my pants and asked what it was. When I told him, he jerked away, emphatically stated his repulsion, and refused to kiss me anymore that night. So, being a human that menstruates is gross? Got it.

And don't even get me started on the lengths I would go to in order to have flawless skin from head to toe. Acne creams of every variety for my pimples. Nair hair remover for my bikini line and legs. (I can still smell the heavy chemicals in the back of my throat.) Then, there was the continual appearance of warts on my hands, elbows, and knees. Some I froze off. Some I used duct tape on. Some I coated with clear nail polish. At least one of these tactics worked for all but one stubborn wart that remained on my left wrist. I got creative hiding it under tight bracelets in the summer and long-sleeves during the fall, winter, and spring. If the natural functions associated with my body of pooping, monthly bleeding, and growing hair grossed guys out, I wasn't about to take chances with that wart, lest it further decrease my desirability.

Desirability was also tied to a specific definition of sexual purity. If a guy believed me to be defiled, then I was no longer desirable, at least not for a serious romantic relationship. "Purity" was monitored, too. My mom told me about how when she married my dad, she was instructed to wear a blue wedding dress. White was off limits. When I asked why, she said it was because she'd already had kids. Hearing that story shifted something inside me and confirmed how essential it was to remain "pure," before I even knew what sex was.

Regarding my sexuality, early on I internalized the misbelief that I existed for the pleasure of men. The only things I knew about sex were learned through experience. I mean, for a long time I didn't call body parts by their correct anatomical names. Penis was "peeper," and I didn't know the difference between a vagina and vulva. I couldn't talk to my mom about any of this because I felt neither comfortable nor safe doing so. She'd slapped me for joking about a pickle looking like a dildo, though I wasn't really sure what a dildo was. That slap, in part, deterred me from wanting to ask my mom anything about sex.

My mom had also acted awkwardly when I asked her what a virgin was. I'd heard the word virgin in a song we sang about Mary, the mother of Jesus, at Christmas. Then, I heard the word again in a movie I watched with an older cousin. The movie was *Wish Upon a Star*, starring a young Katherine Heigl, and it was one of my favorite movies. When I asked my mom about the definition of a virgin, she wouldn't give me a straightforward answer. She eventually landed on telling me that a virgin was someone who wasn't married, which I accepted at the time.

*****

Back when Stephen and I were dating and I met his friends, I was fully my extra self, or "TMTH" as Stephen liked to say. Too Much To Handle. Donning my signature cowboy boots and a different earring in each of my six piercings, I stepped into the spotlight to spontaneously perform at the gathering.

Out of the corner of my eye, I caught a glimpse of Stephen ducking a bit. Was he embarrassed of me? This was the first time I let his body language affect my own perception of myself. My confidence to be myself was put to the test because of my codependent tendencies. I soon began to self-consciously wonder if I needed to change myself for Stephen's comfort, so that I could be a more improved version of myself. Maybe the self I was wasn't who I should be anyway.

At Entrench, I often heard how lucky, or #blessed, I was to be with Stephen but never heard the inverse. The implicit message in this was that I better be grateful a godly man like Stephen chose me. I needed to be careful to prevent him from waking up one day and realizing he could do better. It felt good to hear that one of Stephen's friends wondered, "How did he get her?"

A few months later, I invited Stephen to the big 4th of July party at my aunt's house on the lake. This was only the second time Stephen had been around my extended family, and it was his first time meeting my cousin Jessie's husband, Kyle. Unlike many people there, Kyle actually carried on conversations with Stephen. Unfortunately, they were conversations where Kyle relentlessly mocked him. Looking back, we understand why Stephen's preferences could be abrasive to someone who didn't agree with his decisions. These decisions included declining alcohol. At the time, he didn't drink. He'd never tried it and didn't desire to. This was strike one against Stephen's "masculinity."

Strike two came when Stephen told Kyle he would go to an all-men swimming pool if it was an option because he thought it would help me not feel insecure. Kyle insisted Stephen was "a homosexual," as Stephen insisted he wanted to "value and respect" me. Kyle went on to brag about the open relationship he and his wife had, all while she shook her head to indicate he was lying.

My own insecurities in my relationship with Stephen were intensified by a book of lies I read that I have since thrown in the garbage where it belongs. The author argued that when men are attracted to women, and those women wear tight clothes, men picture those women naked. Men then store the image to refer back to. How could I ever compete with a rolodex of images?

Around this time, a group of newly engaged and recently married women from Entrench gathered one night for a discussion. We were instructed by an older woman in the church that we could not tell our husbands "no" to sex. We were told that we could say either "yes" or "convince me." (Oddly enough, Stephen was not being told he couldn't tell me "no" to sex.) Imagine instilling in new wives or soon-to-be wives that the most basic boundary setting word is off limits with their husbands. This didn't alarm me, though, because the most basic boundary-setting word was already off limits with the boys and men from my former life.

Aside from the horrific consequence of excusing marital rape, this line of reasoning teaches that men want sex more than women. That is rarely the case for me and Stephen. Much later, I would encounter the Dual Control Model (DCM) through the work of Emily Nagoski and her book *Come as You Are*.[26] The DCM is made up of the accelerator and the brake. It usually doesn't take much for my accelerator to get going, and my brakes aren't typically that sensitive. For Stephen, the reverse is often true.

Rather than contradicting dehumanizing, misogynistic claims, Caroline, my mentor at Entrench Church and our pastor Jake's wife, exacerbated the situation. She instructed me to hide my cleavage by pressing my shirt against my chest when I bent over. She also explained that I shouldn't wear spaghetti strap tank tops and had to be vigilant to not let my bra straps show. The real downer was I needed to get rid of my strapless shirts because they resembled a towel wrapped around me, which would make men think about me getting out of the shower. To top it all off, she told me about a man who was "tempted" by his sister because of how she dressed. The responsibility of preventing men from lusting after me was placed directly on my shoulders. I received the message, "Cover up," instead of men receiving the message, "Stop objectifying her."

Caroline also gave me some copies of Carolyn Mahaney's "Modesty Checklist." Carolyn Mahaney is the wife of C.J. Mahaney (yes, that C.J. Mahaney of Sovereign Grace Ministries/Churches). Caroline wanted me to distribute these copies to the women I had contact with at Entrench. Dutifully, I did. And I got serious side-eye from some of the young women who were already light years ahead of me in understanding that they were not responsible for the thoughts of others. Ignoring the women who weren't buying the modesty message, I focused my energy on those who were. Together, we gossiped about the women who were "immodest" and fed off each other's insecurities.

Everything Caroline told me about modesty checked out that summer when I wore my favorite vintage-y red tank top with the funky brown beads. The one Stephen asked me to change. One benefit, if you want to call it that, of adjusting my wardrobe was that dressing in a frumpier and less form-fitting way meant paying less attention to how my body looked. That didn't stop me from being enveloped by worries. Was Stephen going to be satisfied with me? Was he going to leave me? My induction into this ideology taught me that every woman was a threat, which is a terrible place to live from. Underneath all this was the implicit belief that women can taint the purity of men, as if we are the reason for their lust, even when we are in no way trying to flirt with or make ourselves sexually appealing to them.

Rather than wrestling with these trappings of purity culture, I perpetuated them by heaping burdens on other women that they were not meant to bear. One example of this was in enforcing the "Billy Graham rule." Per the Billy Graham rule, men are told to never be alone with a woman they aren't married to, as if being alone with us will inevitably lead to them being "tempted" sexually or initiating an affair. Some men take it a step further by completely ignoring us, as if simply being in our presence compromises their "purity." One man on Twitter took it all the way to the extreme by stating he won't even be alone with his own mother, and I have a lot of questions about that. (P.S. There are plenty of men who are proponents of the Billy Graham rule as part of their public persona while assaulting people privately.)

For years, I shamed women for what they did or didn't wear on their bodies. My judgment and suspicions, left unchecked and unconfessed, festered to the point of making them responsible for the behavior of someone else, whether that was a man who "lusted" after them or the insecurity I projected onto them. To be clear, they are in no way responsible for my behavior or the behavior of another person. Rather than repenting of the harsh judgments I harbored against other women, I delivered messages that I deemed from the Lord. This was to mask the fact that I really just wanted to mold their modesty to mirror mine. I self-righteously and erroneously assumed my standard was worthy of imitation.

Another layer to all of this was that I continued believing a falsehood I picked up in childhood due to being sexually abused. I believed that men lack self-control and couldn't be trusted to not assault us if they were tempted nor to decline a woman who made an unwelcome sexual advance. These, too, are dehumanizing assumptions. For the men I know who have loved me and other women well, they've raised the bar and demonstrated they are not lustful and ravenous beasts. In line with the damaging beliefs about sex, though, when Stephen and I were dating, Jake and Caroline reminded us that "it is better to marry than burn with passion" 1 Corinthians 7:9 (ESV).

* * * * *

Most weddings are not without their fair share of drama, but when you add purity culture into the mix, it's an added layer of complication. This came to bear for our engagement photo shoot. For the occasion, we borrowed black pea coats from some friends and headed to Manchester Meadows. This was the park where we took walks when we dated. Most of the pictures were your standard engagement lineup, but there was one where I'm showing off my ring with my mouth wide open in excitement. The open mouth was one of my signature poses. Stephen told me not to, but I ignored him and loved the photo. (I always insisted that I still looked so cute even with my mouth agape.)

Then, we headed downtown sporting argyle sweaters. I bought Stephen his. He bought me mine. We were adorable! We were laughing, smiling, and having a great time until we were instructed to take a couple of photos that led to Stephen feeling uncomfortable. His discomfort stemmed from the close contact of our bodies. There was one picture where I was told to get on his back. In another, he was holding me from behind with his arms right under my breasts. His squirmy reaction to those two poses was yet another reminder that my body was a "temptation" that Stephen needed to avoid at all costs until after we were married. Do you know how stressful it is to feel like the source of someone's moral compromise (since that person believes it's impure to even think sexual thoughts about the person they're engaged to)? The tension simply escalated when I had my lingerie shower.

Women from every area of my life came with bags from Victoria's Secret and the like. In my body, I was holding conflicting emotions of exhilaration and embarrassment while opening bra and panty sets in front of a room full of women, including my mom. My mom came with my childhood best friend and my friend's mom. They brought something for Stephen. To clarify, it felt like all of the items were for Stephen in the sense of it was my duty to entice him and spice up the bedroom, but my mom had something specifically for Stephen to wear.

It was a type of underwear with a sleeve for his penis to go through. Sitting above his penis would be a pair of glasses and a mustache. The thought of a detective penis was too much. I could've fainted. The outrageous sexual "toy" from my mom confused me because just a few years earlier, she'd slapped me for saying dildo. Sex seemed really scary during the lingerie shower, but I tried to laugh off my anxiety. Stephen was also getting nervous and wanted to avoid any talk about sex with me. He didn't want to hear a word about the lingerie.

Aside from paltry sex ed in ninth grade, most of my sexual knowledge came from experiences, some non-consensual. Stephen had little knowledge. Following the lingerie shower, we had a conversation with Jake and Caroline about sex as one of our final premarital counseling sessions. The first few minutes were spent together. Jake reminded us what a gift from God sex is, but that it's meant to be saved for marriage and would only be enjoyable within that context. Yes, when Stephen and I were alone, our dating boundaries were proving much more difficult to hold. There was an urge, a pull. Shame clouded the feelings because we were being told they were bad, not to fantasize, and certainly not to act on them. I don't judge myself for how I felt during the times when I desired sex while we were engaged because I now recognize that these were totally normal desires.

Jake did encourage us to take things slow and directly addressed Stephen needing to foster open communication and dialogue with me so I could express discomfort. I appreciated that Jake emphasized that there was no need to rush. After that, Stephen talked in one room with Jake, and I met with Caroline in a different room. Caroline shared about how painful sex would probably be (for me) in the beginning, sex being understood very narrowly as penal penetration of a vagina. Okay, I did not sign up for pain, and there are other ways to cultivate and heighten sexual pleasure that don't hurt people with vulvas. But we didn't talk about those.

As the wedding quickly approached, Jake was consistently there for us. He was even present, quite incidentally, a few days before the wedding when Stephen and I needed help picking out condoms. It's true. We were in Walmart shopping for honeymoon provisions, which, naturally, included condoms. Aimlessly wandering the family planning aisle, we were overwhelmed by the sheer volume of choices. That's when we saw Jake walk by. We made eye contact. "We're getting these to use on our honeymoon," I blurted, because, you know, purity culture.

Stephen admitted, "We don't know what to buy," as he gestured toward the bounty before us. Jake came to the rescue.

With a "value pack" of condoms and lubricant in our cart, we were ready to check out. Jake headed that way, too. I then told the unsuspecting cashier we were getting married in a few days, introduced Jake as our pastor, and explained that he assisted us in picking out our inaugural condoms. Stephen tried to reel me in, but I had no filter.

* * * * *

Purity culture extended far beyond the blatantly sexual, however. Remember the fire that destroyed our apartment and most of our possessions? In the months following that event, I spent a lot of time and care restocking my wardrobe. One day, Stephen asked me why I had so many gray shirts. Without skipping a beat, I was chipper as I told him, "I like gray." And I really believed that I liked gray. There's certainly not anything wrong with the color gray for clothing, but I'd convinced myself that I liked gray more than the bright and vibrant colors I'd once worn. There were 50 shades of gray in my closet (sorry, I had to) as I became obsessed with "modesty."

This also meant that even though I loved jewelry, I stopped wearing as much. After hearing numerous teachings on 1 Peter 3:3-4, my entire wardrobe went through some changes. I memorized the words, "Do not let your adorning be external — the braiding of hair and the putting on of gold jewelry, or the clothing you wear — but let your adorning be the hidden person of the heart with the imperishable beauty of a gentle and quiet spirit, which in God's sight is very precious" (ESV). My clothing became less form fitting as I sought to conceal my body and not draw attention to myself. And where I once wore six different earrings, bangle bracelets on both wrists, an anklet on my left leg, multiple rings on my fingers and toes, and necklaces, I slowly phased the excess of jewelry out. I literally toned down my wardrobe and accessories so that I could let my adorning come from within instead of being external.

My own passion for modesty continued spilling over into my interactions. Just as I'd passed along the "Modesty Checklist" to women in the church, I used my position as a fill-in for the kids' ministry director to further spread these beliefs about modesty. Typing up a list of standards for the volunteers to agree to regarding clothing, I included things like not wearing short skirts and being careful when bending over. During the volunteer training, I read out the requirements. Then, I added, "Do y'all understand that, men?" We all laughed because we knew the instructions were for women. Instructions I'd written and read aloud.

Also, you remember how I had that lingerie party with so many people? Well, I'd received so much sexy clothing that it filled a wicker chest. That wicker chest sat at the foot of our bed. Our bed had been burnt to a crisp during the fire, along with the wicker basket and all of its lacy contents. Never fear, though. People stepped up and bought more. Don't get me wrong, I was grateful for replacement lingerie. However, the very existence of lingerie, and the buying of it after going through a devastating fire, reinforced the expectation that I needed to be both sexually available and appealing all the time. Even following a traumatic event. And that oversized box of condoms we'd purchased with Jake's help before our wedding? It was also gone. But no one bought us condoms, and we never bought more. Never. Which I'm sure has something to do with the fact that the counting and "pull-out" methods were free.

My whole life, I was taught that my power as a woman was in my sexual desirability, and Stephen was taught his power was in his sexual prowess. I got the new lingerie, but post-fire Nicki still desired sex more than Stephen. The conclusion I came to was that I simply wasn't desirable. When we had sex, it was wonderful. Stephen was tender and generous. He tried his best to ensure my sexual needs were met. He wanted it to be pleasurable for me every single time. Our communication and dialogue about what felt good and didn't was open, but there was nothing he could say to assuage the feeling in me that I wasn't attractive enough for him. The fears were made worse as I continued to view other women as competition.

* * * * *

The first few years of marriage, I gained 20 pounds and struggled with how my body looked with the additional weight. This led to insecurity on my part because I was told that maintaining my pre-marriage figure is what would keep Stephen attracted to me. (It's important to note the fatphobia here as well as the racial origins of fatphobia, which sociologist Sabrina Strings, Ph.D. explains in her book *Fearing the Black Body*.[27]) The fear of Stephen not finding me attractive grew, especially as I heard about the insatiable consumption of pornography and subsequent shame of men at Entrench. Their "addiction" to porn or "temptation" to look at porn was never dealt with in a way that led to healing. (For the record, my judgment is reserved for the unethical exploitation of people, not for the people who are often exploited in the production of pornography. There is a separate conversation to be had about ethical production and consumption where no one is exploited.)

This all relates to the larger conversation about manhood because of the misbeliefs attached to masculinity, such as a voracious sexual appetite. Plus, there was the never-ending, ensuing cycle of shame people in the church felt when they admitted to viewing porn. Though Stephen wasn't watching porn, the underlying current still fed my insecurity that I wasn't meeting his sexual needs and he would have them met elsewhere. Then, a woman hit on Stephen, in front of me, and confirmed my misbelief that women couldn't be trusted.

We were at a music event in the building Entrench rented. As a result of volunteering for these concerts, Stephen and I had been spending time with a woman who was employed by the department that organized the shows. She was newly divorced. To witness to her, we took her dinner and kept her company several times. It was during the last installment of the concert series that she made her move. She was intoxicated, and her speech was slurring, but she came up to Stephen and pulled him close to her. When she tried to rest her head on his chest, he removed her arms from around him, but the damage had been done. That was the last time we talked to her. Because of her behavior, I made the exception the rule and decided once and for all that every woman was scheming about how to steal Stephen from me because he was such a catch.

* * * * *

My wardrobe posed an ongoing issue. I planned a trip with some friends — Aubrey, Sam and Willow — to Alabama in October 2018. We were going on, what we termed, a "Justice Pilgrimage."

Arriving in Birmingham, we unloaded our belongings at the most charming Airbnb. Trudging to the second floor of the house, Sam and I each got one of the rooms, Willow the living room, and Aubrey blew up her inflatable mattress in the spacious landing at the top of the stairs. We had tickets to visit The National Memorial for Peace and Justice and the Legacy Museum the next morning.

With the rising of the sun on Saturday, I shimmied into my blue and green speckled romper and was mortified by my bra playing peek-a-boo. I hadn't thought to pack my strapless bra because I assumed my romper's straps would be wide enough to hide the bra I was wearing. Sprinting down the stairs, I had to find Willow. Everyone else was gathered on the front porch. Working up the courage, I asked Willow if I could borrow the black cardigan she'd worn the day before. She was planning to wear it again but was hesitant to tell me no, so Aubrey bluntly intervened on Willow's behalf. Gulping back tears and resisting the urge to launch an explanation, I said I was going to finish getting ready. Once I was out of sight, I fled upstairs and called Stephen, crying as I relayed what had happened.

My experience with direct purity culture teaching began at Entrench with everything Caroline instructed me to do. She'd told me that I couldn't wear tank tops and had to be careful about my bra straps not showing. Now my bra straps were showing. With every shaking fiber of my being, I didn't want to be a distraction to the men at the museum and memorial. Obviously this line of reasoning was quite demeaning to the men I would come into contact with, to automatically label them as lacking self-control and powerless against the glimpse of my undergarments, but I didn't understand this then.

Aubrey, Sam, and Willow all came upstairs and discovered I was crying. I fumbled over my words as I attempted to illustrate my conundrum. We talked, and I realized that Aubrey and Sam didn't think the same things Caroline taught me, which further contributed to my confusion. "No one will be paying attention to your straps," they assured me.

I still thought Caroline was right, and by extension *I* was right. So, when they exited my room, I slipped a black t-shirt under my romper. The remainder of the trip was heavy. Seeing the six-foot monuments suspended in the air above me as I walked and reading the descriptions of the circumstances surrounding various racial terror lynchings, each step became laborious as I lugged my groaning heart. How privileged and self-centered of me to enter that experience consumed with thoughts of myself and my clothing instead of directing time and energy toward preparing for what I would encounter.

* * * * *

There was a leader at Entrench who once shared that vasectomies "turn a man from a lion into a kitten." Well, fast-forwarding a bit, once Stephen and I moved toward mutuality, Stephen did end up getting a vasectomy. Five months later, when there was no sperm detected in Stephen's sample, we had sex. On Sunday, December 11, 2022, I had the best orgasm of my life up to that point. (Yes, I made a note of the date to include it in this book.) It's amazing how much more magical sex was for me when I didn't have to worry about getting pregnant again. What's disappointing is that even if Stephen told "kitten/lion" guy about how transcendental our post-vasectomy coitus was, it wouldn't matter. To men like him, sex is about his prowess, not his partner's pleasure, his dominance, not his partner's delight.

This toxic idea of a man taking a dominant role in sexual intercourse even shows up in the language I was taught surrounding the fertilization of my eggs. Passive words like "present" were used to describe my egg, whereas active words like "penetrate" were used to describe sperm. Turns out, sperm aren't powerful swimmers defeating all odds to get through my cervix to my egg. Instead, my reproductive tract assists the sperm in their journey by doing things like contracting to move the sperm more quickly. My egg even emits a "chemical signal that acts almost like a GPS, so that the sperm have a good indicator of which fallopian tube to go to."

Then, my egg "uses chemicals to select" the sperm that will fertilize it. Did you get that? My egg is not penetrated by the sperm that assaulted its way into my egg. My egg decides which sperm will fertilize it. My egg is so *not* passive.[28] Being taught that my egg was being acted upon, rather than my egg being an active agent in the fertilization process, reinforced the notion that I am to be a passive recipient during sexual intercourse. For someone who already thought I didn't have agency and autonomy, I did not need to be taught the "science" of dead white men who brought biased assumptions to their critiques of my reproductive organs.

It's sad and disappointing, but not surprising, that complementarian Christians in particular are still responsible for peddling this harmful rhetoric. In a recent article put out by The Gospel Coalition, a writer compared Christ penetrating the Christian Church to a husband penetrating his wife. Yuck. He went on to describe ejaculation as a sacrificial offering, as if Stephen is serving me and pointing me to Jesus when he "bestows [this gift] upon the altar within [my] Most Holy Place." You can't make this stuff up. The article was removed,[29] but not before Julia and Jeremiah of the *Sexvangelicals* podcast read and responded to it.[30]

The same man who feared becoming a kitten if he got a vasectomy also refused to cultivate healthy friendships with women. He cited avoiding an affair, or the appearance of an affair, as his reason. A recent public example of this whole "men and women being friends" conversation took place when Matt Chandler temporarily stepped down from his pastoral position at The Village Church in Flower Mound, Texas. [31] Here's the thing, though: men like Chandler becoming friends with women can't happen in an authentic way because they still think they're supposed to exercise authority over us. They can't fathom submitting to us when they think we're the ones who should be doing all the submitting. Everything happening with Chandler isn't an example of "why men can't be friends with women." It's instead an example of why men who aren't healing their sexism, misogyny, and misogynoir can't be in *authentic* relationship with us.

Men like Chandler haven't uprooted their dehumanizing beliefs about us. They still view us as existing for their pleasure and consumption, as objects to boost their egos. Until they dismantle the patriarchy inside themselves, they can't be in a genuinely vulnerable and trustworthy relationship with us. Also, men like that are still closely tied to men like conservative political commentators who complain about M&M's not being "sexy" anymore (because even "feminine" candies exist for men and their pleasure). Yep, I'm looking at you, Tucker Carlson.[32]

Having a daughter has also shifted my perspective on all this. I hope she knows her body is her own, that she isn't saving it to one day give to someone else, that it is hers now and forever. To help with her receiving this message, I tell her to put on clothes that make her comfortable. If they feel good and she likes them, wear them. This also means telling her that I will always support her in her choices regarding her body, even if they aren't the same choices I would make. While we're here, I want to lift a middle finger to any ideology that would have her believe she is responsible for others who choose to harm her in any way. It's been a winding journey out of complementarianism, and I will not raise her in the confines of purity culture, a culture that heaps crushing burdens on girls that were never theirs to bear.

I will equip my daughter to call out sexism, misogyny, misogynoir, and patriarchal double standards. Any conversations about modesty will come from the wisdom of people like the late Rachel Held Evans, who wrote, "It seems that most of the Bible's instructions regarding modesty find their context in warnings about materialism, not sexuality...I've heard dozens of sermons about keeping my legs and my cleavage out of sight, but not one about ensuring that my jewelry was not acquired through unjust or exploitive trade practices."[33]

Here's to cultivating and nurturing my daughter's confidence and freedom. Honestly, I hope each of my kids know all of this.

THOUGHTS FROM STEPHEN

One underlying problem for me when it came to gender roles was that I didn't fit into the stereotypical definitions of what it meant to be a man. I wasn't an outdoorsy, adventurous alpha type who wanted to dominate others and fight for a woman. I knew this was who I was expected to be, though that characteristic of domination was in opposition to what I was taught God wanted me to be. As a man, the patriarchy had been embedded in me from childhood, demonstrating that it was right for me to rule over girls and women. However, when I encountered teachings about Jesus laying his power down and being a servant leader, I wrestled against the desire to dominate.

This wrestling wasn't because I wanted to value women but because I thought dominating others wasn't how God wanted me to be. I didn't want to disappoint God. During a small group book study my junior year of college, we talked about the book *Wild at Heart* by John Eldredge. Either during this study or at a retreat, someone shared about how every girl is waiting for a hero to come rescue her. It was our job as men to be those rescuers as we protected and led.

Then there was the trope about all men wanting sex and that is all we think about. Outside of the church, that message was prevalent in popular culture and media. I was surprised when this belief was touted in a Sunday morning church service. During the sermon, the pastor started talking about sex and how good sex is. One of his points was something along the lines of, "This church stands for sex, sex, and more sex." There were "amens" and cheering from the men in the congregation, which reinforced the belief that sex exists for men only. The pastor's words, his delivery, and the rowdy reception were completely disorienting.

That Sunday, my then girlfriend, who normally attended a different church, came to church with me. I felt excited that we were attending together. Of all the days for her to visit, it had to be the day of the sex sermon. This topic felt taboo and sacrilegious. Growing up, sex wasn't talked about in the sermons (or maybe I was asleep during those sermons when I was a kid). For a broader evangelical norm, sex was off the table in terms of discussion. But with the church planting movement, churches were trying to be relevant in the topics they addressed. So, they "took sex back" to follow "God's design."

If the women had been the ones cheering when the pastor said, "This church stands for sex, sex, and more sex," how would the men have felt? Why *weren't* the women cheering? Does it have anything to do with the way we've conditioned men and women to fit into a certain box with respect to sex? Is it because women weren't getting pleasure out of their sexual experiences? If they aren't satisfied, why is that? The lack of women cheering should have been an indication that there's a problem, but it wasn't considered a problem. It was both expected and accepted that the men would cheer and that the women wouldn't.

On top of all this, the English Standard Version (ESV) of the Bible that I read supported complementarian theology. If you just read the words from that version and don't know the context, then it is really easy to twist those verses to support complementarian theology. For example, the word *ezer*, translated as "helper" in Genesis 2, was taught to me as if women are supposed to be secretaries for men. Then there were the texts that addressed the roles of men and women in the Bible, such as Ephesians 5, 1 Peter 3, and 1 Timothy 2.

I learned that this is what the Bible teaches and this is just the way God wants it to be. I'd heard in sermons that this didn't make women less valuable. It was just a difference in roles. There seemed to be an airtight explanation for why an egalitarian interpretation of texts like Ephesians 5:21 and Galatians 3:28 was incorrect. I was essentially complementarian because I thought that's what the Bible taught, and I was seeking to be faithful to what I thought was God's design.

It has felt disorienting to have so much of what I was once so certain of turned on its head. I feel like I've been a pawn, doing someone else's bidding to "keep people in line." I feel manipulated by the system. I feel sad for the ways I've hurt others and benefited from their burdens. I also feel freed from the deception now.

The heaviest belief burden I've unloaded in becoming egalitarian is one I heard through the teaching at Entrench. I was told I needed to stay a certain size, look a certain way, and not neglect Stephen in any way, even while rearing littles, lest he find attention elsewhere. And should he leave me, I would inevitably have played a part in pushing him into the arms of someone else. Well, I'm calling BS.

There are plenty of evangelical Christian women more attractive by arbitrary standards than me. They did all they were told to do to keep their husbands "satisfied." Yet, none of it prevented an affair. If a husband who claims to follow Christ leads his wife to believe his commitment hinges on her physical appearance, he is acting as nothing more than an entitled, immature, and misogynistic sexist.

Here's the thing: when Stephen and I were engaged, the advice and counsel we received from Jake and others at Entrench fueled anxiety, self-doubt, and division in our relationship. This isn't the fruit of walking in healing and wholeness.

Today, I've found my partnership with Stephen is better now that I can say, "I trust you to not objectify women." And if he does objectify a woman, that's not my fault. The objectification is not evidence of a deficiency in me. I've found my partnership with Stephen is better now that I am not wary of myself and other women. I've found my partnership with Stephen is better now that he can say, "We're on the same team. I want you to exercise the fullness of your gifts so we can offer our best selves to one another." I've found that my life is fuller now that I am not concerned with maintaining any system of oppression within the institutional church.

Chapter 6
Pregnancy and Parenting

Complementarianism communicated that motherhood is the highest and holiest calling. I wanted to be pregnant so badly because I wanted to be part of the "Mom Club" at Entrench. Once I had my first child, though, I didn't feel like I thought I would. The messages Stephen received failed to equip him to deal with his emotions in a healthy way. Complementarianism cuts us off from our emotions, and both of us were living disembodied lives. We tried to carry out the familial roles we were told we were supposed to but kept bumping into each other. We were trying to force ourselves into the boxes prescribed by complementarianism instead of doing what came naturally.

The Sleeping Arrangements

Nicki's Perspective

I decided to interview a friend from Entrench for my blog. She talked about how wives should still be putting their husbands first, even when they become new moms. There I was, exhausted, face-to-face with her, and this was her top-notch advice. I hadn't told her that Stephen was sleeping in the room with our newborn and bringing the baby to me in the guest room when she woke up. However, my friend *did* know about another mom whose husband slept on the couch so that she and the baby could share a bed. My friend was appalled by this.

She insisted that we, as wives and moms, needed to dig around under the bed to find our wife hats, dust them off, and put them on. Our husbands were more important than our kids. The marriage relationship was more important to nurture. Needless to say, that section of the interview didn't make the cut and is not featured in the post. And I never felt comfortable telling her about our sleeping arrangements, which probably doesn't come as a shock.

The Sleeping Arrangements

Stephen's Perspective

The transition to having our first child was good for me. I enjoyed being a dad. Though it was tough adjusting to the stress of having our lives turned upside down, I thought of myself as a good dad. Nicki often told me I was and gave me the "#1 Dad" shirt to prove it. The transition to having our second child was much more difficult for me. I struggled with paternal postnatal depression and experienced deep emotions of great irritability. I didn't know this was a form of depression at the time. I thought it was my sinful selfishness being exposed. Nicki now had two children to care for on her own while I was at work. So, when I was at home, I felt I had to do what I could to relieve her and alleviate her burden.

One way I could do that was to help her get as much rest as she could at night. The first go round with a child, Nicki couldn't sleep well with the baby in our room. So, the second time, Nicki thought it was best for her to sleep in one room while I slept in the room with the newborn. When the baby woke up, I could just take her to Nicki to nurse. I didn't always have a willing spirit or attitude about this. I thought, after all I was doing, what more could I give? I believed I had the harder role of having to work and then come home to jump in with the kids.

This is what happens when there is a hierarchical structure. My perspective was misguided. We were a team and needed to function like a team. We eventually made it through that season and continued in our complementarian mindset, but that was the year this belief system had its first rumblings of change.

Our commitment to complementarianism truly solidified when Stephen and I first became parents. In many ways, being complementarian was easier as I adjusted to becoming a mom. When so much of my brain and body power needed to go toward sustaining babies, it helped to be a stay-at-home mom (SAHM) with Stephen being the only one of us working. It helped to have him handling all our finances. It helped to have him making major decisions. It was working for us, and I was woefully unaware of the amount of privilege that allowed it to work for us. Because it was working for us, I was convinced that it would work for anyone else, if they just let it. I was naïve, judgmental, and self-absorbed.

Just like I wanted to get married to be accepted by the community at Entrench, I wanted to become a mom. At the age of 25, I was on the fast track to becoming one of the thousands of fundamentalist-adjacent women who is perpetually pregnant. Yes, we are grown women who are technically making our own choices. However, when perpetual pregnancy is presented as the only option to glorify God, or the option that most glorifies God, it can lead to trauma for women. This trauma is exacerbated by husbands pressuring their wives to have more children when their wives want to be done giving birth.

My kids were born in November 2014, June 2016, and October 2017. There's nothing inherently wrong with giving birth in rapid succession if it's your choice. However, as the adage goes, "If you can't say no, you aren't free to say yes."[34] To be all the way clear, Stephen never made me feel like I couldn't say no. The theology I was taught at Entrench told me I couldn't say no. When I breathe in the innocence, fierceness, and steadfast love of my kids, I wouldn't have it any other way. But, truth be told, I was having babies when I should have been in therapy, growing in self-awareness and healing my own trauma.

* * * * *

Part of our complementarian indoctrination included reciting that Stephen and I were equal in dignity, value, and worth, but our roles were not equal. Our roles were complementary and intended to display the "gospel." I'm not quite sure how Christ's love, the love that Stephen

101

was supposed to demonstrate towards me, translated to leadership. Love and leadership are not interchangeable, but interchange they did.

If marriage was the norm to aspire to at Entrench, motherhood was the "highest and holiest calling" for women. This mantra, intended to esteem mothers, inevitably drove a wedge between women. It excluded anyone who didn't have children and diminished their contributions. Producing one progeny after another was part of the "quiverfull" culture. Though I don't want to, I'll quote the ESV because that's what Jake used. Jake seized each opportunity to reference Psalm 127:3-5, "Behold, children are a heritage from the LORD, the fruit of the womb a reward. Like arrows in the hand of a warrior are the children of one's youth. Blessed is the man who fills his quiver with them! He shall not be put to shame when he speaks with his enemies in the gate."

Quiverfull is the idea that truly godly families "believe that God knows how many children are right for them."[35] Oftentimes, this "trusting the Lord" with family planning leads to large families. Those who adhere to Quiverfull dogma think they are birthing babies to add to the Lord's army, children to disciple and discipline in the knowledge and admonition of the Lord. They fear the "culture" or the "world" corrupting God's people. Therefore, the reaction is to birth children into the ideology. It's usually easier to indoctrinate a small child who relies on their parents for everything than to convert new people to a harmful belief system. Publicly, it's often framed as "Children are a blessing from the Lord, so have lots of them."

Jake even taught, through a literal interpretation of the story of Adam and Eve, that Eve was created to be Adam's helper. According to Jake, the best way Eve helped Adam was in fulfilling the "creation mandate" to be fruitful and multiply. Naturally, he concluded, the best way his own wife could help him was by bearing their children. Reducing a woman to her reproductive parts acting as an assembly line is part and parcel of the Quiverfull tradition.

Remaining a DINK (dual income, no kids) family was regarded as selfish. This was made abundantly clear by Jake in private conversations with us and some of our friends. If the reason for postponing children was to better prepare financially, the remedy was to trust that God would provide. Jake made his opinion on this topic public knowledge when he was on a panel during a parenting conference. The panelists were asked questions from the audience. One participant was curious about whether or not it would be wise to add another addition to a family when finances were tight. The moderator handed the question off to Jake, as the pastor on the panel with the largest family. Jake matter-of-factly boiled it down to a lack of faith. God wants us to reproduce, after all, so God will make a way. We just have to be obedient.

It was always presented as selfish to not get married. Once married, it was presented as selfish to not have children. Those relationships of marriage and parenting were meant to make us more like Christ. "If you don't want to be made more like Christ, then what's wrong with you?" was Jake's whole attitude. For those of us who did have children, no one talked about how harmful it was to bring children into our unhealthiness when we weren't in therapy and were neglecting our emotional well-being. No one talked about how irresponsible it was to cajole young people into having kids that we were not financially or emotionally ready for. No one talked about the realities of being queer in a community that was homophobic or dared mention being infertile. My single friends didn't feel safe approaching the pastors to share about the full scope of their experiences as unmarried women.

Not everyone agreed with Jake, though. There was pushback from a couple of older women at Entrench who encouraged me to use birth control when I offhandedly mentioned that Stephen and I were ready to have children whenever they came and that we were doing very little to prevent pregnancy. These concerned, kind, and wonderful women urgently insisted that I should use birth control, finish my degree, and then have kids. I ignored them, though, convinced they were wrong. They were disagreeing with Jake and an author I admired who wrote that anyone who told us to control the size of our families via family-planning strategies was believing lies and not trusting God.

I redirected my efforts to trying to convince Stephen we should adopt a child from Haiti or Nepal. That we — as newlyweds without much money and with me still in school — were fit to be parents and should adopt. He was resistant to the idea. There was a lot of white saviorism within my reasoning. It was dangerous for me to think that we were the best solution for Black and brown children, internationally or domestically.

Any money we were going to use to adopt a Black or brown child could instead go toward helping reunite a family, supporting a Black or brown family in their adoption journey, or something similar. I was nowhere near thinking this way back then. No, back then, I was praying for Stephen to change his mind because that's something I was allowed to do. I was not allowed to bring the issue up repeatedly, because that is nagging, and it's "better to live on the corner of a roof than to share a house with a nagging wife" Proverbs 21:9 (CSB). No nagging. Just praying for God to "soften" Stephen's heart to what I thought was clearly God's will.

* * * * *

Stephen and I were married for almost four and a half years before having kids. We weren't trying to be a DINK family, but that's the way it was for much longer than we expected. The disappointment of not getting pregnant was only made worse by the misbelief that it was my duty to bear children as the best way to be a helper to Stephen. We didn't wait to have kids because we wanted to have more money in the bank, a house, or more time together. We did think back when I was still in college that it would be ideal to have children after I graduated, but we were seeking receptive hearts to what we were being taught was the Lord's will.

Naturally, Jake made it seem like God's will was a "quiverfull" of children. When Stephen and I decided to actively try to get pregnant, over a year passed by with no baby. So, Stephen and I stepped up our game. I received medical advice, personal advice, and unsolicited advice, to no avail. Thinking of Hannah from the Bible, I initiated her strategy of entreating God. Hannah's entreating led to 1 Samuel 1:27, "For this child I prayed, and the LORD has granted me my petition that I made to him" (ESV). At the time, I thought we were having to wait so God could teach me a lesson, the lesson that this god was in control of my womb. There was a whole slew of Bible verses to back up this claim, but it's such an insensitive claim. What kind of a jerk wants to use the pain of infertility to teach a lesson? The god I was taught to fear while needing to say that he is good. That's who.

Soon after Stephen's 30th birthday, the time had come: I was pregnant with our first. It was my second year as a third-grade teacher at Hunter Street Elementary. Teaching was a profession I'd thrown myself into completely. It was the norm for me to stay at the school working until 6:00 p.m. when the janitorial staff were locking up. Every weekend I spent hours planning engaging lessons and grading student work. The Winthrop faculty-in-residence at Hunter Street said I was on track to being named Teacher of the Year if I kept it up, though she didn't know I lacked a robust social life outside of work and church. The Teacher of the Year dream was within reach if I just kept grinding. I'd already been asked to present at conferences, including one in New Orleans. Standing in front of a group of educators and sharing strategies that had worked with my students was invigorating.

After a few more years, I'd be ready to be a mentor teacher to a Winthrop intern. Nothing was going to stop me from achieving my goals as an educator. That is, until I took a pregnancy test and saw two lines. Typing in the first day of my last menstrual period, I received an estimated due date of November 1, 2014.

Our firstborn, Joshua, made his way into the world on his due date. (Even from the womb, he knew his Momma was a planner and liked to keep a schedule.) It was determined by my midwife that I required stitches after she'd needed to cut an episiotomy. So, after an exhausting labor and delivery at home, Stephen and I made the drive to the hospital, newborn baby Joshua in tow. After a traumatic hospital experience (that I detail in *As Familiar as Family*), we were finally home and together a few days later.

During one of our first meals, we had Joshua in a bassinet beside us as we ate in the kitchen. Stephen looked over at Joshua and started crying, which made this the fifth time I'd ever seen him cry. (First was after the fire. Second was when he was laid off. Third was right after Joshua was born. Fourth was at the hospital.) As he cried, he said to Joshua, "I don't know how I ever could have thought you would be a burden," meaning financially.

Throughout the next week, I wrestled with anger and disappointment. I felt like my body betrayed me, that I couldn't even successfully complete the thing I'd been told my body was made to do. When I thought about the hospital administrator who had threatened us, I felt cheated out of the joy of being a new mom. When the administrator was in the room, I had felt powerless and helpless. I hate that feeling. This was the only chance I got for a first birth experience. There are no do-overs. Plus, I had to keep my legs squeezed together, it stung when I peed, and I didn't sleep for more than an hour at a time for days. In addition to the physical recovery, I was emotionally traumatized by the treatment I'd received at the hospital.

To top it all off, I felt nothing when I gazed at Joshua. Focusing on mustering up the over-the-moon love everyone kept droning on about didn't manifest it. Then, there was the guilt I was carrying because I'd begged for this baby. I could hold the product of my invocation. 1 Samuel 1:27, right? "For this child I prayed, and the LORD has granted me my petition" (ESV). But I didn't even want to hold him. Feeling more (emotionally) burdened than blessed, shame plunged me further into desolation because of the thoughts that preoccupied my mind.

Adding the label of mother didn't bring me any closer to knowing who I was, but in my context, I wasn't supposed to be concerned about having my own identity. I'd been a third grade teacher for two years, but now I was going to be a SAHM. Engrossed in being a wife and mother was how I was meant to live. Or so I thought. Besides, I believed that any inclination that tempted me away from my "highest and holiest calling" was surely an attack of the enemy meant to distract me. I couldn't let my guard down for a moment lest I, like Mother Eve, be led astray. To suffer in childbearing and become a mother over and over again until I could conceive no more was my lot in life. That was the most important task entrusted to me to help my husband. I knew I might as well hurry up and be content with it.

One mom at Entrench challenged me to journal "the hard things" about being a mom at the end of each day. She then encouraged me to thank God for those things. There was no room for me to express anything but gratitude when talking to other moms. Meanwhile, Jake challenged the congregation to pray a big prayer during the service. In the front of my notebook, I wrote my prayer. I prayed for God to use me to proclaim the gospel to thousands of moms. In response to my prayer, I started a blog about the stresses and joys of life, specifically as a mom. I was trying to embrace my new role with everything I had but still wanted to dream a little for myself. Journaling was something I'd always done. Through writing posts for a blog, I found a creative outlet that I could line up with the expectation for motherhood to be my whole schtick.

* * * * *

Each night when Stephen got home from work, I felt like I had to give him a rundown of everything I accomplished while he'd been away. There was an internal pressure to report how productive I'd been so that he would value what I was doing in our home and not resent me for my lack of income. Turns out, I was also depressed; I just didn't know it. One night during Joshua's newborn months, I left Joshua with Stephen and went to my best friend Anne's house so we could watch another episode of the television show *Parenthood*. Anne's house had become my preferred place to be, even over my own home. She asked me, "Do you think you could have postpartum depression?" I was sure that I did not. Reformed theology's version of toxic positivity had me thinking that because I had Jesus, I couldn't be depressed. The thing is, I didn't want to be alive anymore. I hated my life. But there was no one I could admit that to.

Meanwhile, I was shocked to learn that Stephen and I shouldn't have vaginal intercourse during the six-week postpartum period, and maybe even for longer, considering my surgery. I was told that I wouldn't have full control over my vagina and rectum for up to a year, and that the full strength of the muscles might never return to what it was prior to the surgery. This meant standing in our kitchen and peeing because I couldn't squeeze tightly enough. While I stood there crying, Stephen tenderly changed my pants because I was still too sore to lift my legs. Way to kill a mood, Nicki, if there was any chance of setting a sultry one.

When I was interested in some type of intimacy, I suggested oral sex. Stephen was so freaked out, and I told one of my mentors. She assured me he'd be changing his mind soon enough. Her advice for him was to "just get through it" and use peroxide on his toothbrush. This wasn't the first time she'd talked with me about just getting through sex. Granted, in my relationship with Stephen, I was the one who was almost always ready to have sex. However, if I wasn't, I did not need the message to "just get through it."

Stephen and I were often too exhausted for sex anyway. There was nothing that could have prepared us for the sleep deprivation that comes with a newborn. When the time changed in the spring and Joshua consistently started sleeping through the night, it was amazing what a few nights of uninterrupted sleep did for us. We'd been bickering constantly. I was so annoyed with Stephen's ability to quickly fall asleep, and stay asleep, while I laid there with my eyes open waiting for the baby to wake up. I was unable to sleep because of all the goat-like grunts coming from Joshua's little body. Then, after I finally drifted off, I had to be the one up with the baby. The contempt began in those early weeks when I couldn't get out of bed easily, due to my surgery, to nurse Joshua in the middle of the night.

Nudging Stephen (seriously, how could he not hear the baby crying in the bassinet at the end of the bed), he would sit straight up. I'd ask him to get the baby. He'd mumble, "Oh, yeah, okay," and then recline on his elbow before settling back under the covers. He'd instantly be back in a state of deep slumber as if I'd never awakened him. This meant either doing the whole thing over again or just pressing through the pain to get the baby myself. Most of the time, I just got the baby myself. From there, the contempt continued to build between us. Every little thing we did got on the other's nerves. Stephen felt like I thought he couldn't do anything right. I wouldn't say I felt like he couldn't do anything right, per se, but I did struggle since he wasn't doing things my way.

The work of motherhood sometimes seemed like it was out-weighing the joy, until one night when I carried Joshua into his room and something began to shift. The air was lighter, yet somehow full of possibility. Curled up in the padded blue hand-me-down glider, I sensed a hint of hope. I unclipped my light gray nursing tank to start the next round-the-clock feeding session, acutely aware of Joshua's chubby cheek pressed against my bare breast. With his free hand, he reached for my cheek before resting his open palm on my chest. We locked eyes, and I completely melted into the dark brown puddles that stared up at me. When he finished milking me dry, he was still hungry. So, I stood up and passed him to Stephen.

Stephen slowly, gently, rocked Joshua, back and forth, back and forth, while feeding him a bottle. Sitting on the footrest, I swayed in tandem with the rocker. Out of nowhere, the flicker of hope I'd felt earlier flamed as Joshua began laughing. And he just kept laughing, a surprisingly satisfying belly laugh that rose from the depths of our little baby's squishy body. The more he laughed, the more we laughed. The more we laughed, the more he laughed. Time stood still as we collectively basked in the simple pleasure of each other's presence. It was the anchor I didn't know I needed.

* * * * *

My initial reaction to having two under two, two in diapers, two sweet babies completely dependent on me, made me weak in the knees. It wasn't long before doubt and fear crept in and consumed me because of my experience with Joshua's birth. The traumatic final minutes of labor and delivery coupled with the hospital stay, followed by postpartum depression, tainted my excitement. I knew I wanted to have another home birth and needed to select a midwife. Stephen and I met with Nova, the midwife who assisted Joshua's birth.

When we talked around our oblong wooden kitchen table, Nova patiently answered every question and assuaged every fear. She spoke of how this was a new birth. Joshua's was done, and I could do this. On June 18th, at 3:41 a.m., our Emma Kate entered the world after a brisk labor. One reason we chose the name Emma Kate was because we could shorten it to EK. As far as birth goes, hers was amazing. It was everything I wished my first birth experience had been. But maybe EK's birth seemed so phenomenal because of the difficulty associated with Joshua's birth.

In the following weeks, I kept thinking about how unreal it was that I got to be EK's mother. I wondered what she would be like as she grew. Would her personality match Joshua's or would they be polar opposites? The second time around, I didn't even mind the night feedings as much. Comparing how I felt after EK's birth with how I felt after Joshua was born, I could already tell that the postpartum period would be vastly different. Don't get me wrong. EK's labor was still labor, but it was a whole new experience. Joshua's birth was redeemed in a way as EK's arrival ushered in the healing of some wounds.

As I was adjusting to life with two littles, Stephen began serving at Entrench as the lead deacon for the first slate of deacons. It was while Stephen was attending one of those deacon meetings that I developed mastitis, which led to a revelation about how I couldn't keep living like we were living. I had limits and needed to not only acknowledge that but embrace it. There was no way I could continue prioritizing everyone else above myself.

Though I no longer felt the pressure to have dinner on the table when Stephen arrived, I now felt the pressure to make sure the kids were well-behaved and quiet (during the worst hour for wee ones), have make-up and a smile on my face, wear "real clothes," and welcome Stephen warmly, all in the name of ensuring our home was his sanctuary.

* * * * *

As parents of young children, we made sure to implement something we'd heard discussed before we even became parents. We did not call our kids "sir" or "ma'am." The publicly declared reason was because we wanted them to understand that these honorifics were reserved for showing respect to adults. The more honest reason was because we didn't view them as whole humans worthy of respect. Also, we didn't want to destabilize the hierarchy by making our kids think they had any authority in our home.

In a hierarchical system, everyone in the hierarchy wants to have someone to dominate. Husbands (and the whole family) are dominated by a god who looks an awful lot like the pastor. Then, husbands dominate their wives and children. Wives don't want to be on the bottom, so they dominate their kids. It's no wonder that the sons, in particular, go on to dominate others, including their siblings as children and their own families in adulthood.

A few years ago, I read an article titled "Your Child Is Your Neighbor" by Jen Wilkin. I regret to say that the source of where I found this was on The Gospel Coalition (TGC). Though I no longer align with much of what is elevated within TGC, I am grateful for the ways I was transformed after reading this article.

Wilkin wrote, "If you asked me the single-most misleading statement I've heard with regard to parenting, it would be this: The Bible is relatively silent on the topic of parenting. On the surface, this statement appears true…Until we remember that children are people. Because if children are people, then they are also our neighbors. This means that every scriptural imperative that speaks to loving our neighbor as we love ourselves suddenly comes to bear on how we parent."[36] It should not have been a revolutionary revelation that my children are people, but it radically changed the way I viewed them.

The narrative I had been taught about children included that they were to be seen and not heard. Pastors taught that children were to be controlled because they weren't mature enough to be trusted to make their own decisions. Even the more benevolent evangelical teaching that emphasized removing shame to get to a child's heart, instead of focusing on altering outward behavior, still commanded that spanking be part of the disciplinary process. The same older woman who told me I couldn't tell Stephen "no" to sex also taught that it was crucial to teach the children I didn't even have at the time that they must obey me the first time I told them to do something.

First-time obedience hinged on the principles of obeying right away, all the way, and with a happy heart. While there are certainly circumstances related to safety where children should listen and act quickly, I realized this wasn't my primary motivation. Instead, I was treating my children as an extension of my ego. If my children misbehaved in public, I thought that provided evidence of a deficiency in me as a mom. I thought that onlookers would think I was failing as a parent (because that's how I viewed other parents when their kids didn't listen to them right away, all the way, and with a happy heart).

Well, rather than seeing children as less than full humans for me to dominate, and rather than seeing myself as the authority figure that they must acquiesce to, I began to see children as truly equal to adults. When I see the children around me as my equals, I treat them with dignity. I respect their boundaries, independence, and bodily autonomy. As a mom, I am now teaching my kids the power of no. I don't withdraw love from them when they tell me no. I am helping them establish healthy boundaries for themselves, with me, and with others, and giving them opportunities to practice implementing their boundaries in safe community.

However, during our Entrench days, Stephen and I certainly elevated ourselves above our children. We positioned ourselves as their authorities in all matters, including spiritual matters. We did catechisms with the kids, though Joshua was not even two years old and EK was a baby. The catechisms were usually done, inconsistently, around the dinner table. Stephen had to be the one to lead our family devotionals, even though I was the Early Childhood Education major and it came more naturally to me to plan engaging lessons. It wasn't acceptable for me to take over because then I'd be usurping Stephen's authority. Around this time, I participated in a book study at another local church. We were learning about the impact mothers had on men who were considered church fathers within white evangelicalism. It was affirmed that, as mothers, we would have a spiritual influence on our children, and that influence could be quite strong, but it should not overshadow our husband's influence.

Looking back on that time period, I think about how our family devotional time would have happened consistently, not sporadically, if I'd been in charge, because I was stronger in this area than Stephen. But Stephen would've felt like a failure and inadequate. This begs the question: was the goal for our kids to learn about God or to be indoctrinated into patriarchy?

* * * * *

Retreating further into myself, I noticed the difference in my demeanor when our chiropractor suddenly and unexpectedly passed away. When we tried out and talked with other chiropractors, I didn't ask a single question. The same person who used to sing her food orders in restaurants sat silently in offices six years later. Lacking the energy to do almost everything outside of caring for Joshua and EK, I wanted (and needed) Stephen to take more initiative and still wanted him to be more assertive, including with my parents.

One day, a cousin was meeting EK, a visit she'd arranged prior. There was a knock at the door. I knew it was my parents, even though they had not called. When my cousin overheard me telling Stephen that's who it was, she said, "They wouldn't just show up."

Oh yes, they would.

And they did.

Here was Stephen's moment to shine, to let them know that in the future it would help if they made plans with us ahead of time. Instead, he dully sat there.

My dad was working in Rock Hill around this time as well. I took the kids to see him at work and have lunch with him once. Foolishly, I hoped he would arrange more visits to stop by to spend time with his grandkids after work. He did not. He only came by once, and unannounced at that. My friend Tessa was chatting in the living room with me while Joshua and EK napped. My dad came in and took my recliner. Within a few minutes, he said, "Let 'em have another. That'll break 'em." This was in reference to me, Stephen, and our growing family. The realization hit me then that there were people who wanted to see me broken. Even worse, some of them were people who should have been rooting for my wholeness and healing.

Little did Stephen and I know, we *were* going to "have another." When I saw the lines indicating a positive result, Stephen just hugged me. He let me sob on his shoulders, as the weight of a third child hit me. Then I remembered the New Year's resolution I'd made during a service at Entrench before ringing in 2017. "Resolved to plead with God to live like motherhood is one of His ordained means of spiritual growth in my life and to enjoy Him as I mother." I had penned these words in the front of my journal. Rather than being distraught, I was reminded to practice gratitude.

Every Sunday, we struggled out the door to get to church on time. There was another blowout diaper, a nursing session that went long, or any number of things that can slow down progress with two little ones. Stephen and I argued all the way to church until putting a smile on our faces to walk inside the building. We called it "spiritual warfare," attacks from the enemy who wanted to discourage and defeat us, to keep us from going to be with God's people. Who could've guessed that these reactions stemmed from the activated nervous systems of two humans who were stretched too thin and needed to experience some calm stability?

Over the following months, Stephen and I planned for Pappas Baby #3. As Joshua was talking more and more, we taught him the correct anatomical names for his body parts, as we went on to do with all of our kids. I wanted them to be ahead of where I was at their ages. I was already thinking about how to foster safe, open communication with them, communication that would not one day result in me slapping them for saying "dildo."

For almost four years, I'd been perpetually pregnant or nursing. The fact that homeschooling was right around the corner with Joshua almost ignited a panic attack in me. Stephen was adamant that we needed to homeschool our kids (and by we, it would really be me). There was even a mom at Entrench who said, "I've never heard a reason for not homeschooling that wasn't selfish." I didn't want to be selfish. However, it was getting more difficult to remind myself that any resistance I felt was a result of the enemy keeping me from living a faithful life devoted to God's ways that are higher than my ways.

Our midwife, Nova, referred to my third pregnancy as our "wild card." Throughout the final three weeks, I experienced prodromal labor, labor that starts and stops. I was convinced this was the pregnancy that would never end. Each time the contractions began, I would get excited and think the baby would be born some time that very night. The next morning, the sun would gradually brighten our room. I would wake up, disappointed, and cry some more.

After crying and talking with Stephen, tranquility would return, and I would appreciate the time I still had with just Joshua and EK. Nova offered additional support and encouragement as I battled fears and frustrations. I was 42 weeks pregnant when Levi arrived. The relief I felt was indescribable as I uttered, "Thank you, dear Lord Jesus" and nestled against a pillow that padded the iron bed frame. With three under three in tow, my true self continued to slip further out of reach.

Stephen and I had no idea that a whole lot was going to be changing in our lives very soon, but surely we would always be complementarian, right? I mean, we couldn't question complementarianism because the marriage roles of complementarianism equaled the gospel, and the gospel couldn't be critiqued. But I was tired, okay, because pregnancy is hard on a body. I was finally tired enough to start questioning the complementarian foundation our marriage was built upon.

THOUGHTS FROM STEPHEN

In the years leading up to parenthood, I really wanted to get it right. I wanted to be a strong man of God so that I could lead my future kids and family well. That meant attending the "Man Up" conference Entrench hosted and rigorously taking notes. Thankfully, there wasn't too much of the "to be a man you have to be a wild outdoorsman" in the messaging, though there were plenty of those types of men at Entrench. Each time one of them talked about adventures camping, kayaking, or backpacking through mountain ranges or using tools in their fully fitted workshop to build some new creation out of wood, I felt inadequate.

My days were spent behind a computer looking at spreadsheets. The solace was that even *that* could be done for the glory of God. Plus, the work paid well enough for us to get approved for a home loan. We knew that when we had kids, Nicki would stay home with them, so when we applied for a loan, we only factored in income from my jobs. Following the "Man Up" conference, I got together with a small group of guys to read a book on manhood. It felt good to have that community and camaraderie with like-minded men.

The first Father's Day after Nicki found out she was pregnant, she bought me a dark blue short-sleeve t-shirt with the message "#1 Dad" on it. She was so encouraging as she told me I was already the #1 Dad. I told her that I would feel presumptuous wearing it before the baby was born, and that I would probably still feel that way wearing it in public even *after* the baby was born. (When I tried to find her a #1 Mom shirt the next year for Mother's Day, there weren't any in stores. I'm sure they can be found online, but I have yet to see a single #1 Mom shirt in a store.)

When Joshua was born, Nicki needed me. And Joshua needed me. It felt nice to be needed, when I was able to meet the needs. When I wasn't able to meet the needs, those familiar feelings of inadequacy crept in. Like when Nicki was in labor, and the midwife couldn't detect the baby's heartbeat. I was so scared our baby wouldn't make it that I buried my head behind Nicki's. The relief I felt when we realized he was alive is indescribable; I cried tears of relief and joy. This was probably the third time Nicki had seen me cry.

My heart still breaks when I think about holding Joshua as Nicki was in surgery at the hospital the day he was born. It had been hours since he last ate. He wanted to nurse and needed his mom. We hadn't brought any formula with us because we hadn't expected to be stuck at the hospital that long. All I could do was weep as he cried that hungry, helpless, newborn cry. Rocking him, I tried to soothe him until Nicki returned. He eventually wore himself out and fell asleep in my arms. It felt like an eternity waiting for Nicki to get back to the room after surgery. A doctor came in around 10:00 p.m. to inform me that Nicki had made it through surgery, but the tears were worse than anticipated. We would need to stay longer for her to recover.

The next day, we were told by a hospital administrator that Joshua looked jaundiced. Trying to be helpful, I took Joshua for a drive to get some sun on his skin. I'd heard this was a good idea. Getting to a sunny spot, I parked the car and unzipped his clothes so the sun could shine on him. After some time sitting in the car, I put his onesie back on, buckled him, and drove to the parking garage. Once I parked and went to unbuckle him, I noticed that he seemed very lethargic. I began to panic and questioned what I had just done.

Picking him up out of his car seat, I was careful to support his head. I carried him back into the hospital to return to Nicki's room. As I walked through the hospital, all I could think was that I had done something that would lead to his death. Instead of helping him, I felt like I made things worse. I felt scared and like a failure. No way was I the #1 Dad. When I entered the room, Nicki and her best friend Anne were there.

Crying, I shared that I thought I hurt him and made him worse because he was more lethargic now. Nicki calmly took him, gave him a bottle of the formula Anne had brought, and made everything better. Joshua immediately perked up after downing the formula. Here Nicki was, after spending nine months pregnant, enduring a long, painful labor and giving birth the day before, having major reconstructive surgery the night before, not getting any sleep, and holding me together. She was definitely the #1 Mom.

I didn't know what to do to take care of Nicki when we were in the hospital or how to advocate for her and Joshua. When the administrator had threatened us, I just sat there. But I held Joshua and bonded with him over those few days. I can still feel his tiny frame in my arms as I slept in the recliner in the hospital room. You couldn't put him down in the plastic crib box because he'd immediately wake up, so he slept in my arms night and day. It's a miracle I didn't drop him while I slept. When we got home, it was time for me to step up even more so that Nicki could rest her body after surgery. The heightened emotions and lack of solid sleep caught up to me, and I was teary-eyed often. Like the time I looked over at Joshua in his bassinet in the kitchen and cried while eating dinner with Nicki. Prior to him being born, I only thought about kids and planning for them in economic terms. As I looked at him that night, I told him through teary eyes, "I don't know how I could ever view you as an expense." Joshua was my little buddy, then and forever.

I only had a week off work following Joshua's birth. Then, the organization where I worked had Leadership and Board Meetings. I was involved in the planning and coordination of the meetings, so I felt like I needed to be there. Also, I didn't have the PTO to take more time than that. The transition was difficult for Nicki, so I definitely should have figured out how to take more time off. I think it was so hard for her because of the isolation that came with trying to put a baby on a schedule and having to be home at certain times so he could sleep in a darkened room with the sound machine on. When she was told, "Don't try to put a newborn on a schedule" by one mom at Entrench (which contradicted the advice of other moms at Entrench), I couldn't keep up with what to do and when to do it.

Nicki would leave the house to go spend time with Anne in the evenings, and I could finally relax and try to do things the way I thought worked best, or at least test something out without the stress of Nicki telling me why it wouldn't work. I had heard from many older people who had been through this before that I needed to enjoy this time. So, I tried to keep that mindset, not wishing it away; however, it was hard with the stress of a rigid schedule for Joshua. I wanted to just be with him, hold him, go with the flow, and comfort him, but that's not what Nicki was reading. It was a stressful time trying to adjust to this new way of life with no clue what we were doing.

Things weren't all bad though. The night of the 2015 Super Bowl, instead of going to a friend's house to watch the game, I stayed home. While putting Joshua to bed, I was holding him in the rocker in his room after reading a story from his *Jesus Storybook Bible* and feeding him a bottle. Nicki had come in to join us, too. Joshua started laughing at something. We, in turn, began laughing. Our laughing fed off each other until I was laughing so hard that tears streamed from my eyes. It was a very special moment for me that I would've missed had I gone to watch the game somewhere else. Things got a lot better when Joshua turned four months old and began sleeping through the night. Getting good, restorative sleep makes a world of difference. As Joshua grew each month, he increasingly became more engaged and loved to smile. I can still see that toothless grin with his little bit of hair parted to the side and hear his contagious laugh. In my very biased opinion, I think he would have made a good baby model.

It was becoming more fun to have him and be able to do things with him without being so stringent. Then, a bit of a shock: Nicki called me at work to tell me she was pregnant. I couldn't believe it. There was no way I had it in me to go through everything we'd experienced with Joshua again, but this time with a new baby and a toddler. Plus, our best friends, Anne and Jeremy, told us they were moving. Nicki wouldn't have that friendship to help her through the tough times ahead.

* * * * *

Adjusting to two under two was hard. I learned from Joshua's birth experience that I should take more time off work and did. Nicki was more relaxed the second go round, but she was still particular about the kids' schedules. Her preferences took precedence. It makes sense, since she was the one with them more than me, but I wanted a say in what was done. When Nicki took four-month-old EK with her for the weekend to spend time with Anne, I really enjoyed the weekend I got with Joshua. I didn't throw his schedule out the window, but I wasn't as rigid in implementing it as Nicki.

Something I noticed in myself was building resentment, and not just toward Nicki. Also toward EK. As I dug deeper, I realized that maybe I was resenting that Nicki and EK didn't need me as much as Nicki and newborn Joshua had needed me. Nicki and EK were bonding, and I missed out on the level of bonding I'd gotten with Joshua. Just as Nicki struggled with postpartum depression after Joshua's birth, I struggled with paternal postnatal depression after EK's birth and wasn't sure what to do about it. I had only ever heard of postpartum depression as it relates to mothers and didn't have this language available to me at the time. All I knew was that I had moments of intense irritability toward the new baby. I knew something was wrong but was too scared and prideful to admit to others what I was feeling.

Finally reaching a point where I had to talk with someone, I set up a meeting with Jake. Fearing what he would think of me, I shared with him what I was experiencing. Surely he would be able to relate to what I was feeling, seeing as how he had five kids. He told me that he had never gone through anything similar. His response was, "I hope you get the help you need." He didn't follow up, either.

There was another friend I told. He listened and was empathetic, but he wasn't sure what to do. I was crying out for help in the only way I knew, but I wasn't getting the support I needed. It didn't cross my mind to seek out a qualified professional because I thought, "I have Jesus. I don't need a counselor/therapist," though I probably would have gone if Jake had recommended one. I at least would've met with Jake if he had made himself available for some sessions or offered any type of support. It took a lot for me to be vulnerable and admit that I was struggling. To then feel even more alone on the other side of my request for help was disconcerting. With everything I was giving to Entrench, you would think I'd get something back when I needed it, but I started to feel like I just needed to "man up," like we were taught at that conference at church. I just needed to push through. The church needed me.

Yes, my family needed me, too. However, I internalized the message that, even though I was supposed to be the leader and provider for my family, our kids were Nicki's primary mission field. My wife and kids should still look to me as their spiritual authority, but I had important things I needed to get done for Jake at Entrench, though I would have ultimately said I was using my spiritual gifts to do it all for God and God's glory. Never mind the fact that it felt like my family and my church were pitted against each other when my family should have come first. That gnawing feeling in my gut could be explained away by reminding myself that my church was also my family, and my church family was God's family. I was supposed to love God more than my family, and I loved God by obeying God. To obey God meant to serve God's people. It was easy to get swept up in that reasoning and forget that the people right inside of my home were God's people, too. They should have gotten the best of me, not the leftovers.

In the background leading up to my paternal postnatal depression, I was the volunteer coordinator. Nicki and I were at Entrench early each Sunday to set up; we greeted everyone, and we stayed late to break down. Being a staff member meant attending monthly staff meetings. I was also the church's bookkeeper, which meant weekly bank deposits and balancing the books but also having to constantly ask Jake to fill out the reimbursement form and not just give me a bunch of receipts. On top of this, I completed a few months of elder classes.

      With no formal theological training, the men of the church could go through a yearlong discipleship process with the pastors. In the sessions, we learned all the major and minor points the pastors wanted us to adhere to with the possibility of one day, maybe, becoming an elder. I didn't necessarily want to be an elder in fulfillment of feeling "called" to it. Maybe I wanted to be one because of the relationship and connection it offered me and a feeling of approval. Regardless of my motivation, Jake encouraged me to sign up. So, I did.

      During the months when I participated, we read a book in which the author gave a "biblical defense" for spanking. It was required reading for the course. The next assignment was to write a paper detailing my position on divorce and what the Bible allowed. Basically, the necessary position the elders were looking for was that it is never acceptable, under any circumstances, to get a divorce. That's what I wrote and got good feedback on. It's what I believed at that time. I was completely bought in, as I came to interpret the biblical texts in that way.

Taking care of our kids and home was my full-time and only job. Yet, there was the expectation that I not talk about the kids with Stephen when out on a rare date. Several different sources communicated to me that I needed to avoid the topic of our children when we were having one-on-one time away from them. Even Stephen (not to be confused with the early aughts Disney show *Even Stevens*) voiced this sentiment to me. His reasoning was that he wanted something beyond our kids to bond us.

Why was it that the thing I spent all my time doing was not something to burden or bore Stephen with? For all the "highest and holiest calling" language, it sure felt like an erasure of my contributions, a minimization of what I filled my days doing. Stephen could talk about his job with me. If I got bored, I felt compelled to feign interest and nod along while he rattled off QuickBooks jargon. But the work I did as a mom wasn't worthy of the same admiration. I needed to find something else that was more interesting to converse about with him.

The lie that motherhood is *the* highest and holiest calling detached me from an individual identity. Motherhood certainly is important work for me, but it is not my only important work. Over the past few years, I've been dedicating time to discovering who I am and what I want for myself. My kids, and Stephen, need to bear witness to me taking risks to try new things and flourishing outside of being a mom.

Recently, I was able to articulate to Stephen that our kids do bond us. And that's beautiful. No, I don't want to be defined solely by my role as a mother. But I also don't want to censor myself from talking about the three humans we made. So, I'm going to talk about them during our dates, evening walks, and whenever else I want to, while Stephen does the same. We never should've been instructed otherwise.

Chapter 7
Home and Finances

Complementarianism categorizes certain roles in the home as masculine and others as feminine. Stephen and I tried to live out our complementarian beliefs by adhering to "rules" about what we should do based on being a wife or a husband. I handled most of the interior of our home, Stephen the exterior. In addition, he took care of our finances. However, as the pressures of living up to the unattainable standards of complementarianism took a toll on me as a wife and mother, something had to change.

If Stephen and I had stayed committed to living out the tenets of complementarianism via gendered chores, it surely would have destroyed me.

The Gospel Mats

Nicki's Perspective

One day on the way home from my teaching internship, I stopped at Walmart to purchase memory foam bath mats. One teal. The other beige. When Stephen saw them, he wanted me to return them and instructed me not to remove the tags. I removed the tags. He bemoaned my action as he opened the hall closet. He showed me that he had already purchased some mats for me as gifts for our anniversary. Then, he announced that he would be taking back the mats he'd purchased. His reasoning was because I apparently couldn't just trust him by listening when he'd told me not to remove the tags. Regret swallowed me as my eyes filled with tears. He'd been so thoughtful. I was overwhelmed by shame. At the time, I chastised myself for, what I considered, defying him.

Stephen held me in his arms as I profusely apologized for my defiance. He told me I could keep all the mats and didn't have to wait until our anniversary. We shared this story of what we called our "gospel mats" with our community group. In the story, I was the wayward sinner who couldn't patiently wait to be blessed, who instead sought to satisfy myself on my own terms by ripping off price tags. Stephen represented God in the scenario. He had a closet full of blessings for me…if only I could be content until the right time. When I challenged his authority by cutting off the tags, he would have been just in his decision to load up the mats he'd purchased and return them to Anna's Linens. Instead, he richly lavished undeserved blessings on me by allowing me to keep every single mat. (Insert vomiting emoji here, am I right?)

The work continues for me to heal from the damage caused by thinking of myself as ungrateful and defiant.

The Gospel Mats

Stephen's Perspective

It was Nicki's last semester of college. Some of her scholarships had ended because it was her fifth year. We didn't want to take out loans for her tuition costs, so we were on a monthly payment plan. Because of this, we didn't have excess money for non-essentials. Our second wedding anniversary was approaching. Nicki had been wanting memory foam mats for our bathroom. I had the great idea to get her a floor mat for our anniversary, but it was our second anniversary, so why get just one? I splurged a little and got one for the kitchen and one for the other bathroom. Excitedly, I took them home and hid them. I couldn't wait to see the surprise on her face!

It turns out, Nicki had this great idea, too. Being the go-getter she is, she went ahead and got some. When she walked in the door with the bag of floor mats, my heart sank. I couldn't give away the surprise and tell her I just purchased some, so I told her to take them back. After all, I was the head of the house, so she would need to do as I said. Nicki told me, "No, I'm not taking them back."

I felt betrayed and that she couldn't just trust me. Following a tense exchange of trying to get her to take them back and her continuing to resist, I only had one option. Revealing my secret, I showed her all the mats. She felt badly, and I felt justified in my pride. Nicki offered to take back the ones she purchased, but I ended up just saying she could keep them. We were taught in the church we were a part of to try to see the "good news" of Jesus in everyday life. So, we shared with our community group this real-life example of "the gospel" at work.

I represented God, who had this great storehouse of blessings to shower on the beloved. Nicki represented people, who couldn't trust God to give them what they needed or wanted and who took matters into their own hands. I would've been justified to return the mats I purchased and not give them to Nicki, letting her miss out on the joy of the gifts. But I didn't. Just as God gives us grace and bestows gifts upon us that we don't deserve, I thought I was giving grace and bestowing gifts lavishly on her (albeit, we are just talking about floor mats you stand on).

We thought we were so mature being able to see the gospel in this situation. Our community group ate this up. So did my ego. I was the one representing God. Nicki was representing sinners. I didn't even think about how this impacted her, telling this story to others.

Stephen and I didn't have any conversations about household roles. Without talking about them, we broke chores down along stereotypical gender lines based on what we'd seen modeled. As the man, Stephen handled the exterior of our home and the garbage. As the woman, the interior of the home was my responsibility. To make it sound more godly, I was told that the interior of the home was mine to "steward." My "stewardship" included doing things a grown man was perfectly capable of doing for himself, as he had done before we got married. I folded and put away Stephen's laundry for a decade. He never told me I had to, but he also never said I should stop.

When we were engaged, I'd learned from a mentor at Entrench that it was my duty to make our home a sanctuary — for Stephen. Everything from the minute decor to the grand design needed to be done with Stephen's comfort, convenience, and preferences in mind. Since the apartment that I moved into when we got married had previously been his apartment, I left the layout alone. He liked brown and blue, so the sofa slipcovers were brown and blue.

Another aspect of making our home his sanctuary centered around being told that I was the thermostat. This meant I "set the temperature." Talk about pressure. Imagine instilling in new wives or soon-to-be wives that we not only needed to manage our homes but also manage the emotional well-being of our husbands. This didn't raise any red flags, though, because I'd been managing the emotions of boys and men my entire life. For the first few years of our marriage, I tried to make sure I was in a good mood, with a smile on my face, ready to hug and kiss Stephen when he walked in the door. If I was upset with him, I needed to set that aside so that he could come into a happy home. The message inherent in this was that if our home wasn't happy, it was my fault (and he'd be justified in looking for happiness elsewhere).

To take the cheeriness up a notch, I decided to implement something I heard on a podcast episode. There was a woman who sang, "Oh my man, I love him so. He'll never know. All my life was in despair, and then he was there," getting more guttural and animated as the song went on. This was her greeting for her husband when he got home from work. When I told a friend about it, she laughed about how her husband would love it if she sang to him, but she would never do that. Well, I was doing that for Stephen, and hearing her laugh about it led to me feeling embarrassed. She wondered aloud why we as wives are expected to praise our husbands for being decent humans. Good question.

*****

My mom handled all of our family's finances when I was growing up. Often, I passed by the sunroom and saw her hunched over the table, balancing the checkbook. She seemed concerned about how much money was spent on unwarranted items. Witnessing how stressful this was for her, I decided I never wanted that kind of stress for myself.

At 15, I started working. I paid for my own gas and clothes. In a way, I wanted that, partially because I didn't want to be a burden and partially because I wanted that independence. When I was 18, I moved out on my own. I was living with a few friends, paying all my own bills. My limited income from Chick-fil-A covered groceries, gas, and living necessities. Each pay period, I tried to have a little money left over to go out when I could. I had a good handle on my finances. I only overdrew my account once, and I did it with full knowledge it would happen. While waiting for a paycheck to deposit, I was in desperate need of groceries. So, I swiped my card and hoped for the best. That one overdraft charge hovered over me, and I saw it as a source of failure and not being careful enough. Reflexively, I assumed it was proof that I was actually bad with money.

Soon after, Stephen and I got married, and I was told that he was going to be my provider. He was older than me, living on his own, and frugal. I assumed he had never overdrawn his account. Though I'd watched how much my mom struggled and seemed not to trust anyone else enough to turn things over to them, I inherently trusted Stephen when it came to our money.

When I came into our marriage, I was debt-free. I'd paid off my own vehicle and received scholarships and financial aid for school. I was proud of all this. But with our union, Stephen's debt immediately became mine. And buddy had a lot of student loan debt. My jaw is still on the floor from when I found out how much he owed. This new knowledge didn't deter me from putting my monetary hope in him, though. I knew we'd be okay. The challenge of insurmountable debt before us just came with the "two become one" territory.

* * * * *

The fall following the fire at our apartment when we were new-lyweds, Stephen and I were invited to a Halloween party. With Stephen as frugal as he is, we would not be spending money on costumes.

We went to BCM and rummaged around in a closet until he found something he could wear: a blue M&M outfit. When we got home, I looked through my clothes and decided on a pink checkered plaid shirt, faded blue jeans, and pigtails. It was the best I could come up with to portray Mary Ann from *Gilligan's Island*. Naturally, no one knew who I was. One guy asked, "Who are you? No-effort-girl?" Stephen and I still talk about how funny that was. We ended up having a nice time, and the party provided a sort of escape from the aftermath of the fire. But I knew it was my duty as a devoted Christian to bring up the fire to illustrate God's goodness whenever I got the chance.

In one of my classes at Winthrop, we were assigned a project to share a story that highlighted our family values. Since Stephen and I formed a new family when we got married, I chose to present about us and shared about the night he proposed. I chose this story because I wanted to make sure to share the gospel with the class, which was synonymous with complementarianism in my mind. Then, I told my fellow classmates about the fire and how we'd lost everything, but our hope was in Christ. Explaining the lyrics from the song Stephen wrote to propose, I hammered home how it was his responsibility to love me and mine to respect him. My utmost desire in that presentation was for all the women to see what an embodiment I was of submissive femininity so they would aspire to be the same.

The next time our class met, one of my classmates caught up with me afterwards. She handed me an envelope with $800 cash because she wanted to help us out. Then, she told me how she was waiting for a man like Stephen and knew the kind of woman she needed to be in order to be worthy of someone like him. (I wish I could take back so much of what I said in that presentation and counteract the narrative I put forward that she needed to do or be anything other than the kind person she was.) Things were going well, for God's glory, until something happened in a different class.

Human Experience was the name of the class, or something like that. The curriculum centered around seeking answers to questions such as, "Who am I?" and "Why am I here?" Lucky for my classmates, I knew the answers. Or at least I thought I did. We existed to bring God glory, of course, and who I meant by God was quite a narrow interpretation. Without recourse, I was allowed to share the gospel each time I opened my mouth. The free expression of our beliefs was encouraged. No one ever pushed back. Plus, most of us had a Christian background, so rarely did anyone say anything I disagreed with, except for the day a student talked badly about being a SAHM.

The guy proclaimed he didn't want to marry someone who lazily lounged around the house while he worked. The beloved late Rachel Held Evans wrote about this when it came to that feeling of something that's important being devalued.[37] She believed that motherhood, and everything associated with it, is important. She wasn't trying to devalue motherhood when encouraging others to find meaning and identity outside of the role of mom. In that moment in class, though, I doubled down on defending how valuable it was to be a SAHM.

I countered that a SAHM wasn't lazily lounging but instead shaping future generations, working tirelessly to upkeep a properly functioning home, and that she should be honored for those contributions to society. The thing is, I took that student's critique personally because I knew it was expected of me to be a SAHM. I desperately needed the role of SAHM to be seen by people outside of Entrench as important work, as something that was just as important as a corporate job. That day was the first time I felt what would become normal to feel in conservative Christian circles: a false sense of persecution.

All along, I peddled the prosperity gospel of complementarianism that assured women that if they submitted properly, they would be rewarded with a husband who would love them well. Every single wedding card we gave to new couples was filled with the message that we hoped their marriage would reflect the gospel with the groom loving his bride as Christ loves the Church and the bride submitting to her hubs as the Church submits to Christ. (Spoiler alert: I don't care how holy he is, that man ain't Jesus. Double spoiler alert: I wouldn't care if he *was* Jesus, but that's a whole tangent I won't get into right now.)

* * * * *

Stephen and I slowly slid into egalitarianism naturally and, perhaps, accidentally. As we had more children, roles and responsibilities shifted out of necessity. From there, for a good four years or more, I just couldn't get myself out of bed in the mornings. This was especially true on weekdays when my one adult interactee had to leave for work. I was depressed. I've experienced episodic depression throughout my life, but when I became a mom, postpartum depression was a different, yet familiar, layer.

The thing is, I was told I was supposed to meet Stephen's needs above my own, and above our newborn baby's needs. He was to take precedence. Instead of demanding that, Stephen did the thing that complementarians say he's supposed to do by being "like Jesus" and sacrificing for me. He did this willingly and without complaining. He was so patient with me and didn't require more of me. Joyfully, he picked up all the slack. Instead of telling me that I could either say "yes" or "convince me" regarding sex, he respected me when I had no energy. He did this without making me feel guilty because as a human being I am to be valued for more than my body. If Stephen had put his foot down to flex his "headship" and demanded that I cook all the food, wash all the dishes, fold all the laundry, and, well, you get it, I don't think I would be here today.

Russell Moore, the former President of the Ethics & Religious Liberty Commission, lamented that many complementarian marriages are functioning more like egalitarian marriages. He specifically said, "What I fear is that we have many people in evangelicalism who can check off 'complementarian' on a box but who really aren't living out complementarian lives." The deeper underlying distress he expressed was that complementarianism is *"simply going to go away."*[38]

I find it interesting that someone who was over a committee that is supposedly dedicated to ethics would be opposed to marriages being true partnerships, but we know it's not about liberty for all ethics and religions, or even liberty for all interpretations within the Christian tradition, is it? It's about the preservation of a narrow view of marriage that is between one cisgender, heterosexual man and one cisgender, heterosexual woman where the man is the head. It's about religious liberty for complementarians to avoid being critiqued for how their system harms others. It's about hierarchy. Men like Moore repeatedly demonstrate that they are more concerned with the threat of their ideology's death than the absence of abundant life inherent in their ideology.

I've heard things like, "They just don't make 'em like they used to," but I'm not sure the elusive "they" ever did. A world run by patriarchy, historically and currently, leaves no space for men like Stephen. Yes, I realize I am #blessed as I read a text message another mentor sent me about Stephen: "He's one of the good ones." But it's past time for Stephen to be an anomaly. The bar is set unbelievably low for him compared to the scrutiny I've experienced as a wife, and then as a mother. Stephen could teach classes if that would help, but I just don't know if it would. So, "man manufacturer," if you read these words, could you ignore Russell Moore and make more of 'em like Stephen?

* * * * *

Bubbling under the surface after EK's birth was the still unresolved point of tension about Stephen not leaving work at 5:00 or communicating with me when he'd be working late. Once we had kids, I wanted to know when he'd be home because I'd been with the kids all day. I *needed* to know when another adult would be home. Plus, Jake and Entrench occupied so many of Stephen's evenings and weekends.

It's impossible to tally up all the times I had to be with the kids while he had staff meetings, deacon meetings, and elder training meetings. My responsibility as a supportive helper was to keep things at home running smoothly so he could fulfill his responsibilities to the church and his jobs. (He worked full-time at a missions organization and half-time as Entrench's bookkeeper.) Even when my breast was burning because of mastitis while Stephen was at a deacon meeting, I wasn't allowed to complain. As one friend explained, "We're expected to sacrifice our husbands on the altar of Entrench Church."

In addition to "stewarding" our home, it was silently understood that most of the child-rearing and caretaking of our kids were in my "sphere of influence." Don't get me wrong, Stephen did a ton with the kids, much more than a lot of men from the church. I'm thinking specifically about the one who refused to change a poopy diaper. That's right. His wife had to leave events early if one of their diapered kids pooped. The kid had to sit in feces for half an hour until the mom got home to do the diaper change. (That husband went on to hold a prominent leadership role in the church after we left.)

Back then, I would tell myself, or hear other women say things like, "Well, at least Stephen is so helpful," or "At least your husband doesn't work nights." The "at least list" could go on and on. The only winner of the "at least" game in this situation is the patriarchy. "At least" minimized what was difficult for me and propped up the joyful women as the ones to aspire to be like, the real role models.

In that kind of "quiverfull" culture, women are reproducing left and right, year after year, and exist to cheer on their husbands in their personal endeavors (he needs his PhD; he wants to start a business; he wants to be a church planter). Having expectations of your husband is frowned upon. Instead, be grateful he works hard to provide for your family. Then, do all you can to make that easier for him. You're responsible for making your home an oasis — for him. Don't have any expectations from him in the home. He's exhausted (as if I'm not). Plus, the home is part of your "sphere of influence." My true self slipped further out of reach with each diaper change, midnight feeding, and temper tantrum. I felt guilty each time I momentarily entertained thoughts of pursuing something outside of motherhood. My kids were my mission field, or so I'd been taught. I shouldn't have been distracted. But I was. So, I was becoming an outlier at Entrench and felt like if I expected anything at all from Stephen, I was expecting too much.

* * * * *

In the spring of 2018, a women's ministry was started at Entrench. We were going to be studying the Bible intensely together. I couldn't get to the sign-up sheet fast enough. While sitting at a table with a friend during an early meeting in May, she texted me a three-part blog series titled "Toward a Better Reading: Reflections on the Permanent Changes to the Text of Genesis 3:16 in the ESV" by Wendy Alsup and Hannah Anderson. This was big, as we were told the English Standard Version of the Bible is the most accurate translation. The ESV was *the* prized translation at Entrench.

In dealing with Genesis 3:16, the footnote written by the translators of the ESV perpetuated the interpretation that women want to usurp the God-ordained authority of men by existing in opposition to them. In the three-part blog series, Alsup and Anderson offered a more liberating interpretation. For starters, my mind was blown that there was another valid interpretation of a Bible verse that I'd only heard taught one way. My tiny world tilted on its axis a little bit when I concluded that the ESV interpretation wasn't even valid because the translators lacked integrity, my words not Alsup's or Anderson's. (If you're interested in checking out the blog posts, I want to provide a warning that the content in the posts is complementarian and what is called "nonaffirming" of LGBTQ+ folx.)

For context, Genesis 3:16 is part of what's recorded as words from God to Eve. "Your desire shall be contrary to your husband, but he shall rule over you." The word in question is what was translated as "contrary to" in the latest revision of the ESV. Originally translated as "for," Alsup and Anderson examined the Hebrew preposition *'el.* Without venturing too far into the weeds, *'el* "shows the direction something is pointed or headed." It could be translated as to, for, toward, and against. Even when *'el* is against, it denotes direction. The example the authors provided was in the English language, we can say, "The rake is lying against the tree." So how did we end up with *'el* being recorded in the ESV as contrary to?

Alsup and Anderson wrote, "The easiest explanation for why translators changed the 'for' to 'contrary' is that they moved from translation to commentary, projecting the negative meaning of Genesis 4:7-8 back into Genesis 3:16." The commentary they were referencing dated back to the 1970s when some woman who was opposed to feminism partnered with the patriarchy — my words not theirs — to malign women who were fighting for equality. As Alsup and Anderson expounded, "The only way translators can justify rendering *'el* as 'contrary' is to assume something negative about the woman's desire based on the use of desire in Genesis 4:7-8. But such a novel change relies solely on commentary, not on accepted definitions to the Hebrew *'el*."[39] I'd been duped and didn't know it. Further, the changes the committee made to Genesis 3:16 and 4:7 were being touted as permanent, meaning the committee would not revisit these verses, regardless of any additional information brought to their attention.

What happened to the standards of hermeneutics to ensure accurate biblical interpretation? Healthy hermeneutics go right out the window when an ideology, like complementarianism, becomes more important than approaching a biblical text without bias. What else had I been lied to about, whether by commission or omission, when it came to the Bible?

Turns out a lot.

The next post I read was from "The Week of Mutuality" series by Rachel Held Evans. It was #BecauseOfRHE that my beliefs about gender and gender roles began to shift as I opened up to questioning the complementarian theology I'd been taught. I just happened to find the series as I was studying other passages about women and women's roles. Soon after, Stephen and I went out to dinner for our anniversary in May. He didn't say much as I unleashed everything I'd been learning. I had no idea that, as Evans explained, "Peter and Paul were putting a Christian spin on what their readers would have immediately recognized as the popular Greco-Roman 'household codes.'"

Evans illuminated, "Where typical Greco-Roman household codes required nothing of the head of household regarding fair treatment of subordinates, Peter and Paul encouraged men to be kind to their slaves, to be gentle with their children, and, shockingly, to love their wives as they love themselves. Furthermore, the Christian versions of the household codes are the only ones that speak directly to the less powerful members of the household — the slaves, wives, and children — probably because the church at the time consisted of just such powerless people."[40]

Evans also pointed out that, "If Christians are to use these passages to argue that a hierarchical relationship between man and woman is divinely instituted and inherently holy, then, for consistency's sake, they must also argue the same for the relationship between master and slave," which we know many white Christians did when they enslaved African Americans and their descendants. Evans was egalitarian, so I wasn't ready to embrace what she shared, but she sure did give me a lot to think about.

To celebrate our anniversary that year, Stephen also gave me the most thoughtful gifts: 10 coffee cups from Target I'd been eyeing every recent trip. To top it off, he wrote a clever card using the text from the mugs.

Hello Gorgeous!
Did you know *you're my person*? I know it is hard to get out of bed, but maybe *motivation in a mug* can help. The to-do list hits you first thing, *but first coffee* is needed. I know I can be frustrating, but please continue to *bear with me*. You are a great wife and manage our home *like a boss*! With your wild side in Target, people are apt to mistake you as the *caffeine queen*. I'm glad you chose to move up the alphabet from *W* to *P*. I'm so humbled and honored to have you as my *wifey*! Happy 8th Anniversary!

This gesture from Stephen was reminiscent of our playful, flirty days. Since we'd stifled that lightheartedness early on when dating, Stephen's card resurrected the joy by making me laugh. The gift and card also made me feel special. It demonstrated to me that he'd listened. He'd paid attention to something I desired. Then, he financially invested in the gifts to brighten my world. I was deeply touched in a way that took me back to those pre-dating days.

Though Stephen still perceived me as the "manager of the home," we were each thinking more and more about how to partner *with* one another. This was especially true as we considered the amount of work, with little to no recognition, moms with young kids were doing in their homes and at Entrench.

Moms with young kids made up a quarter of Entrench's members. We were doing the work of a deacon without the title in our community groups, in church ministries, and every Wednesday morning. To save money and remove the cleaning duties from Jake and Daniel, the worship leader, members divided up the jobs at the church building. We swept, cleaned carpets and chairs, scrubbed toilets, and disposed of bulky trash bags at the dumpster in the far corner of the property. Moms with babies strapped to their backs maneuvered commercial-grade vacuums with ease. But when the church was asked to nominate new deacons in June 2018, moms with young kids weren't considered, at least not at the same rate as fathers with young children.

* * * * *

Today, division of labor is still a consistent topic of discussion for me and Stephen. I was recently sharing with him a Facebook post in one of the groups I'm in: all the moms were complaining about their husbands not helping around the house in any way. Stephen said, "You'd never let me get away with that." The truth is, Stephen isn't the kind of guy who would just come home and do nothing. Even way back when I first spent time with him, he cleared my tray at that BCM retreat. Before he met me, he was that person who cleared people's plates at family gatherings and started washing the dishes just because.

This backstory brings me to a point of tension for us, though, because becoming egalitarian doesn't mean everything is now easy for us. A few months ago, Stephen and I were arguing about how I shared something "critical" with a friend of ours, something that didn't paint him in the best light. He rapidly responded, "I don't get it. You're always talking about how wonderful I am and how much I do, but then you complain about wanting me to do more."

Calmly, I took a deep breath to reply, "Two things can be true. I can be grateful for you and need more support sometimes."

Pent up frustration continued to build until Stephen complained, "We shouldn't even be writing a book together. We aren't practicing mutuality. We're just arguing all the time." That last statement was an exaggeration informed by the argument we were having at that moment and another recurrent argument about finances.

As a self-preservation dominant person, Stephen is more stressed in general about finances. This has intensified since 2021 when we had a home makeover and exceeded our budget. There are some line items still in the negative two years later. When I spend money that is allocated for one of those areas, Stephen spirals and thinks I don't care about the budget that he so meticulously tracks. However, when he spends money from one of those areas, it's totally fine. We sat down to talk about this so I could voice that the double standard isn't fair to me.

It's hard to remove the hierarchy in a relationship when there's someone who isn't bringing in much, if any, money. I think that if I were working full-time and Stephen were a stay-at-home dad without a steady work-from-home or side job income, there would be some possessiveness I would have over the main income. This tension between us was exacerbated by the fact that I'm not monetizing much of my work. I'm donating 100% of the profits from *As Familiar as Family* and don't bring in money from the *Broadening the Narrative* podcast. So, even though I'm doing things I could monetize, I haven't monetized those two things.

Stephen has mentioned a few times that it would be nice if I could make money from something that I'm doing. The thing is, if I did make money off the things I'm doing, I'd be reluctant to put it toward a line item that doesn't directly benefit me because it would be such an insignificant amount of money. How does that mindset fit into a framework of mutuality? I don't know. The other thing was, I didn't even know what I'd do for income. I knew I did not want to go back to teaching, and I don't want to work a job I don't like just to make money.

Long story short: I don't like that feeling of being a burden and of only spending money but not bringing it in. In the past, I thought the guilt I felt just came with the SAHM territory, but no more. Back in our Entrench days, however, I had none of this language or even a model for a new way of being.

As time went on, though, more and more light was coming through the crack that was forming in the once shatter-proof image I'd constructed of complementarianism.

THOUGHTS FROM STEPHEN

Growing up, my family wasn't wealthy. I knew my parents struggled and that there was conflict between them, most often about overspending. My dad was in the dark about what was taking place, and my mom handled everything related to the finances. There was a lot of credit card debt. We didn't go without, but we were getting things we really couldn't afford.

Seeing that as a kid affected me. I started working when I was 16 so I'd have money for things. I didn't spend a lot. I used my money mostly for car insurance and gas, and I didn't want to be a burden for my parents. Once Nicki and I got married, I didn't want history to repeat with us. We continuously heard that finances are the number one reason people get divorced. The message was clear: we're supposed to share everything because we are one now. That said, I took complete ownership over our budget.

My job was bookkeeping, and it was logical for this to translate back at home. The complementarian messaging of the husband as the provider and the leader was then layered on. I felt at the time that if you're not knowing what's going on, it means you don't care about the state of finances. If you don't care, why would you be involved in the financial decision-making? So, I didn't get Nicki's input in the creation of our budget, but I did want her to take an interest in our finances.

* * * * *

It was the fall of 2021. We had a yard sale. Someone Nicki knew came over. I was meeting her for the first time. Instead of asking, "What's your name?" she asked, "Are you the head of the house?"

In the past, I would have answered in the affirmative; however, I had been on this journey of trying to dismantle the hierarchical view of husbands and wives for a couple of years at that point. Because of this, I answered, "I wouldn't consider myself the head. We're a team. We're a partnership," and I just left it at that. I knew what she was asking, and I knew based on the question what she believed. It would have been easier in some ways to answer in the way she wanted or to not respond the way I did. But I chose to not cave to the pressure internally of avoiding conflict. I'm sure that her being a woman contributed to me feeling more freedom to answer the way that I did, which shows that I still have work to do.

It's interesting that this person's question to me was about my position in my marriage. It goes to show the deeply ingrained patriarchy and view of dominance of husbands over their wives and families within the complementarian space. Her use of the word "household" highlights that she expected me, as the husband, to be the head, not only of Nicki but also of our kids. All this links back to the way Genesis 3 is taught, where Adam was held accountable for sin entering creation, and the idea that husbands throughout history to present day will have to give an account for the way they led their families.

This is way too much pressure on somebody. I don't want to carry that weight anymore. Now, we work together. We are one family. What we do impacts and affects each other. If I want respect, then I need to behave and act in such a way that earns it. I am not entitled to or automatically due that respect.

* * * * *

Nicki and I were recently chatting about this story: A wife was calling her husband out on the patriarchal stuff inside of him. His response was, "I do more around the house than any husband we know." He displayed the work he did as a badge of honor and evidence that he doesn't have to dismantle anything. She replied, "That's the problem. You think you're better than not just other husbands, but you think you're better than me. You're superior, and I'm inferior."

This story hit me, to be honest. For our whole marriage, I have done all this stuff around the house. I've changed diapers and helped out in ways that are not like "these other guys." From what I hear, "these guys" don't do *anything*. I don't just come home, sit on the couch, watch TV, and drink a beer. I'm serving at home. Yet, it still feels like it's not enough. I believe I have the same mindset as this other husband, the idea that I'm better than "these other guys" in a certain sense. Maybe I'm even a bit resentful of Nicki for the fact that I "have" to do these things. Having that called out was very interesting, and something I'm exploring.

Recently, I developed a fear about the vulnerability of being at the mercy of someone else to provide for me. This angst stems from witnessing "upstanding" Christian husbands abandon their wives or otherwise punish their wives for divorcing them. I talked about this fear with Stephen. I worried about how I lacked a predictable, dependable income. He expressed concern about me not trusting him to not do something like this to me. Squaring myself to face him, I explained this wasn't about not trusting him. This was about not trusting patriarchy. The complementarian system we'd operated within denied women financial autonomy, by design. As Miriam Delaney Heard shared on *Broadening the Narrative*, "A woman who has marketable skills, can support herself, make her own way in the world — that's freedom."[41]

Over the next few months, I started bringing in some income by working for the Charlotte Murder Mystery Company, but I still didn't have an equal say in how Stephen and I spent money. Truthfully, I didn't really want to be involved because there was no invitation to have an equal voice in our budget. For most of our marriage, I had to justify any amount of money I spent. To avoid the scrutiny (and subsequent shame), it was easier to leave all things money in Stephen's hands.

When Stephen was working on our taxes in April 2023, he recommended I open my own bank account. His reasoning was so that we could keep my book income separate from the rest of our income. He meant it more for his convenience when it came to budgeting and tracking. I was resistant because I'd come to depend so much on Stephen handling all things money. Also, I didn't trust myself to budget and track my spending. With the help of a friend in the banking industry, I opened an account on May 22, 2023 (our 13th anniversary). The account is in my name and doesn't have Stephen's name attached to it in any way. I didn't realize what a game changer that would be for me feeling empowered. I didn't realize how restricted I'd felt until I tasted that financial independence. Then, I decided to retroactively provide myself with back-pay from our emergency money for the years when I'd contributed financially but did without "frivolous" or "indulgent" purchases. I'm now using this money to invest in myself.

Chapter 8
Advocacy and Amplifying

Complementarianism maintains control by squashing curiosity. In our marriage, the questioning of hierarchical systems began with whiteness and led us to questioning complementarianism. Learning to self-reflect on the ways I personally perpetuate white supremacy and uphold the patriarchy changed everything.

The Spiritual Abuse

Nicki's Perspective

In July 2018, Stephen and I set up a meeting with Jake following a round of deacon nominations at Entrench. This meeting would forever alter the trajectory of our journeys. (Not to be dramatic or anything.) The air felt heavy with the now familiar suffocating quality I'd come to associate with Entrench. Silently, I sat beside Stephen on a lumpy couch in Jake's office as Stephen relayed his frustrations. "The lack of women in the top five nominations is indicative of a church culture that doesn't value women," Stephen explained.

Jake cocked his head and replied, "It *could* be an indication of that." My chest tightened. My breathing became shallow. My high hopes were on the decline.

"It is," Stephen rapidly responded. "People aren't even thinking of women as they nominate."

Not budging, Stephen explained examples of sexism in the church. Jake didn't think any of the stories were a big deal. So, I brought up an incident that involved Jake. With an eerie coolness, he nonchalantly expressed he didn't remember what I was talking about. Gently, I reminded him of how he'd defended an athlete's sexist comment. Then, I asked, "What do you believe about women?"

He countered, "What do you think I believe about women?"

Caught off guard, I smiled a lopsided grin as I replied, "Well, I need you to answer the question because I have some follow-up questions depending on how you answer." Then, he seemed to snap. It wasn't a full-on blow-out, but he pointed his finger at me as he declared, "No, you aren't going to pigeonhole me, put me in a box, and label me a sexist. I'm not answering your questions."

The clock stopped ticking. The suffocation in the air thickened. I began hyperventilating. Ignoring my gut reaction to walk out because of the codependency in my relationship with Jake, I silently begged God for wisdom and clarity to bounce back and finish the conversation well. Stephen moved to block Jake from my line of sight. Jake grabbed a box of tissues and muttered the empty words, "I'm sorry for making you cry," without probing to uncover the why behind my tears.

Being spiritually abused led to more questions about complementarianism, patriarchy, and hierarchy.

The Spiritual Abuse

Stephen's Perspective

I entered the familiar church building with Nicki. We were hopeful that this conversation with Jake would be the catalyst to change and growth at Entrench.

After opening our time together by asking Jake how he and his family were doing, I planned to pray. We wanted to pray for them during a difficult time in their personal lives. He was pretty closed off from the beginning and didn't open up about ways he was struggling. I felt hurt that he wouldn't share his burdens and let us support him, especially since we served together and I was the lead deacon at the church. My role was to ensure the people of the church were being cared for. I prayed for him and his family. Then, we started sharing our concerns.

Stunned, I sat there processing Jake's reaction as Nicki began to cry and hyperventilate. This was not how I envisioned the conversation going.

Comforting Nicki, I tried to help her calm down while my conflict avoidant alarms were sounding. My heart was racing. I was completely caught off guard. Instead of using my male privilege to interrupt Jake's accusation and protect Nicki from further harm, I just sat there, not saying a thing. I knew Nicki truly cared for Jake and wanted Entrench to be the best church it could be. She was my beloved wife of eight years. Yet, I also felt deep loyalty to Jake. He had mentored me, performed mine and Nicki's wedding ceremony, and accepted me in spite of my past. My livelihood was, in part, tied to my bookkeeping role at Entrench; it made up a fifth of our income.

I knew we were trying to help the church grow in reflecting the beauty of the gospel and being a manifestation of the manifold wisdom of God. However, as the conversation took a sour turn, I began gaslighting myself.

I wish I could go back and speak up. I would set a clear boundary and tap into my internal wellspring of energy. I would not stand for Nicki to be treated this way. Instead, it took another six months and another traumatizing meeting to get out, and even that was because of Nicki.

As 2017 began, Stephen and I didn't know that welcoming a baby wasn't the only way our lives would be changing. One of our friends endorsed Be the Bridge, an organization dedicated to equipping people to be "authentic racial bridge-builders." I got involved. This was coming on the heels of 2016's election, an election where I felt uneasy about the options for the first time. At community group one night, a couple of us were talking about voting third party. One man in our group, who I'll call Dean, explained that we needed to vote for 45 (a.k.a. Trump) because of the Supreme Court and abortion.

Stephen defended our decision to vote third party. We'd been doing a ton of research because we couldn't vote for Hillary Clinton. During that election period, I thought back to when I read Clinton's *It Takes a Village* my freshman year at USC-L and how my life could've gone very differently. Instead, as you know, I got so involved with BCM and Cru, and then Entrench, that I doubled down on my disdain for Clinton. All of this culminated in the misogyny to not vote for her simply because she was a woman. Sure, back then I could hide behind her pro-choice stance on abortion; but, at the end of the day, John Piper and others like him made sure to hammer home how this wasn't a position a woman should hold. If Wayne Grudem exercised caution about women as church treasurers, how much more as a nation's president?

To cultivate transparency, I don't hide the fact that I did decide to cast my vote for 45. I despised the Donald. When he bragged about his ability to sexually assault women and get away with it, my stomach churned. I kept waiting for the men at Entrench to denounce 45, or to at least declare that what he said was unequivocally out of step with the gospel. None of them did. They didn't say anything to criticize 45's behavior. Though I'd planned to vote third party, I aligned myself with 45 when I stepped up to the voting booth. I will regret it for as long as I live, and maybe longer. I did it because, as educator Louiza Duran has explained, white women (who are different from women who happen to be white) will choose their whiteness over their own female liberation. That's why 53% of us, myself included, voted for 45 in 2016.

When 45 was declared the winner, Dean sent me a celebratory message on Facebook. Though I was relieved that Clinton didn't win, I couldn't muster up happiness to celebrate that 45 did. But I believed male headship was God-ordained, so there wasn't much I could do about that. Then, I set the election, and everything that came with it, aside. I had the privilege to be able to do that. Well, when I got involved with Be the Bridge, the election, and everything that came with it, was brought to the center again.

My small group for Be the Bridge only met a few times before we disbanded, but Be the Bridge is what helped me start my lifelong anti-racism journey. I am not an expert, or an antiracism educator, and I never will be, so I want to clearly state that. When I looked around at Entrench, the church didn't reflect the racial demographics of the city. I came to realize this was because our majority white congregation expected anyone who *wasn't* white to assimilate to be part of the church. Over the next few months, I reflected on how all of my church experiences were in white churches.

* * * * *

My involvement with Be the Bridge also started my introspective journey toward understanding sexism. Binging podcasts recorded by Black women, I learned about the connection between white supremacy and patriarchy. It was around this time I really began to understand that there was a double standard put forth by conservative evangelical leaders. Like that one guy who said Christians should be focusing on our families (cough cough, James Dobson), but then he endorsed a man who represented the antithesis of those prized "family values." That guy declared that we should cut 45 some slack regarding his commitment to being a Christian. I found it odd how protective we were expected to be of these supposedly tough, aggressive men.

It reminds me of this quote I recently read by Melissa Febos: "It is a shared technique of abusive partners, corporations, cult leaders, despotic governments, and many who benefit from unequal power structures and wish to continue benefiting from them: to convince the disempowered to identify with the needs of the powerful instead of their own."[42] It took over a year for me to begin perceiving the double standard, but I eventually understood how Hillary Clinton's Christianity was scrutinized as constant doubt was cast on her commitment to God. Her faith, according to the conservative evangelicals, was for show politically. That sentiment never escaped their lips about their man 45. (Sidenote: I'm not advocating that liberal white women are the answer to our nation's problems. We liberal white women still have *a lot* of healing to do.)

* * * * *

In the fall of 2017, Entrench moved into a new building. Jake's vision became one of extending and building a bigger auditorium for the people who would flock to his beacon of fundamentalist dogma. While the congregation was settling in, I was getting restless. My journey into understanding antiracism, white supremacy, and the patriarchy continued. I emailed the pastors to say that we as a church needed to be taking more of a stand against racism. We needed to make changes to not just say, "People of color are welcome here" but to create an environment where people of color would actually feel welcome.

Stephen had sent an email to the church leadership a few months before regarding systemic racism. Nothing had been done. For some reason, I thought adding my voice would propel the pastors to action. Silly me.

The reason I contacted the pastors was because of Jake's sermon from Ephesians 3. He had explained that in verse 10, the word manifold in the phrase "manifold wisdom of God" meant "multicolored." Because I assumed the pastors wanted to nurture a multiethnic congregation, I shared resources with them and provided many suggestions. One of the resources was a podcast series from *Truth's Table* about multiethnic churches. I asked them to listen and said that Stephen and I would love to meet with them afterwards. In passing, I mentioned that we could also talk about sexism in addition to racism, as I had noted examples of sexism in the church, too.

Roger, another pastor at Entrench, emailed back the next day. He requested patience as the pastors would need time to listen to the multiethnic church series. He also referenced the importance of the guidelines for dealing with sin recorded in Matthew 18. He asked if I was able to address the individuals I referenced who were sinning by their racism and sexism. He said the next step would be to provide specifics so the pastors could talk to the individuals.

The next day, I emailed back that the instructions in Matthew 18 were for someone to deal with sin directly committed against them. Since racism was not a sin against me, I could not be expected to be the sole confronter of racism in the church. I would continue exhorting others as opportunities presented themselves, but this was not something for me to do alone. Then, I explained it wouldn't be wise to advise people of color at Entrench to privately confront other church members about their racism. Discernment is necessary in figuring out how to apply Matthew 18 for individuals instead of legalistically saying the text must be followed in this manner for each scenario.

Since Roger asked about the sexism I'd briefly mentioned, I provided context for why I had not confronted the individuals. Only one of the recent events I'd alluded to involved a comment directed toward me. I knew the person who spoke it would not think it was sexist because… well…patriarchy. Again, I said it would be a terrible idea to expect the women of the church to go alone to confront men about this issue. For starters, more time would be spent trying to explain why the comments or actions were sexist. There's also more room for shaming the victim, usually for being "too sensitive."

At Entrench, the pastor as a shepherd metaphor was often used. I explained that, from the way I thought about it, shepherds give each sheep attention and care. There are some sheep in need of more protection than others. Defending the most vulnerable sheep looks different than caring for less vulnerable sheep. Now, I don't actually know a thing about sheep or shepherds, so take that with a grain of salt.

When it came to my identity as a woman in the church, I told the pastors that many women under their care were looking to them to be like fathers and brothers. It didn't seem like the fatherly, brotherly, or "shepherdly" way to love the women of the church to send us out to address sexism that ultimately needs to be dealt with from the top down. I concluded that the women of the church needed them to say, "I see you. I hear you. I am for you. I will fight for you to be seen as a fellow image bearer."

* * * * *

It didn't seem to matter how many times I emailed the elders. They appeared unmoved by the gravity of the dishonor that women were experiencing in the church. I told them about the time that Stephen and I had been searching for empty seats during a Volunteer Appreciation event. An aspiring-to-eldership church member overheard Stephen ask me where I wanted to sit. The man who would later be installed as an elder interjected, "We don't ask our wives where to sit. We tell them." The men surrounding him laughed at my expense while my cheeks turned red. Let's just say I did not feel appreciated at the very event meant to show volunteers appreciation.

There was also the time Dean (the guy who celebrated 45's win) shamed his wife via Facebook by writing, "My wife made some blatantly ignorant comments about guns today. Lucky for her she has a loving husband to correct her." This husband in the church, who I'll briefly call "gun guy," wanted to be an elder like the "we tell our wives where to sit" guy. "Gun guy" publicly humiliated his wife to put her back into the place he thought she should be in. According to his worldview, that place is obviously below him because she certainly didn't have the freedom to reverse the situation by posting about him in that manner.

As these types of comments were allowed to flourish, I witnessed harsher comments, like a wife who heard from her husband on multiple occasions, "I will listen to anyone before I listen to you." That husband did not value his wife. He believed that in "ruling over her," he never had to listen to her. Her opinion did not matter to him. Without holding back in one email to the elders, I named the church culture as one that contributed to the harmful verbal abuse in marriages like the one my friend was in.

I noted that the larger "Church" is suffering because of damaging stereotypes against women. With the budding knowledge I was gaining and a sprinkling of sarcasm, I wrote, "Eve was deceived, after all, so women can't be trusted to make an intellectual and wise decision, right? Husbands now rule over their wives as a result of the fall, so women just need to be ruled because they are just bent towards being obstinate, right? That's what is consistently communicated by evangelicals. Eve's deception becomes my perpetual deception, though Adam's sin doesn't discount men. We have receipts of wise and discerning women throughout the Scriptures and throughout history, but those women become the exceptions. We don't apply Nabal's foolishness to all men, though. Nabal is the exception for men rather than the rule."

When the elders asked me to reveal the identities of the men I'd emailed about, I reluctantly did so. The reasoning given for wanting me to disclose this information was so that relationships could be repaired. Over the next year before we left Entrench, I didn't experience restoration. Instead, my relationships with the men of the church became even more strained than when I'd first contacted the elders.

* * * * *

When the church was asked to nominate new deacons, nary a woman received enough nominations to appear in the top five. Stephen offered to allow a woman with young children to serve in his place. Jake's response was that if Stephen stepped down, they would simply replace him with the nominee who received the next highest number of nominations. He explained that Stephen wouldn't like that because it was another white man.

With the deacon nominations (and more) as the backdrop, I wanted to meet with Jake. Desperate to make sense of what was happening, I turned to a group message I was part of. A few of us lamented the lack of women in the recent deacon nominations. In response, Roger's wife Sam asked, "Don't you trust your leaders?" By replying to our pain like she did, Sam became another person I didn't feel safe with. She also told us Roger was more of a feminist than her, though I'm not sure how patriarchy, "soft" or not, squares with feminism.

Things were a little awkward with Sam when we attended a women's conference, but I just avoided any critical talk about Entrench. At one point, a few of the women in the jam-packed van talked about their experiences when their husbands were in seminary. One mentioned a class that was led by the wife of the seminary's president. She'd been excited about the class initially. Her excitement evaporated when one of the lessons was on how to pack your husband's luggage.

Apparently, wives should be prepared for their husbands to travel and do Super Important Work for God's Kingdom. Since wives are simply players in their husbands' games, helpers in their husbands' simulations, they should learn to do any and everything that can alleviate stress for their husbands. This includes, but is not limited to, mastering the most efficient way to fit underwear, outerwear, and toiletries in a suitcase. This was the first time the thought crossed my mind, "Why do we need to baby men if they're supposed to be the 'leaders'? Are we their moms or their partners?"

A few weeks later, Roger came over to our house. His eyes softened and he leaned in as I expounded on a litany of grievances. There was the lack of care for women from the pastors. There was also the culture at Entrench that contributed to people not nominating women as frequently as men for the role of deacon. This was especially hurtful considering we were fulfilling the responsibilities of a deacon by being community group leaders. Imagine my shock when Roger informed me that women weren't considered community group leaders. It was apparently the official position at Entrench, but it was news to me. For years, I had given so much of myself to ensure that our weekly meetings ran smoothly. Everything from writing the discussion questions to organizing the meals and cooking, while hosting. Yet I'd apparently never be considered a leader.

Roger encouraged me to talk with Jake about all this. At his urging, I scheduled a meeting. That meeting would mark a pivotal shift in my relationship with Jake and Entrench as well as my relationship to complementarianism.

* * * * *

Disenchantment had been setting in for myself and Stephen because of Jake's silence about dismantling white supremacy at Entrench. Still, I naively believed I would be listened to and understood. Sitting across from Jake, Stephen expressed his concerns about the patriarchal church culture. When Jake dismissed him, Stephen brought up "we tell our wives where to sit" guy and "gun guy" (Dean).

Jake shrugged the sitting situation off, even as Stephen shared his regret at not actively disrupting the patriarchy in that moment. When Stephen mentioned Dean's Facebook post about his wife, Jake quipped, "You know he was only joking, right?" A husband in the church publicly humiliated his wife, and the pastor excused it. Like it literally wasn't a big deal to him. It wasn't even a little deal.

Unable to sit in silence any longer, I echoed one of Jake's oft quoted seminary professors, "What you say you believe plus what you do shows what you actually believe." When I reminded him about something his own wife had recently shared, his retort was, "She can think whatever she wants to," a bold statement from a conservative complementarian. Surely he doesn't mean *whatever*.

The tension continued building until Jake directly spiritually abused me. He used the power imbalance between us to his advantage as he accused me of labeling him a sexist. Every suppressed emotion I hadn't dealt with rose to the surface and spilled over in the form of an embarrassing bout of hyperventilation. With each struggling breath, I sank deeper into the couch and berated myself for doing the one thing I'd promised myself I wouldn't. Though the women of the church didn't appoint me to speak on their behalf, I realized I was representing them all and had resolved I wouldn't cry. I didn't want Jake to perceive me as weak because I knew from my childhood that this is how "emotional women" were categorized by so many men.

As my shock wore off, Jake attempted to smooth things over without delving into his accusation against me or addressing his behavior.

He proved common ground between us as he said, "We're both complementarian. Y'all are just broader in your application than I am. My approach is narrower concerning what I believe women can do in the church." I asked Jake if we could start a group at Entrench to meet with him ahead of the sermon each week, especially when the subject material was sensitive. His reply was simply, "I don't have the time for that, but feel free to keep sending me things."

Stephen and I decided to tell Jake that the advice he and Caroline gave about Stephen not talking to other women hurt our marriage. Jake defended their advice while pinning the blame on Caroline and what he referred to as her "insecurity." Like Caroline, I'd been insecure in the early years of my marriage to Stephen. Unlike Caroline, I no longer felt that same intense level of insecurity. Why, after 20+ years of marriage, was her anxiety about Jake being tempted and having an affair growing? She'd told me numerous times about friends of theirs in ministry who were getting divorced because of the husband's adultery. With wide eyes, she would tremble as she anticipated this outcome for her own marriage. It seems that mischaracterizing women as temptresses that men are powerless against only increases insecurity. It certainly does nothing to get to the root of the reasons for feeling insecure.

The night I was directly spiritually abused by Jake was when I realized that Entrench wasn't rooted in mutuality but in a hierarchy that defaulted to Jake's preferences. While Jake preached we are supposed to "count others more significant" and to "look to the interests of others," he was somehow absolved from that. Our meeting concluded cordially a couple of hours later at midnight. We thanked Jake for his time and walked into the humidity of a South Carolina summer night.

Climbing into our trusty black Honda Civic, my head thudded against the headrest. All I could say was, "That was not good." Stephen and I didn't speak on the 10-minute ride home. Hindsight is 20/20. I should have trusted my intuition and listened to the message my body sent me to get out of that church. If I could do it all over again, that night would have been the end of my time at Entrench.

While we still had a bit of road ahead of us, that night did mark the beginning of my leaving Entrench in stages, and I'd already started the path toward leaving complementarianism. I just didn't know it yet.

* * * * *

In the fall of 2018, I attended a Truth's Table event that was hosted at Christ Central Church. During the Meet and Greet portion, the hosts of the *Truth's Table* podcast, Michelle Higgins, Ekemini Uwan, and Dr. Christina Edmondson, answered questions about all the things. My jaw dropped a little at Dr. Christina Edmondson's response to a question about complementarian theology.

She calmly explained, "Complementarianism was a reaction to feminism. I don't want to teach my daughters a reactionary theology. I want to teach them a biblical theology, which includes that they are fearfully and wonderfully made." Turns out, it wasn't until 1977 that George Knight III published his seminal work on the now-called complementarian view on gender. It was titled *The New Testament Teaching on the Role Relationship of Men and Women.* If you're like me when I heard this the first time, you might be feeling surprised. Here's the thing: I didn't realize how recently the complementarian take on biblical passages was developed. I was taught this theological interpretation as if it's been the only option since the inception of the Christian Church.

Simply hearing that complementarian theology was a reaction to feminism helped me feel less disobedient for questioning it. Was it truly possible to love God deeply and reject the confines of complementarian theology? These brilliant and bold women were demonstrating it was possible to have a far more embodied faith than I'd ever had under the constraints of complementarianism.

After the Meet and Greet, we made our way to the sanctuary. Pastor Howard Brown welcomed everyone and vocalized his enthusiastic support of and gratitude toward the women of *Truth's Table*. My eyes misted as I listened to a man publicly praise the three Black women on stage for the ways they helped him grow. Pastor Howard's humility and tenderness drew me in and were a balm for my wounded heart.

The next day, I devoured all three of Pastor Howard's sermons under the title "Does the Bible Promote Misogyny?"[43][44][45] Tears slid down my face as I listened to a pastor gently handle the horrors of the rape and dismemberment of the unnamed concubine in Judges 19. I had to know more about this church not too far from us seeking to bring justice regarding racism and sexism. "We have to visit this church," I implored Stephen. He was reluctant because it felt like a betrayal to Jake, to Entrench, to his livelihood and only community, but he could sense my urgency and agreed.

Stephen and I loaded up our traveling circus to see for ourselves if this church was all I cautiously wanted it to be. Within minutes, I was once again shocked. The band that morning was predominantly women. Pastor Howard's wife was leading worship. She opened with a prayer for the Jewish community that had been targeted by antisemitic white supremacist violence at the Tree of Life synagogue in Pittsburgh. These were the kinds of traumatic events many of us had been desiring for leadership at Entrench to comment on, yet our church was blaringly silent. We wouldn't have to request for leadership at Christ Central to voice concern over tragedies if this were our home church.

From listening to Pastor Howard's sermon series, I believed he genuinely cared about women. That didn't prepare me for what he did the morning we were there. After approaching the pulpit, he thanked the women in his life for their contributions. He said, "Y'all wrote that sermon and helped me preach it. I found myself not in charge or ahead of that message but needing to be changed by it." He went on to explain how he "got checked the other night" regarding something he said after the ladies of *Truth's Table* spoke.

Pastor Howard displayed such humility as he acknowledged his wrongdoing and gave credit to the women who helped with the writing of the sermons on misogyny. When we left Christ Central, I paid attention to what I felt in my body. I was light, not weighed down like I'd been feeling at Entrench. It dawned on me that being appreciated and valued at church shouldn't be an "every once in a while I'll throw you a bone" occurrence.

* * * * *

Though Jake and Roger did not know we had visited Christ Central, a few weeks later I emailed them the Judges 19 sermons from Pastor Howard. I started researching more about how words are translated in the Bible. This led me to a blog post by Daniel Hill. In the post, he examined the verse in Acts 17:31 from the New International Version (NIV). "For he has set a day when he will judge the world with justice by the man he has appointed. He has given proof of this to everyone by raising him from the dead."

Without venturing too far into the weeds, I read about how the word justice in that verse of the NIV was translated as righteousness in other translations and in other verses across translations. What followed in the post was a thorough exploration of the history of the word *dikaiosune*. This word was consistently understood as justice until it started being translated as righteousness. Hill asked the question, "Is it possible that somewhere along the way righteousness was seen as a more valuable spiritual attribute than justice?" He answered, "It would certainly seem so."[46]

Then, I read Dr. Martin Luther King Jr.'s "Letter from a Birmingham Jail." Through King's work, I realized that the tactic of disparaging those who seek justice was as old as the Civil Rights Movement, and as old as the construct of white supremacy itself. As Bryan Stevenson, the founder and executive director of the Equal Justice Initiative, explained, "So many of us have become afraid and angry. We've become so fearful and vengeful that we've thrown away children, discarded the disabled, and sanctioned the imprisonment of the sick and the weak — not because they are a threat to public safety or beyond rehabilitation but because we think it makes us seem tough, less broken."[47]

One of the people who was "concerned" about my Social Justice Warrior (SJW) status was Dean. Dean joined the "two-thirds of white evangelicals [who] said they're 'excited' or 'satisfied' about the outcome," according to a poll after the 2016 election. The researchers reported that "64 percent of white evangelicals 'completely' or 'mostly' agreed that 'society as a whole has become too soft and feminine.'"[48] That was part of their reasoning for being able to support a man like 45.

Like those poll respondents and every "tough on crime" advocate, Dean was worried that society was too soft and feminine. He also often harped about the "sissification of Jesus." One night during community group, he seemed to relish in the passage from the book of Revelation about Jesus coming back as a conquering warrior. His voice deepened as he declared that Jesus is a "man's man" who will return to rightfully and violently squash his enemies. (The conflation of manhood with violence wasn't lost on me, but I didn't say anything.) The blood and gore of the triumphant coming Christ did not deter Dean. And honestly, his obsession with the violent military return of Christ makes sense considering how much military language is in the Bible. Even the "people of God" are instructed to embody the ethics of war, all the way down to the armor of God Christians are commanded to put on and battles they're instructed to engage in against "the desires of the flesh."

I bring all of this context into a book about coming out of complementarianism because it's vital to painting the picture of what many complementarians think about manhood.

THOUGHTS FROM STEPHEN

Once Nicki joined Be the Bridge and read something called "Whiteness 101," arguments between us ensued as she began talking about white supremacy and white privilege. Taking a deep breath and asking, "Why am I feeling defensive?" really helped. As I sat with what came up, I realized that maybe there was some truth to what she was sharing. Otherwise, I wouldn't be so defensive. It was at least worth exploring. I didn't think there was any harm in that.

As Nicki's journey continued, I loved witnessing her excitement about what she'd read by Rachel Held Evans. That didn't stop me from thinking, "Whoa whoa whoa, slow down with the gender stuff." It was easier to spot racism and white supremacy than it was to spot patriarchy in myself and the world around me because, from my point of view at the time, "male headship" was God's design.

* * * * *

I owe a lot of my journey in understanding and dismantling systemic racism to Nicki and a Black man named James who was part of our community group. They patiently had conversations with me. I began seeking to change my ways and undo racism within me and within systems in this country because of my faith in Jesus.

In 2015, I had spouted racist remarks to my father-in-law about the Civil Rights Movement pastors' sermons. I'd insisted that their messages were more about surface issues rather than the deeper, true gospel issues. A couple years later, I was trying to convince our community group and church to take a clear stand denouncing white supremacy. Naively, I thought everyone else would have the same reaction if they just knew the things I knew. Boy, was I wrong!

This led to our community group bleeding members and long-standing relationships being fractured. I believed firmly in what I was learning and felt betrayed that I was 33 years old and just learning these things.

As I became more involved with Be the Bridge and continuing on my own journey, I wanted to use my position at Entrench to encourage the church leaders, all of us, to confront racial injustice. Without giving it a second thought, I emailed the pastors, community group leaders, and deacons about Entrench releasing a statement regarding racial justice and, more specifically, denouncing white supremacy. Turns out, it came across to the pastors as me trying to go above or around them. After the next monthly prayer and dinner night, I was talking with two of them and one expressed that he wished I would have had a conversation with them confidentially before sending out the mass email. This is the culture of white supremacy: to sweep things under the rug privately rather than expose them publicly. The Bible is even used to reinforce this framework. I felt sorry for what I did, since I sensed displeasure and conflict from them. From there, things didn't get any better.

As a community group leader, I wanted to talk about things that impacted the people in our group. I'd had many conversations with James and really cared about him. One week, I asked if he would be open to sharing about his experiences at Entrench. This topic went along with the previous Sunday's sermon about the "manifold" wisdom of God, in which Jake explained that the word manifold could be translated as "multicolored." James said yes and asked a couple of his friends to participate, too. We informed our community group via a late Facebook post about the plans, but we didn't check to make sure everyone saw the post.

That evening, as we sat around the living room at a long-time friends' house, I shared what we would be doing. We had sent questions ahead of time to James so he knew what to expect. I thought our group would be receptive to hearing from someone they knew, had eaten many meals with, and had worshiped alongside every Sunday for more than a year.

Safe spaces, code-switching, and color-blindness were addressed. Multiple white people engaged in the discussion. One white woman even communicated how some of her high school students had explained to her the problems with the color-blind approach. Those students had told their teacher, "If you don't see our skin color, you're not seeing us." From what I could tell, things were moving along fine. Group members were respectfully listening. When they did speak, it was from a place of curiosity. Then, someone said, "Can I raise an argument?" That someone was Dean.

Prior to our meeting, Nicki and I had agreed that we would interrupt anything harmful. The way in which Dean was trying to "raise an argument" when people were being vulnerable qualified as harmful. I hesitated in order to avoid conflict. Before I could say anything, Nicki interjected, "No. We're white. Our voices have been heard for a long time. The point of this gathering is to listen, not to argue."

Would I have spoken up if Nicki hadn't?

Things stayed tense, but I thought everything was fine overall when we wrapped up for the evening. I soon received a text from Jake to all the community group leaders. In the text, he instructed us to inform the pastors if we weren't going to be discussing Sunday's sermons during the weeknight meetings. When I read the message to Nicki, she somehow knew it was directed toward us. I thought, "No way. If it was, Jake would talk with me directly." Plus, we were discussing the Sunday sermons in a real-life matter. We weren't doing anything wrong. In a separate message, I replied to Jake to confirm if this was the case, which led to a phone call. Turns out, Nicki was right.

According to Jake, someone in our group contacted him. This person reported that we were going through Be the Bridge curriculum and silencing white people. Though I was not one to raise my voice in general, and especially not to someone I saw as an authority figure, I loudly demanded him to tell me who told him this. He responded that he'd never heard me that passionate before, which Nicki later scoffed at. I was clearly angry, but Jake labeled it as "passionate." Jake wouldn't disclose the person's identity, but we knew. There was only one person it could have been: Dean. Jake encouraged me to call him and resolve this, based on "not [letting] the sun go down on your anger" Ephesians 4:26 (ESV).

Though I really didn't want to, I called Dean. Our conversation was unproductive, as he remained focused on convincing me I was being led astray and forsaking the gospel.

$$* * * * *$$

As time went on, I learned more and more about being an Enneagram 9, "the easy-going mediator." Peace is a top priority for me. As someone who craves the stability of peace, I couldn't handle the chaos around and within me. Shifting beliefs, strained relationships, and a lack of support were contributing to me feeling like I was on shaky ground. There were two forces pulling me. One was telling me not to rock the boat. The other was telling me that the boat needed to be rocked. I didn't know what to do, and then Nicki said I should read "Letter from a Birmingham Jail."

Something happened inside of me when I read Dr. Martin Luther King Jr.'s words as he addressed the "white moderate who is more devoted to order than to justice; who prefers a negative peace which is the absence of tension to a positive peace which is the presence of justice; who constantly says, 'I agree with you in the goal you seek, but I can't agree with your methods of direct action'; who paternalistically feels that he can set the timetable for another man's freedom."[49] That realization that peace*making* is not the same as peace*keeping* was the push I needed to begin questioning complementarianism as I began to understand that no one was truly benefiting from me keeping the false "peace" that came with complementarianism.

It took a long time for me to be open to receiving the truth about systemic oppression. As Audre Lorde explained, the closer you are to the mythical norm, the harder it is to change.[50] Listening to others who had different life experiences than me has led me to perceive the good news of Jesus in a different light. Jesus actually came to turn the systems of oppression on their heads, exalting the oppressed and bringing down the oppressors. This has freed me to pursue emotional healing and health, allowing me to get to know my emotions, especially my anger, and strive to practice curiosity and compassion toward it so that I can change.

There was a single mom at Entrench who was financially, emotionally, and maritally struggling. Witnessing the way the church as a whole responded to her stirred something inside of me. I began wondering, "If being a SAHM is the ideal path for mothers and homeschooling is what God wants us to do, why isn't the church helping her do that?" (I'm not saying they are correct. It was just another "aha" moment of realizing there was an inconsistency between what the church preached versus what they practiced.) By this time, a few other moms from Entrench were breaking the mold and enrolling their kids in public schools. Stephen was still determined for us (read: me) to homeschool, but I was open to pursuing other options.

Then, James, the only Black man in our community group, shared something that further peeled back the complementarian curtain. He brought up how there are many white male pastors who ridicule Black churches that have women as pastors. He pointed out that when white people waged war on Black communities under the guise of a "war on drugs," the mass incarceration that followed swallowed up countless Black men who could have been pastors. With Black men being put into cages, Black women filled the void in their churches. White evangelicals then had the audacity to express disdain for the Black women who were fixing a problem the women didn't create. These women were holding their churches and communities together. Instead of being supported by white churches, they were mocked.

The SAHM and women as pastors revelations were two more steps toward understanding that if a doctrine (complementarianism) that supposedly is commanded by God can't be universally applied, then maybe it's not from a "Divine Being."

SECTION 3

In the Garden of Eden Eve showed more courage than Adam...when the serpent offered the forbidden fruit. She knew that there was something better than paradise.

-Cesare Borgia

Chapter 9
The Beginning of the End

Following being directly spiritually abused by Jake, Stephen and I were wrestling with how to be faithful complementarians while also providing space for the women in our community group to exercise their "spiritual gifts." I was certain I could convince Jake that white supremacy and patriarchy were problems in the church. He just didn't know what he didn't know. Once I enlightened him, we could work together to expose the systems of oppression at play. In doing so, we would alter the way things were done at Entrench and get our spheres of influence one step closer to "on earth as it is in heaven" Matthew 6:10 (CSB).

With a renewed commitment to changing the culture of the church, I decided to move forward. Jake was, understandably, too busy to add another meeting to his schedule. However, he *had* said he was open to me sending him information to review. Therefore, I decided to reach out to Daniel, Entrench's worship leader, about beginning a group with him to study the scriptures together and email our insights to Jake. I stepped out onto the patio. The sun-soaked tiles warmed the soles of my feet. Scrolling through my contacts, I arrived at the "D"s. I crossed my fingers as the ringing commenced. Unable to sit, I paced around the backyard as we talked. I didn't tell him about the details of what happened in Jake's office.

A few minutes later, I launched into the reason for my call. Daniel was all in. He said he would talk with Jake as soon as he could. The hope that can feel like both my gift and my curse swelled in me. I was sure that everything was going to work out. Jake would be grateful for a group like this that could email him and utilize our "spiritual gifts" without infringing on his time with his family or other responsibilities. This plan was going to work because it had to.

When I got to talk to Daniel at church the following Sunday, he didn't report what I was expecting. When he had pitched the idea for forming a group to give input prior to sermons, Jake told him no. Jake said he needed Daniel focused on other tasks and he wouldn't use anything the group sent him. I couldn't reconcile Jake's disregard for the insights of members of the church with my belief that every person was a valuable part of "the Body of Christ." Why didn't Jake think he would benefit or be able to implement anything?

That afternoon, my eardrums were vibrating with each thump of my heart as I pulled the computer out from under the bookshelf by the bed. The volume of the pounding increased as I typed an email to Jake. Second-guessing each sentence, I put myself in Jake's position as I requested a follow-up meeting to debrief our previous meeting. I asked for Roger to attend, too. After days of deliberation, with shaking hands, I pressed send. Then, I waited.

Two days later, I received a reply that the dates I listed wouldn't work. Anticlimactic, I know. Jake wrote back that coordinating a time was a priority, but days passed without another email. Then weeks. The dearth of support from Jake caused me to question if he even realized there were any problems between us or problems at Entrench.

* * * * *

My journey toward egalitarianism, or mutuality, accelerated when my friend Aubrey texted me the *Almost Heretical* podcast series on gender.[51] Why was there even a conversation around what women can and cannot do in church? It no longer made sense to me. My mind was a mess, busy making connections as new-to-me information overloaded my brain. Every passage about women I'd been taught by complementarians could be examined through an egalitarian framework. Plus, the concept of mutuality was more traditional as a belief held by Christians.

There was one episode where a group of women were being interviewed about their experiences and how they'd been harmed by complementarianism. The fact that their stories were being treated as important was a balm to my weary soul. All I wanted was to feel like my stories mattered to the men at Entrench. As I listened to the two white male podcast hosts hold the women in high regard and expound on egalitarian interpretations, I thought, *God doesn't hate me for being a woman after all.*

Listening to the episodes, I wanted to simultaneously throw my phone across the room in a fit of anger, curl up in the fetal position to cry, and run victory laps around the house. How is it that I was pushing 30 and had never been taught a whole different world of Christian theology concerning women? Enraged by the power white evangelical men think is theirs by God's good design, I yelled and shook my fists. Tears welled up in my eyes and spilled over as I felt fully seen and valued as a woman by God. The scholarship unpacked in the nine-part series caused me to break out in spontaneous bursts of elation. Why aren't more complementarian pastors open to this? Oh right, because they fear the slippery slope. Well, I strapped on my skis and don't regret the decision to speed downhill for a single second.

The god of complementarianism prohibits women to teach or exercise authority over men. Therefore, women can't be pastors, shepherds, overseers, or elders. However, this god gives consent for men to read books on theology written by women. The book provides a barrier, as it were, so that the man isn't being directly taught by a woman. You can't make this stuff up. It deeply grieves me that I not only once believed this but also perpetuated it.

Well, I think these oppressive beliefs stem from a few things. For starters, there's a misunderstanding of the word *authentein*, from 1 Timothy 2:12. Paul wrote, "I do not permit a woman to teach or exercise authority over a man; rather, she is to remain quiet" (ESV). The word *authentein* is translated as exercise authority over. Through the *Almost Heretical* series, I learned that this is the only time *authentein* is used in the Bible. It has a violent connotation of domination, domination that harms and removes consent, autonomy, and agency. Well then, of course Paul wouldn't want a woman to violently dominate a man, but please understand he never commands the inverse. Never once does Paul, or any other contributor to what we call the Bible, state that a man violently dominating a woman is God's good design. Anyone violently dominating anyone is antithetical to the teaching of Jesus and the early Christ followers.

Secondly, within complementarianism there is an assignment of certain "spiritual gifts" to cishet men. It's as if only that group of people can possess the gifts of teaching and shepherding for the benefit of a church. However, spiritual gifts know no gender. Additionally, there's a conflation of terms. Elder/*Presbuteros*, overseer/*episkopos*, shepherd/*poimen* (or pastor by another name). These terms are grouped together and used interchangeably when they shouldn't be.

Lastly, within complementarianism, there is an establishment of arbitrary standards. In churches that allow for the possibility of women having the gifts of teaching or shepherding, those women are able to use these gifts, but only with other women or children. This then spills over into a different discussion about when a boy can no longer benefit from the teaching of women in the church. All this also betrays the belief that complementarians think pastors are meant to exercise authority, which has led to numerous problems, including spiritual abuse coupled with a lack of accountability.

Ultimately, the *Almost Heretical* gender series changed everything, though not right away. By the end of 2018, I was convinced that mutuality based on gifts was God's design. The fruit from complementarianism's poor substitute for intimacy and partnership was rotten. However, I was still too nervous to identify as egalitarian. Part of the reason for my reservation was a conversation I had with Roger's wife, Sam, in which she was convinced there was a third option "between" complementarianism and egalitarianism, an option that featured the "best" of both ideologies. Since I still believed in the "inerrancy" of the Bible and the seemingly straightforward prohibition on women teaching men, Sam's offering seemed like a safe alternative for the moment instead of needing to choose. Egalitarians had such a bad reputation from the people at Entrench, so I gave myself some distance from the pressure of feeling like I needed to declare then and there if I was egalitarian.

A couple days later, when I asked Stephen how he viewed me after listening to the *Almost Heretical* episodes, he replied, "I see you as my equal now." Notice he didn't say, "I see you as more of an equal." He was finally, for the first time, understanding that I *am* equal. Under complementarianism, Stephen was programmed to parrot, "Women are equal in dignity, value, and worth." By his own admission, he didn't perceive women as equal to him until after he listened to the gender series. From there, Stephen and I became besties and true partners, though he did wonder aloud, "What if we're wrong?" as we (still very cautiously) headed toward mutuality.

If what Tim Ritter and Nate Hanson were teaching on *Almost Heretical* was true, then not only was it right for me to interpret my experiences at Entrench as unequal treatment, but it was right for me to demand equality. "Equal in dignity, value, and worth" was no longer cutting it for me. Was I not equal in intellect and spiritual gifts, too? Yes, I was. Were cishet white men the standard for all other people to determine our worth in comparison to them? No, they were not. Now that I knew these things, really knew them, I wasn't sure what I was going to do, but I had to act in some way. I trusted myself more and wouldn't accept being treated as lesser. If I accepted this for myself, then I would excuse the oppression of other people, as I had been doing most of my life.

This led to me declaring to Stephen that I wouldn't continue showing up at Entrench and communicating with my presence that it was okay to treat me poorly. Jake and I were not at peace, and I wouldn't be there on a Sunday morning when he was preaching until our relationship was repaired. I naively thought he would make things right between us. Stephen was uneasy about my decision to stop attending church, but he understood.

During this time, I was also using the strategies I'd learned from the women's group at Entrench to repeatedly study Genesis 3, one word at a time in the original Hebrew. Remember, I'd been taught that part of the curse of Genesis 3 with Adam and Eve was that Eve would want to usurp the God-given authority that Adam had over her. Another part of the teaching I absorbed was that we still live under this curse today. Unfortunately, it was another thing I had bought into without picking up on the contradiction. Something cannot be both God's design and a curse, unless your God is very sucky. Widening the lens of my hermeneutical approach also led to a discovery I wouldn't have made if I hadn't more closely examined the history of certain verses.

One of those verses was Romans 16:7. Let's compare the ESV and the NIV translations.

> *"Greet Andronicus and Junia, my kinsmen and my fellow prisoners. They are well known to the apostles, and they were in Christ before me." (ESV)*

> *"Greet Andronicus and Junia, my fellow Jews who have been in prison with me. They are outstanding among the apostles, and they were in Christ before I was." (NIV)*

Notice how one translation (the ESV) establishes Junia as someone "well known *to* the apostles" while the other (the NIV) declares Junia to be "outstanding *among* the apostles." According to adherents to the ESV and similar translations, Junia was not an apostle herself. She was a woman, so how could she hold such a high "office" in the church as an apostle? The ESV rendering is in opposition to the current NIV translation, and others like it, that affirm the apostleship of Junia. Also, did you know that at one point, translators (even of the NIV) decided to completely change the feminine name Junia to the supposedly masculine name Junias to avoid naming the woman Junia as an apostle? The role of a woman as an apostle didn't square with the patriarchy those translators wanted to perpetuate in the late 1800s.[52]

Learning the lengths men were willing to go to diminish women's contributions to the early church was painful. It also felt a lot like Jake diminishing, or flat out ignoring, the contributions women were making at Entrench. It was time for a bit of a change.

* * * * *

On January 1st, I texted my friend Aubrey to commend her for all her growth. She replied with an invitation to come with her into flourishing. The more I thought about it, the more tempting it sounded. As long as my relationship with Jake was strained, I wasn't going to Entrench. Talking with Stephen, I decided I wanted to go to Revolution Church with Aubrey. Just like when we visited Christ Central, Stephen felt like it would be a betrayal to go to another church, but he decided to check it out with me. Was it possible for me to consistently feel what I'd observed in Aubrey?

When Pastor Darryl approached the stage at Revolution, he introduced the new sermon series on the Lord's Prayer. His sermon that day would focus on the phrase "Our Father." Just those two words. Pastor Darryl illustrated the kind of parent God is. Warped views I had of God melted away as the pastor explained that the father in the story of the prodigal son defended his child against the shunning of the community. Imagining God defending me led to weeping. For the first time, I vocalized that God loves me. Me. I'd always told others about God's love for them and knew that God loved me in the way that God had to because, well, it's God. But on that day, I realized what I deserved as a child of God. I realized God loves me with the purest love, love that is free from any taint of narcissism. I wouldn't accept anything less from anyone anymore. I couldn't.

My conceptions about God were disrupted that day. God was not a harsh dictator who demanded my perfection. Instead, God was the one who would run to protect me. If I was wrong about God, then maybe I was wrong about myself. Maybe my autonomy wasn't something to be feared, by me or anyone else. If someone was fearful, maybe that was indicative of an issue that wasn't my responsibility.

A couple of Sundays later, we attended Revolution again. In talking about children, Pastor Darryl tenderly offered the advice that when they mess up big, they need the biggest hugs. This new way of experiencing God was changing me as a person, positively impacting me as a parent. With each Sunday, I felt lighter, unencumbered. Less irritation characterized interactions with my kids. Shifts in my parenting bore witness to how the messages were altering me, like when Joshua hit me during a tantrum. Under the former teaching we'd received, I would have spanked Joshua for his action. Was it any wonder why Joshua hit me? He was simply mirroring me. He took off running to hide. Crouching down, I saw him huddled against the wall under Levi's crib. Attempting to coax him, I held my arms out and asked, "Can you come here?"

Joshua whimpered, "Are you going to spank me?"

"No, buddy, come here," I uttered in a soft voice. He crawled into my lap. I whispered into his hair, "When you mess up big is when you need the biggest hugs." We sat there, me rocking us side to side.

Then Joshua looked up at me and, of his own volition, said, "Mommy, I'm sorry I hit you. Will you forgive me?"

That was all it took for me to stop repeating harmful cycles through wooden spoon spankings. Soon after this interaction, I told Stephen I wanted to stop spanking our kids. His response was, "You're pulling the rug out from under me." Considering all the conversations we'd had leading up to this, it's worth noting that the desire for us to no longer hit our children was the impetus for Stephen to vocalize feeling a loss of stability. It harkens back to the hierarchical structure. As the power around race and gender constructs was being dismantled, power over our children as parents was still considered permissible. But as a mother, I was enjoying my relationship with my kids so much more without the pecking order in place, and I was loving the person I was becoming so much more, too.

When Roger emailed me to (finally) schedule a follow-up meeting with him and Jake, the new Nicki was ready.

THOUGHTS FROM STEPHEN

Just like for Nicki, the *Almost Heretical* gender series challenged, and eventually completely transformed, my perspective on what I'd been taught about gender and gender roles. I'd never been taught the true cultural meaning of head coverings, elders, or the cult of Artemis in Ephesus. I was frustrated that not only had I not been taught the cultural and historical contexts of the verses, but I'd actively been taught incorrect information.

When Nicki asked me how I saw her after listening to those episodes, I remember looking at her to earnestly say, "I see you as my equal now." She was the one to point out to me the use of the word "now," and how that word makes a world of difference. As we discussed the episodes, I confessed that as much as the new information was making sense to me, I was still a bit worried about the path we were on.

* * * * *

We had hoped the meeting with Jake in July 2018 would be a catalyst for change. It was, but just not in the way we were anticipating. It had ignited a fire in Nicki to delve further into what the Bible had to say about men and women, research narcissism, and have the veil lifted to clearly identify power dynamics. During this time, our community group was dwindling in members, but those who remained were committed to racial justice and gender equality.

We were once again hopeful that if Jake could be confronted with the harm he caused Nicki, surely he would ask for forgiveness and seek to make things right with her. We had known Jake for more than a decade and showed we cared for him and his family throughout that time.

After welcoming Jake and Roger into our home in January 2019 for the long-awaited follow-up meeting, we all made our way to the sofa. Nicki began by praying for our time. Then, she asked Jake if there was anything he would like to apologize for from the July meeting. He acted clueless, like he had done nothing wrong. He didn't enact curiosity, ask genuine questions for understanding, or try to make things right with her. Instead, he acted defensively and continued to put up his guard. The tension in the room was thick again. A lot was riding on this conversation I felt pressure and worried. If Jake could just admit wrongdoing and show repentance, we could work through it.

We took a break, and Nicki and I went to our closet. She asked me, almost to verify she wasn't completely out of line in her perception of reality, "You see what he's doing, right?" I affirmed it, and Nicki told me we had to end it. I earnestly told her, "I don't want it to end like this," to which Nicki replied, "It already has." I responded, "I submit to you in this," as a way to highlight the path we had been on and Ephesians 5:21.

The only way I can love Nicki as Christ loved the Church (Ephesians 5:25) is by submitting to her. By this I mean that Jesus came to dismantle systems of hierarchy and oppression by humbling himself. He didn't preserve his status and cultural position of authority but willingly laid it down to show us the way to God, and it's not through maintaining power. This has so many implications and applications for me as a cishet, middle class, able-bodied, white man in the United States. I have so much privilege and power that I must lay down so others who have been marginalized can be lifted up. So, in order to love Nicki as Christ loved the Church, I must get rid of the hierarchy by submitting.

* * * * *

After the meeting that night, I felt crushed and confused about everything that had happened. After more than a decade of relationship, it ended. Not only did it end like an ugly breakup with Jake, but we were losing the community that we had built and had come to rely on. Our lives revolved around this church and the people.

The next several months, I experienced much anger, disappointment, sadness, and bitterness as I grieved the death of this chapter of our lives and the relationships we had built. I felt angry that Jake would preach something from the pulpit but when the rubber met the road, he wouldn't follow his own teaching. I felt disappointment that God had not intervened and helped smooth things over. I felt sad at the loss of my community. I felt bitterness at Nicki for taking us on this journey that led to this point, as if it was her fault. I felt alone; expendable; unneeded. We were now outside the "church family," like outcasts.

It took six months to get a follow-up meeting scheduled with Jake. I thought he would authentically apologize, own where he erred, and commit to making the relationship between us whole. Nothing could prepare me for what was to come.

Looking directly at me, Jake insisted, "You came to me because you think the way we do things at Entrench is sexist, and I," *pound*, "am not," *pound*, "a sexist," *pound*. For added emphasis, he thumped his chest. "And you know what, Nicki?" he rhetorically asked. "I think you just really don't like me, and that's why this is happening."

The power imbalance cannot be ignored, but it was. Jake saw me as a threat, a threat to the complementarian church system he wanted to maintain. Choking up, I was about to repeat the hyperventilation from six months prior.

Rushing through our bedroom with Stephen following closely, I fruitlessly sucked in the air that was escaping in choppy bursts. I felt as though we were repeating the events of half a year ago, but I was a different person now. Understanding my value meant I could no longer accept Jake's abuse, abuse entrenched in unchecked narcissism that chipped away at my dignity while trying to gaslight me to protect his own image.

When we rejoined Roger and Jake, I stood firm because I knew what I deserved. I straightened my torso and locked eyes with Jake to assert, "Our time at Entrench is over. You broke trust with me in July and have done little to nothing to acknowledge and repair that broken trust. So, I cannot submit to your leadership anymore."

Just like that, it was over. I was done experiencing this spiritual abuse. I was done being less than.

I felt free.

Chapter 10
Leaving Church

As Stephen and I processed what we'd just gone through leaving Entrench, I kept thinking about him saying, "I submit to you in this." It shouldn't be some revolutionary idea that Stephen would submit to me at times. It's certainly not a "new age" principle sweeping once "Bible-believing Christians" away. It's something attributed to Paul in Ephesians 5:21 to all the Christians he was writing to. "Submit to one another out of reverence for Christ" (NIV). Based on how wives are the ones constantly and continually instructed to submit to husbands, per the next verse, I guess Jake couldn't fathom that there would be a time when Stephen would submit to me. Jake likely assumed he had our loyalty, especially Stephen's, and that Stephen would never *let* us leave the church.

About a week after we left, a friend from Entrench stopped by our house. What was supposed to be a drop-in turned into a hours-long conversation about women and women's roles. This was when I found out that our friend was egalitarian and had been since studying it in worship school. He then brought up a fascinating point I hadn't considered. Often, complementarians argue that because Jesus (the second person in the Trinity) is subordinate to the Father (the first person in the Trinity), women are simply being like Jesus by being subordinate to men. It was confusing to me how women were being compared to Jesus in this scenario when it suited complementarians. However, husbands were compared to Jesus as the ones wives needed to submit to as the church submits to Christ. Super head-spinning logic going on there.

Then, our friend further pulled the curtain back when he brought up the question of "eternal subordination" of the Son to the Father. He pointed out that if Jesus is eternally in subordination to the Father, that's how men justify the eternal submission of women to men. This "eternal submission as a woman" piece is what scared me the most. These jokers really want a "heaven" where women continue to be submissive because, according to them, that's God's good design.

As my theology shifted post-Entrench, it led to the realization that for all the talk about "total depravity" within neo-Calvinist circles, there is zero ability to reflect on how dangerous it is for men like Jake to accumulate all this power for themselves. Those men are treated as indispensable demi-gods while women are treated as disposable, both at Entrench and to patriarchy as a whole. Women have always been disposable to evangelical Christian patriarchy, as evidenced by the ways evangelicals gloss over the "texts of terror" in the Bible and the ways they flippantly talk about us dying. I mean, evangelical singer Pat Boone himself declared, "I would rather see my four girls shot and die as little girls who have faith in God than leave them to die some years later as godless, faithless, soulless Communists." As author Kristin Du Mez explained, "His audience was thrilled, even if his wife was not."[53]

It makes sense that men like Boone wouldn't care about our death considering the disdain they have for us from the womb. The genitalia of those assigned female at birth is a death sentence, in some places more often than others. There are also so many who are brought home alive just to die inside knowing our dads would have preferred boys. (We didn't miss your fallen face about the pink center of that cake. Also, can we stop the gender reveal parties? For so many reasons.)

∗ ∗ ∗ ∗ ∗

When it came to how the Bible is translated and read by evangelical Christians, another discovery that shook the foundation of my faith was that the word "brothers" could almost always be translated as "brothers and sisters" in the context of addressing a church. The ESV had a footnote that the word *adelphois* translated in the verse as "brothers" could be translated "brothers and sisters." Well, since it *could* be translated that way, I decided to start reading it that way. It didn't detract from the original meaning, after all. Rather, it enhanced the passage. At least for me. Apparently, others were uncomfortable and didn't feel it was necessary. How do I know? Because they told me as much.

Here's what happened. A married couple from Entrench started hosting our former community group. There was a meeting coming up where the group was going to sing worship songs together. A few people invited me to come. I went. We read some verses. Then, I shared the information about "brothers and sisters" and how empowering it was for me to read the Bible in a new way, to really feel like what I'm reading is for me, as an active participant, not a peripheral bystander. One of the women in attendance declared that it didn't matter to her that the verses were translated with the word brothers, without sisters added. I guess she thought her indifference negated my feelings of appreciation. Little did I know, this wasn't the only bone she wanted to pick with me. This person, who we'll call Nadine, was part of an ecumenical group that met for prayer nights once a month. She kept badgering me to attend a prayer night. I told her I'd be at the next one.

I'd been planning on going all day. As I prepared dinner, my mind moved on to other tasks, and I simply forgot. Texting Nadine, I apologized for not making it. It was a good thing I didn't go. Turns out, Jake was also there, which another friend later told me. Nadine had invited him and failed to inform me, despite knowing the whole situation. Apparently, her dedication to "reconciliation" was more important than my well-being. For some reason, I gave her the benefit of the doubt and told her I'd be at the next one. And I was. But I should have skipped that one, too.

My sweet friend Abigail went with me. We settled onto the couch. From there, it went downhill, slowly at first until I was hurtling to a crash at the bottom. There were "little" comments being made, and they were adding up. I couldn't contain the frustration that was being triggered by the freely flowing complementarian rhetoric. There was a middle school boy there who shared about how when he was at church or church related activities, he was "on fire for God." That fire struggled to stay lit when he was at school. At school, he was "tempted" to fit in and do things that he knew didn't please "God" (because we all know that this "God" must be pleased and appeased).

I'm not sure what types of behavior he was engaging in, and I don't think it mattered to most of the people who ended up surrounding him, laying hands on him, and praying for him. Void of accountability for whatever his actions were, this middle school boy had a room full of adults praising God for the "leader" who was being raised up, meaning the boy who'd just hinted at a confession of wrongdoing. In that moment, I couldn't help but think about how differently the situation would be handled if the middle schooler in the center of the circle was a girl. Would the adults be calling her a leader? Probably not.

We got through that round of prayer. If you thought it was a doozy, the subsequent round of prayer would make you dizzy. One man voiced that he wanted to pray for the men in our country. He lamented how men in the U.S. of A are disrespected because sitcom dads are portrayed as buffoons…okay, buddy. There's two things that came to my mind when he said this. One, if you aren't a buffoon as a father, why do you care? Guess what, there are plenty of fathers who are, in fact, guilty of full-on buffoonery. For example, the man who wouldn't change his kids' diapers when they pooped. Insecure men may have their feelings hurt by seeing a man depicted as a buffoon on television, but there are far more serious issues at hand. This leads me to the second thought that came to my mind and out of my mouth.

Twisting to face Abigail, I whispered, "Meanwhile, women in *real life* are being sexually assaulted at alarming rates, but, please, tell me more about dads in *sitcoms*." My whisper was heard by other people. I had zero Fs left to give at that point. Ish really hit the fan when a woman behind me followed up the prayer request for men by asking that we pray for the women in our country. Her plea was for women to joyfully occupy the role of a submissive wife. (Notice how woman and wife are interchangeable in this type of culture, rendering single women invisible.) This woman then recounted how she heard "God" tell her, "Stop trying to lead your family. Flip the table so that your husband is at the head. Then, sit down and shut up." I don't know about you, but I think her "God" sounds like an a-hole. Granted, her "God" was my "God" not too long ago. But yeah, that was the straw that broke this camel's back. (It's me. Hi. I'm the camel. It's me.)

Grabbing my bag, I stormed out the room with Abigail behind me. Cramming my feet in my shoes, I jolted upright when the woman sighed, "Men want respect. Women want love." No, no, no, no, no. Why can't I be loved *and* respected? Further, is it really love if there isn't respect? Then, "sitcom guy" mansplained, "There's a reason Paul wrote, 'Husbands love your wives. Wives submit to your husbands.' It's harder for husbands to love and for wives to submit." Yuck, yuck, yuck, yuck, yuck. But the real kicker was when that guy started talking about head coverings, a topic covered in the *Almost Heretical* gender series. He stated that Paul told women to wear head coverings because it was a symbol of submission to the authority over them. Next thing I knew, I was marching back into the room. Plopping on the couch, I waited until "sitcom guy" was done and unleashed my pent-up fury.

With my finger pointed to the ceiling as if I was a teacher about to impart a life changing lesson, I blurted out, "Actually, no." I talked about what I'd learned from the podcast series concerning head coverings and Paul's instruction to the women of the early church to wear them. The longer I talked, the more settled my body became. I elaborated on how it was forbidden for enslaved women and prostitutes to wear a head covering during the time in which Paul was writing in the Roman empire. It was illegal for them to cover their heads because a veil was reserved for a "woman of honor." The veil was supposed to offer a level of protection to the woman wearing it so that she wouldn't be sexually assaulted. That's right. Women who weren't wearing a veil were considered sexually available to be assaulted.

There's so much more to it, but, from what I understood, by having *all* women in the church community wear a veil, Paul was, first of all, breaking the law, and second of all, communicating equality among the women. There was no hierarchy of women where some were protected and others were not.[54] (Though I didn't say this that night, I think it's important to mention that having "women of honor" wear veils in the Roman empire was not because the patriarchal culture cared about honoring women on the basis of them deserving to be honored. More so, it was because these "women of honor" belonged to the men who were "over them." To assault these women would be an offense against the men.)[55]

As I wound down my mini-lecture that night at Nadine's, I then surprised myself by stating, "I realize that most people here are likely complementarian, and I'm in the minority as an egalitarian." I guess I was identifying as egalitarian, though I didn't mean to say it out loud in that living room and wished I had guarded that information more closely. I knew how quickly that label would discount everything I'd said. The wife of "sitcom guy" spoke up and had us all pray. During the prayer, Abigail and I snuck out. Even though I had some intense regret about how I'd handled the whole situation, Abigail told me that she'd loved it and reminded me that she loved me. There was no shame coming from her. Just lots of compassion and understanding.

When I got home and relayed everything to Stephen, the conflict-avoidant Enneagram 9 in him was flabbergasted. After picking up his jaw from the floor, he simply asked, "Why did you do that?"

"I don't know," was all I could say as I sat on our couch crying.

As we talked more, Stephen wondered if maybe the reason I had gotten so pissed off was because I'd come out from under that complementarian teaching and found freedom in doing so, just to be in a space that I wasn't ready to be in where they were trying to put me back under that teaching. The next day, I messaged Nadine and her husband to apologize to them. Though I stood by my decision to interrupt the patriarchy, I told them that I wished I had spoken with more humility. Nadine messaged back to ask if the two of us could meet. Well, let's just say that this was another thing I should have skipped.

* * * * *

As Nadine spoke with me a couple days later, she began by saying, "I just want to lovingly caution you that in all this talk of mutuality, you aren't finding your identity in egalitarian theology." It was an echo of an earlier conversation Stephen and I had with someone who left our group. That guy wanted to "lovingly caution" us that in all our talk of social justice, we weren't forsaking the gospel. Never once, before this period in my life, did anyone accuse me of forsaking the gospel. Not when I read all the books about being a "biblical woman" as a wife and mother. Not when I spent hours discussing complementarian interpretations, while considering those doctrinal points to be absolute truth. Not when I was completely consumed with a more "spiritually acceptable" topic. They didn't accuse me of forsaking the gospel or finding my identity outside of Christ until we no longer aligned.

For a second time in a matter of days, sitting in Nadine's living room, I was caught off guard. "I have the gift of discerning between the spirits," Nadine explained.

Pulling out the spiritual gift made it harder to push back. I wanted to tell her, "*I have the gift of discernment, too, so was God communicating through me or you?*" Instead, I didn't speak.

"Every conversation this past year has circled back to gender," Nadine continued.

In my mind, I replied, "*I just started studying this seven months ago, so...*"

Nadine slowly said, "What I saw was division as you whispered to Abigail. *That* was the work of the enemy."

I kept the conversation going in my head as I thought, "*Discomfort and tension reveal there is separation. Basically everywhere Jesus went, we're told that people got upset with him. We're told he came to bring a sword to divide the mighty from those they marginalized. It is false unity if I simply sat silently the other night. Concealing my anger is not indicative of living in harmony.*" Nadine didn't know any of this because I, of course, kept it to myself. And still, she kept the low blows coming.

"The old Nicki," she stopped herself to rephrase what she'd just said, but it was too late. The damage had been done. The person

I was becoming was no longer acceptable to her. She wanted the more palatable version of me, the version she felt more comfortable around. I can understand from her point of view that it looked like I had changed. This work of dismantling systems of oppression within oneself transforms people.

Nadine had the opportunity to reach out, but I initiated the initial dialogue. I owned where I erred and asked for forgiveness, not once but twice (because I asked again as I sat across from her one-on-one in her living room). Rather than showing me mercy or asking if I could help her understand my pain, she heaped on shame because I disagreed with complementarianism and expressed differing creeds. Before I left, she asked if we could meet again so that I could tell her more about the trauma of my past, trauma I'd mentioned as to why I was triggered that night during the prayer gathering. Nadine assured me that she and her husband weren't upset with me. Well, her husband contradicted that a few minutes later as I was loading up my kids into the van in his driveway. That joker walked right past me, not once but three times, and did not once look me in the eyes or even acknowledge my presence.

As I drove away, a knowing nestled deep in my bones that I could not come to Nadine with my deepest wounds. She demonstrated that when she called what I did "the work of the enemy." I guess she doesn't perceive that she is just as susceptible to deception as me. Reflecting on Nadine's assessment, I realized that I could spout complementarian theology all day, and I did for a full decade, and never be accused by her of finding my identity in complementarian theology. Nadine thought my views had polarized, and she didn't even recognize me as she pined for "the old Nicki."

* * * * *

Though I had left Entrench and was identifying as egalitarian, I hadn't fully left complementarianism. Revolution still identified as complementarian because, even at a more "progressive" church, dehumanizing ideologies can still lurk beneath the surface. At Revolution, they talked about social justice, prominently featured women on the stage, and had LGBTQ+ folx in the church. I even thought Revolution was affirming. Then, I heard about one of the pastors saying that, though queer people were welcome at the church, they couldn't fully participate and would be told they weren't experiencing God's best for them.

While we're on the topic, a quick note: If you want to attend a church that is egalitarian and affirming, check out Church Clarity. According to the website, "Church Clarity is a crowd-sourced database of local congregations that we score based on how clearly they communicate their actively enforced policies. Our mission is to increase the standard of clarity throughout the Church Industry. We are not advocating for policy changes; we are standardizing church policy disclosure, whatever the policy or type of church in question. People deserve to know the truth."[56]

When I say that women were prominently featured on stage at Revolution, I mean that the welcome and announcements were often done by women, and there were many women on the worship team. There was also the time when the pastor's wife joined him one Sunday. I didn't give it much thought, but now it's deeply unsettling that even these more "progressive" complementarian churches think it's necessary to have a husband on the stage with his wife if she's "teaching." The idea behind this is that the husband's presence provides a stamp of approval for what his wife is saying. Also, the husband is there to stop his wife from going off the rails. He can easily intervene if needed.

So, the pastor's wife joined him that Sunday. It was nice to see a woman on the stage in that capacity, but I wanted more. I got it on June 2, 2019 when Beth Moore taught as part of the summer series. I'd always shied away from Moore before because she wasn't on the list of "approved" women at Entrench. Unsure of what to expect, I was surprised by how much I enjoyed her teaching. She was more humble in her attitude and posture than most men I'd ever seen preach.

Naive Nicki assumed that because the church allowed this singular woman to deliver the message that Sunday, that Revolution was treating women with dignity. I tried not to give too much thought to the fact that the pastor emphasized that Beth Moore was teaching, not preaching. Why did it matter? Why couldn't she be preaching? Also, the Bible verse that complementarians would use to silence Beth Moore reads, "I do not permit a woman to teach or to exercise authority over a man" 1 Timothy 2:23 (ESV). So, it would have lined up more with the theology to say that she was preaching, not teaching. Ugh, my head hurts just thinking about the mental gymnastics.

As I continued moving away from complementarianism, and other toxic religious beliefs, I decided to start an Instagram account on July 4, 2019. I called the account "Broadening the Narrative" and wanted to document my journey by having a space where I could post podcast and book recommendations as well as amplify other accounts.

For some reason, though, I still felt like I needed to run things by Stephen, to get his permission and involve him. He didn't tell me this. It's just that the complementarian conditioning was so deep.

The shame was also deep, as there were certain topics I completely avoided with him because they led to arguments. One of those topics was the inerrancy of the Bible, something I'd been questioning. My research had led me to a blog post titled "An Egalitarian Review of Bible Translations." The authors asked seven questions to analyze various Bible translations regarding gender and women in specific passages. Their conclusion was, "The least gender-accurate translation of both Old and New Testaments, scoring zero for each category, is the English Standard Version."[57]

As I exchanged the ESV for a different version of the Bible, I also began to more closely examine the prominent men who advocated for the exclusion of women, whether that meant excluding Junia as an apostle or Beth Moore as a teacher. These were men like Paige Patterson and John Piper, men I once revered. Not anymore. You have the likes of Patterson, former president of Southwestern Baptist Theological Seminary, openly admitting to counseling a woman to stay in an abusive marriage and pray for her husband. The advice is appalling on its own, but what followed is even more egregious. The woman came back to the church after implementing Patterson's heinous recommendation. She had two black eyes and said to Patterson, "I hope you're happy." The story gets worse.

He responded, "Yes, ma'am, I am happy." The reason for his glee was that he believed his advice worked. It brought her husband to church, but she didn't know it. Standing at the back, her husband had entered the building for the first time.[58] To Patterson, domestic violence was worth it if it led an abusive husband to attend church. Screw that. Seriously, I have all the Fs to give about that.

John Piper also had a violently problematic response to being asked, "What should a wife's submission to her husband look like if he's an abuser?" He declared that if the husband was "simply hurting her," she should "endure verbal abuse for a season" and "endure perhaps being smacked one night." Then, she should seek "help from the church."[59] Not outside legal help or protection. The church — the very institution that empowered the abuser and won't hold him accountable. The multitudes of men like Patterson and Piper who enable abusers do so in part because of verses like 1 Peter 3:1-2. "Likewise, wives, be subject to your own husbands, so that even if some do not obey the word, they may be won without a word by the conduct of their wives, when they see your respectful and pure conduct" (ESV).

Newsflash: women do not exist to bring men to God. Stop using those verses to excuse and minimize domestic violence. And yes, domestic violence and complementarianism are absolutely connected. In a 2018 academic study, researchers explored how adhering to the Calvinist theological beliefs of hierarchical relational expectations and complementarian gender ideology intersected with the acceptance of domestic violence myths. The acceptance of these myths then correlates to an increase in actually carrying out that violence.[60]

* * * * *

As I was experiencing the real-life benefits of leaving a toxic religious institution, I wanted others to experience those benefits, too. This led to me questioning the supposed passivity I'd heard about during my years at Entrench, the supposed failure of men to lead their families and communities well. That's when it dawned on me that maybe these men were struggling with so-called passivity because they weren't meant to be the only ones to lead. Maybe I could lead, too. I was beginning to realize that an overemphasis on Ephesians 5:22 (about wives submitting to husbands) to the neglect of Ephesians 5:21 (about submitting to one another) meant suffering for everyone.

If women in this complementarian culture are expected to submit to men and forfeit our voice, I began to think, thanks to the work of Lisa Sharon Harper, that this expectation was intruding on our responsibility to exercise dominion and stewardship of the earth. After all, in the story of Adam and Eve, the man and the woman were created to exercise dominion — together. Since complementarianism sets up a false gender binary, and then enforces a hierarchy within that system, the "fruit" of said theology is rotten and death-inducing. It is literally producing prideful narcissists who delight in ruling over others instead of stewarding resources together.

We are told that Jesus said, "You'll recognize them by their fruit" Matthew 7:20 (CSB). It's no surprise, then, that complementarianism results in depression, suppression, suspicion, bruised bodies, broken bones, and black eyes. I began to rethink what it meant for a husband to love his wife as Christ. My thoughts at the time were that Jesus doesn't expect us to "go to another place" while he uses us for selfish purposes, as I'd heard wives saying they did during sex. If Jesus didn't do this, then a husband didn't have the right to expect his wife to please him sexually when she didn't desire to. She shouldn't have to go somewhere else mentally. She should — and she does — have the right to simply say, "No." This may be self-explanatory to people who weren't taught the misbeliefs of complementarianism, but this was a breakthrough for me.

Further, it became incompatible to me for people to say, "Christ came so we might have abundant life," and then turn around and say that actually it's just part of living under "the curse" for men to shoulder a heavy burden in leading, while women also live burdened, thinking the worst about ourselves as potential "usurpers."

More and more I was becoming comfortable with the egalitarian label. Meanwhile, some of the still-complementarian men in my life were publicly attempting to distance themselves from men they considered "hyper-complementarians." This line of reasoning is similar to what I had previously thought about the problem not being with complementarianism but instead in how people misapplied complementarianism. In reality, the people "misapplying" the theology are carrying out the theology to an end that makes sense in their worldview.

To the complementarian men who are disturbed by the complementarian fruits of black eyes, bruised bodies, financial abuse, and more: good. You should be disturbed. I'd be worried if you weren't. The discomfort you're feeling knowing that abusive men are also complementarian, and they're using their complementarian beliefs to belittle women, that discomfort is trying to tell you something. If you'll listen. Just like me, I know you've been taught to discount the messages from your body and emotions, but those messages can be so helpful.

If you're a complementarian man who is willing to listen to women who have been harmed by complementarianism and consider our experiences, then you aren't the men I'm uncomfortable around. I'm uncomfortable around the men who won't question it at all, who ignore the pleas of the majority in favor of the submissive agreement of the often-silenced minority. For you men who are willing to listen and consider, by proposing that other men are hyper-complementarian, you prop yourself up as one of the good guys. However, this proposition is the same as "soft patriarchy," and all of it dehumanizes and devalues me. Even the "softest" or most "benevolent" patriarchy is still patriarchy; it still upholds a hierarchy. I invite you to engage in the same work I did of wrestling through not trying to distance yourself from the so-called hyper-complementarians. When you set yourself apart from the "bad apples," you then avoid self-reflecting on the ways you still uphold hierarchy. That self-reflection piece was critical for me in leaving complementarianism and everything connected to it.

The cherry-on-the-complementarian-cake came when I heard that Mark Driscoll, founder of the Acts 29 church planting network Entrench was part of, said that women are penis homes.[61] Driscoll had demeaned women in this way under a pseudonym in 2001, but I didn't read about this until 2019. Goosebumps covered my arms as I read the article and sat with feelings of disgust and discomfort.

Enough with men like Patterson, Piper, and Driscoll. It was time to read more books by egalitarian women, which led me to Rachel Held Evans' book *A Year of Biblical Womanhood*. Some of my favorite passages that spoke to my relationship with complementarianism were:

> "The irony of course, is that while advocates of biblical patriarchy accuse everyone else of biblical selectivity, they themselves do not appear to be stoning adulterers, selling their daughters into slavery, taking multiple wives, or demanding that state laws be adjusted to include death sentence for rape victims…at least not yet. Those who decry the evils of selective literalism tend to be rather clumsy at spotting it in themselves."[62]

> "It seems that most of the Bible's instructions regarding modesty find their context in warnings about materialism, not sexuality…I've heard dozens of sermons about keeping my legs and my cleavage out of sight, but not one about ensuring that my jewelry was not acquired through unjust or exploitive trade practices."[63]

> "Both Jesus and Paul spoke highly of celibacy and singleness, and for centuries the Church honored the contributions of virgins and widows to the extent that their stories occupied the majority of Christian literature…As a Christian, my highest calling is not motherhood; my highest calling is to follow Christ."[64]

> "In Jewish culture it is not the women who memorize Proverbs 31, but the men. Husbands commit each line of the poem to memory, so they can recite it to their wives at the Sabbath meal, usually in a song…We abandoned the meaning of the poem by focusing on the specifics, and it became just another

impossible standard by which to measure our failures. We turned an anthem into an assignment, a poem into a job description."[65]

That final passage about husbands reciting, even singing, Proverbs 31 to their wives at the Sabbath meal unlocked something for me. There were so many ways I'd misunderstood Proverbs 31. Also, there I'd been for years singing, "Oh my man, I love him so," as a greeting to Stephen when he got home from work when it would have been totally acceptable 1) to not do that and 2) for him to sing to me. Instead, I'd been part of a system that expected wives to celebrate our husbands faithfully and dutifully for simply existing and never even desire reciprocation.

* * * * *

When Stephen and I first left Entrench, I hoped to find a forever community at Revolution Church. There was one Sunday when an entire row was filled with people who had left Entrench. Our reasons for leaving varied, but at the root the commonality was a lack of care. Immediately, I began going to the small group that met at my friend Aubrey's house. In May, Stephen and I became members, but we were apprehensive about serving in any capacity. In August, I worked up the courage to fill out Revolution's online form to request help paying for therapy. My hope and faith were renewed. Everything was looking up.

Until it wasn't.

Unfortunately, an experience there led me all the way out of church for a season. That's what happens when unqualified people are first responders to church trauma.

Here's what happened: Stephen and I squealed into the paved lot precisely one minute before our 5:30 appointment. We met care team members Dorothy and Fred at the door and were whisked away to a room designated for private talks. What followed was a tumultuous evening of accusations, judgment, distrust, and pain. The spiritual abuse I'd experienced at Entrench was minimized. I'd expected empathy, people who would support me through my suffering, and to feel loved. This was supposed to be the meeting that turned everything around. But there I was, shoulders slumped in defeat, broken-heartedly resolving to step back from church, perhaps permanently.

I never thought I'd be part of the dechurched club. It's a club

I'd rather not have a membership card for in my wallet. After all, who was I if I didn't walk in a church's doors the following Sunday? Over the next few months, I would begin finding out, and — somewhat surprisingly — I actually liked the person I was getting to know.

* * * * *

After leaving church completely, I felt more freedom to explore what I believed about marriage outside of a complementarian framework. One day while researching, I found an article about a Christian husband taking his wife's last name.[66] For the first time, I questioned this aspect of the patriarchal system that expected me to shed a part of my identity connected to my name to take on a part of Stephen's identity, but that did not expect the same, or anything similar, from him.

Around this time, my wardrobe went through some changes. I wanted to start doing yoga and walking more regularly. Purchasing some athletic tank tops, I felt confident when Stephen said, "You look so strong." When a friend saw me wearing one, she remarked, "I've never seen that much of your skin." It took over a year to get comfortable wearing tank tops and shorts in public again, not wondering, "Is this going to cause someone to stumble?" Even now, I'm hyper-aware of what I'm wearing in certain circumstances or around certain people.

Another change that took place was within me. I began feeling more confident expressing my desires. After much inner deliberation, I told Stephen that I didn't want to homeschool. Since the majority of the responsibility for homeschooling would fall on me, I told him that my opinion carried more weight in this area. It's not that his input wasn't important, but his daily life would not be impacted if I had to homeschool our kids. After we talked through my preferences for sending our kids to public school, we enrolled Joshua for Pre-K. Whoo-hoo!

I also started therapy. With my therapist, for the first time, I voiced that there had been (and still could be) a hierarchy in my marriage. I explained to her that it often felt more like a parent-child relationship than an equal partnership between two adults. In every decision, it all came down to what Stephen wanted and what he thought was best for us. I didn't have an equal voice. This certainly came into play in our finances. My spending has always been more scrutinized. Even though Stephen isn't the type of person who frivolously spends money, there has been more freedom for him to spend money. I think that especially because I'm a SAHM and didn't bring in any income, I felt like the money in our bank account wasn't really money for me.

Stephen's judgment wasn't reserved just for my spending habits, though. There was one conversation where I was telling him about a gory aspect of a show I'd watched earlier in the day. The gore wasn't even shown, just implied. Stephen was disgusted and, no joke, he told me I shouldn't watch that show anymore. My cheeks burned. Later in our room alone, I cried because of the resulting shame. My actions were still subject to his scrutiny. There was definitely a double standard because, a little while later, he watched a movie that I started halfway through with him when I came home from a night out with some friends. While I was watching, someone was thrown into a woodchipper. This violent act was fully displayed. Stephen didn't flinch. He didn't turn the TV off. I went to our room to read a book and cry. Mostly to cry. I wasn't wanting Stephen to stop watching what he wanted to watch. I just wanted him to not judge me for what I watched.

In addition to my spending and TV habits, Stephen analyzed my shifting theology. After we left Revolution, I interrogated my beliefs about hell, the Bible, and so much more. Stephen was worried. After decades of gatekeeping and being warned about the dangers of heresy, Stephen didn't want me to "fall away," as we used to say. We'd be washing dishes while I bubbled over about the latest podcast episode I'd listened to. Stephen's shoulders would pull forward, a sign he was shutting down and shutting me out. There were arguments about me being on the "slippery slope." One night, Stephen was exasperated as he asked, "Do you even believe in absolute truth or sin anymore?"

Finally, I hit a point where I told him, "I'm not going to argue with you. If you want to read or listen, just ask me to send the resources. If you want to talk about them, we can." I'd had all day, if not longer, to mull over what I'd read or listened to. I assumed he wanted to know all about it. Understandably, his defensive reflexes initiated to protect himself from what he'd been taught to perceive as threats. The tension between us resulted in me hiding pieces of who I was becoming. It was lonely not sharing with Stephen, my bestie, but this helped me address my codependency. I am now at a place where I'm going to continue taking the next step that aligns with my values, even if I have to do so alone and without Stephen's approval. It just took a little more time for me to arrive at that resolve and be at peace with it.

THOUGHTS FROM STEPHEN

As I learned more about the misinformation I'd received about gender roles, I felt fearful and nervous. For so long, I was certain that the Bible taught that men were created to lead and women to help. I thought that to believe otherwise would be a misinterpretation of the Bible and lead to eventually forsaking the Gospel; this is the beginning of the slippery slope I had been warned about. I didn't want to forsake the gospel, so I felt cautious about this journey. What if the direction we were headed (toward egalitarianism) was wrong?

Well, the women in my life were proof that the direction *wasn't* wrong. They hadn't talked candidly with me before about how they were spoken to and about and treated in the church. The *Almost Heretical* gender series led me to ask myself why they hadn't felt safe to share their stories with me. This self-reflection was part of what was fueling me to shift how I engaged with my friends who were women.

I admit that I felt afraid of the change. I felt sad about losing our community and relationships that I had built for 12 years. After we left, I struggled with feeling like the only reason Jake had taken an interest in me as an intern was because he thought I would be easy to control and manipulate. I'm sure Jake thought my "headship" over Nicki would keep us at Entrench. But I was witnessing the impact of the spiritual abuse from Jake on Nicki. She and her well-being mattered more. Her mental health suffering was too high a price to pay for the false sense of peace between me and Jake. I had to choose her. It wasn't the heroic or valiant thing to do. It was the right thing to do.

It was tough to leave Entrench, but I watched Nicki begin to flourish again during our time at Revolution. I was cautious about jumping back into a church too quickly because of what we had just experienced. But our time at Revolution was a sort of respite where we could go, be fed, and leave without guilt. The teaching came from a place of the love of God rather than shame. The main teaching pastor also did not shy away from some of the issues we cared about that were such a struggle to get others to care about at Entrench. Revolution was a needed place of healing and restoration on our journey.

* * * * *

Things between me and Nicki were finally in a stable place. We had cohesive direction and more time to connect with one another outside of the responsibilities we'd had in church. We especially enjoyed our time together talking on the back patio after putting the kids down for bed. We settled into new rhythms.

As that time also came to a close, the period after leaving Revolution then had some lifegiving gatherings with friends in our home to share a meal, sing songs, and talk about life. It was a time of great intimacy, similar to what we had strived for at Entrench but never quite captured. I began a new job, leaving a community of people and a familiar work environment, to embark on an adventure in a field in which I had no experience. This also led to loss of stability. Not long after, the people who had been gathering with us in our home found churches to plug into.

Then, the COVID-19 pandemic began. The loneliness of changing beliefs, a new job, lost friendships, and forced isolation added further complicated layers. Some articles I've recently read have centered around a Harvard study spanning 85 years that investigated the key to happiness. The interviewers followed people at different stages of their lives and asked them questions to gauge their happiness. What the study revealed is that happiness has a lot to do with one's expectations of relationships and the reality of their relationships.[67] I am still trying to figure out community and connection these few years later.

Throughout this time after leaving Revolution, I longed for a steady place to stand, but Nicki was running across quicksand. It's true what they say about the slippery slope. Be careful, because one belief is tied to the next. It may all unravel when you start pulling at the strings. Ultimately, I'm glad I got on the slope, despite the bumps. Overall, I am a much more curious and compassionate person than I previously was. I enjoy more freedom in not trying to control everyone else's choices or lives. I still struggle with this at times, but I am working on getting to know myself better so I can heal. I want to be the best version of myself so I can be the best husband to Nicki, dad to our kids, and neighbor to my fellow humans.

As I moved farther from complementarianism, a conversation I had with someone from Entrench continued echoing in my mind. Ms. Donna was a real woman of valor. One afternoon in 2018, she gave me the anchor I've held to ever since when she told me, "We make everything so complicated, but it's actually simple. God wants us to love. It all comes down to love." Because of this insight that Ms. Donna shared with me, the way I've approached my life is informed by love, not fear. I distinctly remember the night I decided that I could be wrong no matter where I "landed" in the complementarian versus egalitarian debate. (This was part of my process then. I no longer worry about "landing" anywhere. In the words of my dear friend and brilliant author Marla Taviano, "Why would I land in any one place for very long at all when I have wings?"[68])

Knowing I could be wrong regardless of my position meant deciding I'd rather be wrong as an egalitarian. Talking with Stephen, I told him, "If when we die we have to stand before God to give an account for our actions, I would rather be able to say, 'I led with love and encouraged all people to exercise their spiritual gifts,' than to continue down the path of complementarianism and ultimately hear God ask, 'Why would you think I'd give spiritual gifts to people that I didn't want them to use?'"

Chapter 11
Undeniably Better

A year after I left Entrench, I publicly marked my departure in the form of a blog post.[69] This was a way to honor myself and my experience. In the post, I addressed various rumors I'd heard through the grapevine regarding my departure from the church as an institution. There was speculation I left because of a disagreement over social justice issues, gender roles, or theological interpretations, that there were certain personal preferences not being met by the church, or that I didn't give things enough time. With a resounding "This is NOT a reason for my departure," I shut that ish down.

A friend recently pointed out how telling it is that the line of reasoning was acceptable at Entrench that Stephen and I left over theological differences surrounding egalitarianism. Even though that wasn't the reason, the people spreading the rumor knew that others wouldn't question it and that Stephen and I would be considered heretical. In that church context, it was regarded as a bad thing that Stephen and I were becoming equal partners. That speaks volumes about the culture.

As Stephen and I were implementing mutuality, the "fruit" of egalitarianism was nourishing each of us as we worked to dismantle hierarchy in our marriage. One practical way we began working on removing the hierarchy was by splitting the finances that would have gone toward tithing. Since we weren't part of a church, we had money that we once would have given to a church. Instead, we split that money down the middle and donated wherever we wanted. By splitting the money, the pressure I'd been feeling of defending my donation decisions was alleviated. That's right, I'd been feeling like I had to constantly beg Stephen to understand why I wanted to donate to certain organizations or individuals. The very nature of needing to defend my decisions sheds light on the power dynamic that was still at play. Splitting the tithing money was a practical way of addressing the hierarchy and trying to function as equals.

During this time, I also joined two Patreon communities and participated in a couple of meetings each month. These groups were important to me because of the authentic community that was nurtured within them. The guilt of leaving Stephen to handle the kids on his own when I had evening or weekend calls was still present. This guilt was there even though I had needed to suck it up for years and do so much with the kids on my own when they were itty bitty to support Stephen fulfilling his obligations at Entrench. For the most part, Stephen was on board with my involvement in the Patreon communities, though every once in a while, repressed resentment he hadn't dealt with would be directed at me.

* * * * *

As I continued healing from the loss of community at Entrench, I planned my 30th birthday party. It was tough to come to terms with the fact that I would not have the 100+ people I'd originally thought I would because of the number of relationships I lost. I don't know if people thought they couldn't be friends with me anymore, if they didn't want to, or if they thought I didn't want to be friends with them anymore. Whatever it was, it left me with less people to invite. That made the people who did show up for me all the more special. For fun, I also bought myself a tiara and have worn it on my birthday every year since.

A couple of weeks after turning 30, I went with two of my closest friends to get similar tattoos. We had the words *eshet chayil*, woman of valor, engraved in our skin to serve as a reminder of who we are and who God says we are. Rachel Held Evans wrote about this in her book *A Year of Biblical Womanhood*, and it ministered to deeply wounded places within me to speak the words over myself. Along with a tattoo, my personal appearance continued to undergo some changes as I brought bright colors back into my clothing options. Phasing out some of the grays, I replaced them with reds and yellows, and I love finding the perfect jewelry to enhance my outfits.

This doesn't mean that I've fully embraced my body as it is. My stretch marks from growing three humans embarrass me. I don't feel confident enough to wear a two-piece bathing suit in public. Last summer, I bought one-piece suits that connected with the stomach and back open, but the bottom portion rose up high enough to cover the tummy that I'm ashamed of. I'm not saying I should or should not be ashamed. I'm just acknowledging that I am and that I have work ahead to continue healing from the lies I still believe about my body, desirability, and beauty.

These are lies I internalized so deeply that I was willing to burn the skin off my wrist with apple cider vinegar to try to get rid of a stubborn wart that had remained since childhood. Each day that I put the drenched cotton ball on my wrist led to more of the skin being eaten away by the acidity. Instead of stopping, I pushed myself to keep going just a little longer. Day after day, I hoped that the apple cider vinegar was killing the wart beneath the top layer of my skin. A literal hole, half an inch wide, formed before I quit applying the cotton balls. I now have a scar that's more noticeable than the wart was. Learn from my mistakes and do not mutilate your skin to try to conform to what is deemed desirable.

* * * * *

As Stephen and I embraced egalitarianism, we were healing from the harm of complementarianism, little by little. We wanted to invite others into the healing, too. In May 2020, we had a conversation on Instagram Live about our journey toward mutuality. Beforehand, I reached out to people and asked what questions they had for us to address. One of those people was Daniel, the former worship leader from Entrench.

He suggested it would be helpful for people to hear why we were so sold on complementarianism initially and then what changed. To discuss what changed for me, I have to quote Daniel from the texts we exchanged. He wrote, "One of my main things for changing my mind was about how following my strict conservative principles for studying the Bible actually led me there. Conservative, expository preachers constantly harp on the importance of studying the historical, cultural, and immediate textual context and doing word studies, but when it came to passages about women, leadership, etc. they all of a sudden decided that that wasn't important because the text 'is plainly understandable' or because 'insert proof text here.'"

Same.

To be consistent in my hermeneutical approach, I needed to apply the same diligence to this topic as I did to other theological topics. As Cynthia Long Westfall explained, "Three hermeneutical principles are shared by most traditions that hold the Bible as authoritative: (1) We do not base a doctrine on one verse. (2) We do not base a doctrine on a verse or passage with interpretive problems. And (3) we give weight to the clearer teaching."[70] I started to realize these principles weren't being applied to many passages about women. Even most complementarian pastors understand this on some level with 1 Timothy 2:11-15. Verse 15 is "But she will be saved through childbearing, if they continue in faith, love, and holiness, with good sense" (CSB).

"She will be saved through child bearing." That's what the text says. Plainly. Yet the complementarian pastors I know understand enough about Pauline theology to know it can't mean what it sounds like it means. There has to be more to it. They dig enough to say that of course Paul cannot mean that women are spiritually saved by having children, but they stop short in their excavation.

Cynthia Long Westfall also examined 1 Corinthians 11:3. "But I want you to know that Christ is the head of every man, and the man is the head of the woman, and God is the head of Christ" (CSB). Westfall wrote, "Most scholars have assumed that the topic of 1 Corinthians 11:3-16 is the authority of men and the subordination of women. This is partly because 'head' is a metaphor for authority in Latin, English, and German, so the meaning of 'authority' has seemed to be intuitive in the history of the interpretation of the passage."[71] Westfall went on to explain how the word *kephale*, translated as head, can also have the meaning of "source." This would make sense in the context of 1 Corinthians 11:3 and the belief that the man Adam was the source of the woman Eve.

Another word that had a fuller meaning than I'd originally been taught is *ezer*, which I'd simply understood as "helper" because of the translation of the Bible I read. This "helper" was taught to me as if I existed to be Stephen's secretary, functioning as an add-on to God's calling on his life. In reading *Half the Church* by Carolyn Custis James, more of my thoughts about marriage, and my role in a marriage, shifted.

Regarding *ezer* she wrote, "Long before I started digging, scholars tallied up the twenty-one times *ezer* appears in the Old Testament: sixteen [of those] times [were] for God as Israel's helper. This created quite a stir as you might imagine, prompting the upgrading from mere helper to strong helper. What followed was a divided (and at times heated) discussion over the meaning of 'strong' — How strong is strong (a debate yet to be resolved)? Putting the facts together, isn't it obvious that the *ezer* is a warrior?"[72] "Warrior" was synonymous with manhood in my mind up until that point. Viewing myself as a strong warrior, rather than a submissive helper, unleashed a deep feminine strength.

In addition, as I began to understand more about mutuality, there was a shift. Verses can be found to support complementarian theology. Yet those same verses, when understood differently based on cultural and textual contexts and with different valid translations of certain words, can then support egalitarian theology. More than this, there are clear and unambiguous passages that were addressed to *all* the people, not just the men, at the churches where the letters were sent. Those passages support mutuality, or a belief that, regardless of individual traits, we must exercise our gifts and respect the exercising of the gifts of others. I'm thinking specifically of 1 Corinthians 12 and Romans 12. These passages are clear and should be used to aid in interpretation. Further, Ephesians 5:21 deals with the people in the churches needing to submit to one another. It can't just be women doing all the submitting if we are instructed to submit *to one another*.

Another key piece for me was rethinking the line in the Lord's prayer, "Your kingdom come, your will be done on earth as it is in heaven" Matthew 6:10 (CSB). I remember having a conversation with a friend about the ways the Bible was used to justify chattel slavery. We talked about bringing God's kingdom to this earth and how chattel slavery was incompatible with God's kingdom because there will be no slavery there. All the ways people are silenced, discredited, and pushed to the margins today, even under the guise of biblical orthodoxy, are incompatible with God's kingdom. Regarding women, I thought, "Wait a minute. If we are supposed to be living into and manifesting God's kingdom here on earth as it is in heaven, and all people will flourish and seek the flourishing of one another perfectly in that place, why would I support anything that prevents that from coming to fruition now?"

The complementarians I knew (and the complementarian I was) fear the "slippery slope." I now understand that designation of a "slippery slope" as an excuse for not exploring a less cruel terrain's interpretation. Yes, once I started to question what I'd been taught about race and understood that I was wrong, it humbled me and opened the door to interrogate other ways I could be wrong. As someone who is near the top of the social ladder in many ways, I recognize that the people around me who held all the power are not the people I want to be like. Further, who I was isn't who I want to be anymore. I don't want to prize my power so much that I pridefully refuse to be held accountable. I don't want to be hardened to the plight of other human beings. I don't want to hurt others and call it being truthful to the biblical text when really it's a way of attempting to hide my contempt, dislike, or even hatred of someone I have othered and dehumanized. Call it the "slippery slope" if you must, but I wouldn't have it any other way.

As I made my way down the slope, I felt lighter. I didn't feel weighed down. The amount of time spent second guessing myself about every little thing was decreasing. My wariness about my motives was diminishing. The freedom to lead in the areas where I was gifted was increasing. Plus, Stephen and I were having more fun together, and I really loved being with him. We were consistently engaging as besties. There was more joy. Our relationship didn't feel as hard for me. More of this, please.

* * * * *

None of the changes Stephen and I were implementing at this time came naturally or with little effort. I had been unintentionally silenced for so long that voicing opposition or trying to forge a path as my own person apart from him was difficult. That is an ongoing journey. Personally, I was finding communication easier. The shame I would have felt as a complementarian if I disagreed with Stephen was abating. I felt more freedom to speak up and to even lovingly call Stephen out if he wasn't exercising humility and was unintentionally enforcing patriarchy in our home. There was a safety with him in a way that was different than before. Though I'd always felt physically safe with him, this was a new level in that I felt more emotionally and mentally secure.

Examining the fruit of complementarianism versus egalitarianism, it was clear we were on a more loving path. Some of the fruit of complementarianism was hindered women who either didn't know what their gifts were or who didn't know how to use those gifts in the church. Embracing egalitarianism meant fully exercising my gifts. As Westfall expounded, "As in the story of the talents in Matthew 25:14-28, women are under a sacred obligation to use all of what God has given them and every advantage to serve [God]. Women must resist any effort to squeeze their strengths, gifts, and abilities into a mold that hides them in the ground and quenches the Holy Spirit."[73]

In the past, there was an expansive crop of quarreling as the men with power were trying to maintain that power. Embracing egalitarianism meant "reject[ing] foolish and ignorant disputes, because [I] know that they breed quarrels" 2 Timothy 2:23 (CSB). As Sarah Bessey so aptly put it, "I'm through wasting my time with debates about women-should-do-this and women-should-not-do-that boundaries. I'm out. What an adventure in missing the point. These are the small, small arguments about a small, small god."[74]

Though Stephen and I were healing, there were still areas that were tough for us to discuss. There was a lot of resistance from him about becoming LGBTQ+ affirming. The resistance wasn't verbal, but I could feel it in my body and witness it in his. There was one time when he flipped through a book I bought that featured contributions from LGBTQ+ artists. There were a couple of pages with some graphic artwork. Again, Stephen tried to shame me. Again, I cried, just as I'd done that time he'd told me I shouldn't watch that TV show. Sometimes it felt like one step forward, two steps back.

* * * * *

About a year into the pandemic, I highly encouraged Stephen to get the COVID-19 vaccine. Stephen's argument against it was that we lean more natural. My rebuttal was that his health ethic can be what it is *and* he can still make an exception for the greater good during an actual pandemic. (Sidenote: I acknowledge there is a lot of nuance in this conversation about the vaccine and appreciate Tina Strawn's questions, "Are you pro-Black BEFORE you are pro-vax? Or are you so pro-vax that you are anti-Black?"[75]) Becoming egalitarian is not equivalent to a flipped script where now I'm on top, and what I say unequivocally goes. However, I told him that even if he didn't get the vaccine, I was going to. I also told him I strongly desired that the kids get the vaccine.

In addition to wanting our family to get the vaccine, I've also wanted us to at least try being vegan. For the most part, we've eliminated meat from our diet, but I'd like to attempt more for the sake of our health and bodies, as well as for the benefit of Mother Earth and all that is in her. Rather than giving veganism a chance, there's been so much pushback about the inconvenience. Stephen isn't too happy about the changes I have implemented to our meal plan (and the kids complain incessantly about the options), so I'm not sure what will happen in this area of our lives as individuals or together.

* * * * *

As my 32nd birthday approached in September 2021, I wanted to have a home and personal makeover of sorts to externally celebrate the internal changes that had been taking place over the prior few years. When it came to our house, there was so much that unsettled me, as I thought about the conversations that took place here with complementarian men who were committed to putting me in my place. The couch and swivel chair we had needed to go because every time I looked at them, I thought about the spiritual abuse, loss, and grief. So, we got new furniture. I loved the way the dark gray couch and the rustic oak modern sliding barndoor farmhouse TV stand anchored the living room in more stability. (Yes, that long description is the name of the item because I checked my order history.)

Then, the popcorn ceilings were scraped and painted eggshell white, which revealed an expansiveness that had formerly been masked in each room. The opening up of our home symbolized the opening up that was taking place inside of us. We let the kids choose the colors for their rooms to be painted. Our kitchen radiated joy in the form of bright yellow. The bathrooms were painted navy blue. The walls in the living room and our bedroom were painted a wispy shade of gray, and I incorporated pops of gold and pink.

For the first decade of our marriage, almost everything we had was part of an eclectic collection of hand-me-down items people had so generously given us after the fire at our apartment. Before the fall of 2021, I'd felt like it would be selfish to buy new things for our home. I also feared it would come across as ungrateful if we didn't keep what people had donated to us. But it was time to release what we no longer needed and welcome in what was to come. Above the mantle, I wove some faux greenery around a 30" round gold rimmed mirror, and my heart skipped a beat. I'd seen this type of beauty in other people's homes, but I never thought I'd have it in my own home. To take it a step further, I didn't think I deserved this beauty because of the (mis) belief that I was a wretched, worthless sinner.

In our room, Stephen and I assembled matching armoires. We cleared out the closet to make space for a desk that I could use for all my writing and podcast recording, which was Stephen's idea. It felt so good to get rid of clothing that we didn't like, want, or fit in anymore. The final steps to transforming our home involved the kitchen and bathrooms. I tackled the kitchen cabinets, a month-long project that required more time and energy than I'd expected. Using a handheld sander, I removed the dark brown stain on the top and bottom cabinets. Then, during the day when the kids were in school, I painted: three coats of white paint on the top set and two coats of navy blue on the bottom. I also sanded and painted the kitchen table and chairs gray and white and love the two-tone look. The last things I painted were the bathroom cabinets. They went from a dark stain to a light gray. Then, I updated the discolored, yellowing sink countertops with white appliance epoxy paint. The finishing touch was a brand-new knob on every cabinet and drawer in the house because I found *the cutest* floral print knobs online.

Each time I completed one of these major DIY projects, I was so freaking proud of myself. Through trial and error and watching lots of YouTube videos, I'd taught myself how to do things that I never thought I could do. Further, in the past I wouldn't have even tried, because I would have thought these tasks weren't "feminine" and that it would somehow impede Stephen's "manhood" if I did these things. The same with mowing the grass. Stephen has horrible allergies and not much free time. I felt like I couldn't help in *this* way, even though I was supposed to be his helper. It just goes to show how arbitrary all of the rules and roles are within complementarianism.

After the home makeover was complete, I wanted to do something to undergo a bit of an outward personal makeover. Because of the work of Dr. Christena Cleveland, one of my guiding questions these days is, "Do I want to do this?"[76] One of my "I want to do this" moments involved me getting my nose pierced on my birthday. Stephen and Levi, our youngest kiddo, came with me. We (jokingly) asked the staff if Levi could get a tattoo with our consent. (If you know Stephen, you know this idea has him written all over it.) The staff silently stared at us until I said, "We're just kidding."

That night, my younger brother called to wish me a happy birthday. After casually mentioning my new piercing, he had a bit of negative feedback.

"Nicki, tell me you're joking. You're not a teenager. You're 31 years old."

Smiling (though he couldn't tell because, you know, the phone), I responded, "I'm actually 32," and moved the conversation along.

Oh, the patriarchy. He thinks he is entitled to an opinion that I should care about and implement regarding my body. It's just like my dad telling me how I shouldn't have gotten my hair cut short or that I couldn't get a second set of piercings in my ears. In the past with my brother, I've let him talk to me however he wants. Not anymore. He called me for Mother's Day in 2022 and first tried to guilt trip me about not visiting home enough. My 31-year-old brother feels no need to operate out of any obligation to our family. However, he is completely comfortable judging me for what he perceives as a lack of familial loyalty as well as for the decisions I make for myself, like wearing a mask, getting the COVID-19 vaccine, and piercing my nose. As he brought up topics I didn't want to talk about with him and gave unsolicited advice, I firmly stated, "This isn't a conversation I'm going to have with you."

The other portion of my personal mini-makeover was getting my hair permed. As a child, I often got perms. I hated having to sit still in the chair while Agnes grouped strands of hair to roll them up for chemical alteration. The smell comes back to me all these years later. By the time I was 32, I hadn't had a perm since I was in high school. Calling a local salon, I scheduled an appointment and was told to plan for the perm to start at $99. "Start at" was the key phrase, but I didn't think it would be too much more.

Well, once the stylist got started, there wasn't anything I could do when she needed to mix an additional perm solution because my hair is quite thick. I'd also originally planned for an hour and a half. Three hours later, I was getting ready to pay for my new look. Hair care products were being pitched that I needed for maintaining the work that had been done. Though there was no price on the bottles, I figured they couldn't be too expensive. When everything was factored in, I struggled to pick my jaw up off the floor. Let's just say each bottle was at least $40. From the van, I called Stephen because I knew he'd received a text message from the credit card company about the charge.

Thankfully, Stephen didn't freak out about the cost. Neither of us could believe how expensive it was, and I probably won't get a perm again, but it was nice to do for myself.

* * * * *

Together, Stephen and I have experienced depths of grief and groaning we weren't prepared for, but we have been strengthened through them. We've been untangling ourselves from damaging ideology we were taught about women, modesty, sex, sexuality, and gender. We've learned about boundaries and practiced establishing them. Even in the midst of residual suffering, we are free and we are flourishing. We won't stop inviting others to join us.

Embracing egalitarianism for me has meant the continual

exchanging of restrictive ideas about modesty that dehumanize for liberative expressions of autonomy and individuality. This has included disrupting toxic generational beliefs about girls. In March 2022, my grandma turned 92. Many family members filled her house for the celebration. When one of my family members was leaving with his family, his daughter came to tell me good-bye. As I watched her, a sudden unexpected sadness overshadowed me. I saw so much of myself in her. Like this teen girl, I used to make my rounds telling each person good-bye, not wanting anyone to feel excluded. After hugging me, she turned to the woman beside me, who looked at the child's ripped shorts and remarked, "I hope you didn't pay full price for those."

Girl and woman laughed. Girl hugged more people. Girl left. When a different girl walked through the living room, her mom told her to pull her dress down. This led to comments about the other girl's ripped jean shorts and spaghetti strap top. One woman declared that if that other girl were her daughter, she'd never let her leave the house in those clothes. Walking away, I went to cry in the spare bedroom as I thought about what I'd just watched. The harmful generational cycle was playing out right before me. I know the woman was thinking that dressing modestly would offer protection to the child, but we know that's not true. Further, no one should be harming her. Weeping, I asked myself, "Can girls just be girls and not be sexualized? Can we stop objectifying a teenage girl and start holding boys and men accountable?"

I was depressed after this. I thought it was just because of the generational cycle I'd witnessed. But as I worked on launching my first memoir, I realized the depression went deeper. A few months after my grandma's birthday, the revelation hit me. My body knew before my brain did that as soon as my book came out, everything with my family would change. Though I knew there would be a strain on relationships, if not a total loss, nothing could prepare me for what was to come.

With Stephen's support, I wrote and self-published *As Familiar as Family*. In September 2022, I got to celebrate the launch with no familial pushback. There was just so much joy. That changed when Stephen got a call from an extended family member who had heard about my book and devoured it in a matter of days. She had found his number online. She told Stephen to let me know that she believed me and that I needed to keep writing. She also let him know that if I wanted to talk, I could give her a call. So, I did.

As we talked, she apologized for not doing anything to protect me, as she explained that she believed me because the abuse I outlined in the book also happened to her at the hands of the same person. She went on to say what a gem Stephen was and how she'd only ever heard negative things about him. This pissed me off. I knew that my family felt like Stephen took me away from them. I didn't know that they were still talking about him. It was easier for them to construct a false narrative that made him the villain than to engage in self-reflection about the reasons I distanced myself. The same night that I talked to the extended family member, I had a missed call and voicemail from my mom. Let's just say it was not a message of congratulations about my book.

Sadly, I haven't talked to many of my family members since.

* * * * *

There's been so much progress for me as an individual as I've realized that my ache of longing to belong cannot be fully healed by Stephen. This has helped me accept that there will be times when my faith shifts at a rate and trajectory that don't match or reflect Stephen's. These days, I don't read the Bible much. (Okay, I can't remember the last time I really read it.) Most of the time, my interactions consist of finding a certain verse. When I do read the Bible, I say "siblings" rather than just "brothers" or "brothers and sisters." This is so that I can practice the inclusivity of all people in my language.

Though more conservative Christians may not think I "value" the Bible anymore, I would say that I do value the Bible, but in a different way now. I value it for what it is, not what I once wanted it to be. Shout out to the book *Inspired* by the late Rachel Held Evans for the guidance provided on this journey.[77] There is so much freedom in not having to try to align what makes the most sense to me with an ancient text. Yes, I became egalitarian using the same Bible that I'd read as a complementarian. Then, I moved away from needing the Bible to justify my egalitarian ethos. Instead of trying to cram my beliefs into a box that lines up with anyone's interpretation of the Bible, I let love lead me.

Full disclosure, I'm not sure what I think about the existence of a Divine Being at this point. On the days when I lean toward a "God" existing, that belief is informed by my experiences of God as a Mother. Molleen Dupree-Dominguez's six-day devotional "The Power of El Shaddai, The Breasted God" was a pivotal resource.[78] Oh, how I wish I'd known sooner that any higher power there might be transcends the boxes and binaries we've created, as Dr. Christena Cleveland has written in her book *God Is a Black Woman* and explained during her "Virtual Pilgrimage to the Black Madonnas of *God Is a Black Woman*." In week four of the pilgrimage, she shared about how the Aramaic transliteration of our father in the "Lord's Prayer" is *abwoon*, birther. So, at this point, I would say that if there is a God, She is a Black woman. To take it a step further, in the words of Dr. Christena Cleveland, "For if God is a Black woman, then She's a Black trans woman. Obviously."[79]

I'm so grateful for the community and the resources that are expanding my worldview. A special shout out to Andrea Miller and the "Liberating Eve" sessions she prepared. Through Andrea's course, I've met other "dissident daughters"[80] who are invested in learning about goddess culture, the Divine Feminine, and our great Mother Moon. I don't want to give too much away because you should sign up for Andrea's courses, but I had no idea the vast history of goddesses. Further, I didn't know that "In ancient times, the snake was not a symbol of evil or danger but symbolized female wisdom, power, and regeneration." I was completely ignorant about how the Serpent was "'Rebranded' in the Genesis creation story as evil, deceptive, or as satan himself."[81]

The lies I was taught about Eve as a "usurper" of Adam's authority, and the demonization Eve had been subjected to within complementarianism, all melted away as I saw myself more fully in what Eve symbolizes for me now. Eve was a seeker of knowledge, as am I. There is nothing wrong with that, nothing sinful about that.

A part of integrating the Divine Feminine into my life includes not being ashamed for having a menstrual cycle. In the past, I would disguise my period by calling it things like "visitor" in my personal calendar on my phone. I didn't want people to get a glimpse of my calendar and be disgusted (like the guy I dated who was repulsed by my pad when we were making out). Now, when I get my period, I don't try to hide it in my calendar. It's called "period," and the color is red. Rather than being ashamed of my menstrual cycle, I'm learning about how I can connect to the lunar cycle, ocean tides, and other rhythms of the earth.

Everything I learned through the "Liberating Eve" workshops paired so beautifully with *God Is a Black Woman* by Dr. Christena Cleveland. Then, I read *Are We Free Yet?: The Black Queer Guide to Divorcing America* by Tina Strawn and the essay "Uses of the Erotic: The Erotic as Power" by Audre Lorde. More unlocked for me as I intentionally began exploring my erotic energy, as defined by Lorde.

> "As women, we have come to distrust that power which rises
> from our deepest and nonrational knowledge. We have been
> warned against it all our lives by the male world, which values
> this depth of feeling enough to keep women around in order
> to exercise it in the service of men, but which fears this same
> depth too much to examine the possibility of it within them-
> selves…Of course, women so empowered are dangerous…For
> once we begin to feel deeply all the aspects of our lives, we
> begin to demand from ourselves and from our life-pursuits that
> they feel in accordance with that joy which we know ourselves
> to be capable of. Our erotic knowledge empowers us, becomes
> a lens through which we scrutinize all aspects of our existence,
> forcing us to evaluate those aspects honestly in terms of their
> relative meaning within our lives. And this is a grave responsi-
> bility, projected from within each of us, not to settle for the
> convenient, the shoddy, the conventionally expected, nor the
> merely safe."[82]

For a time, out of short-sighted self-preservation, I settled
for the convenience of complementarianism. As a white, conservative,
Christian woman married to a nice, white, conservative, Christian man,
being complementarian was conventionally expected and safe. There
was no immediate danger for me. But a lack of danger is not synonymous with abundance. Complementarianism was a coping mechanism.
The decision fatigue that comes with being a mom was alleviated in
some ways by having someone else responsible for making many of the
family decisions. However, as the pressures of living up to the unattainable standards of complementarianism took a toll on me as a wife and
mother, something had to change.

That something included tapping into my erotic energy,
because "the feminine that is not in touch with her sexuality is a lot
easier to control."[83] My erotic energy is feared by men who want me
to take a hospitable, submissive, passive stance to being penetrated by
my husband and him coming into me, per The Gospel Coalition (TGC)
garbage. It's interesting how in TGC's complementarian worldview, sexual intercourse their way points to salvation, but a woman expressing
the etymology of prostitute — the root being prostrate, "one who
prostrates or lays down at the altar, whether she's laying down at the

altar to pray or have sex, who's to say"[84] — does not point to salvation. Double standard much, in the name of patriarchy?

The complementarian worldview keeps women passive sexually, and many women just get through it. They close their eyes and bear it because it's what they've been conditioned to do. It's what's been clearly communicated to them as the role their husbands expect them to embody as wives.

As I examined the Bible, my upbringing, and my social location, I more clearly understood the patriarchal language and culture I'd glossed over and simply accepted, thereby being complicit in my own oppression until I saved myself. And yes, I posit that I saved myself, though not with a "I don't need anyone else" attitude. I absolutely need community. In the words of Tina Strawn, "Find the free people."[85] Put a different way, I am not a damsel in distress and don't need a "Prince Charming"-type hero. I am my own hero, not Stephen. For what it's worth, if it weren't for me, Stephen would still be a complementarian at Entrench. Just some food for thought.

When I think about mutuality, no one is excluded if we operate from a mindset of mutuality. If we all outdo one another in showing honor, look not to our own interests but to the interests of others, and submit to one another (with those who hold the power actively engaging that submission), then we don't have time for arguments over who is out and who is in, who can exercise this gift and who cannot, or who can have this or that gift and who cannot. Mutuality truly equips everyone to flourish, without a hint of exploitation or tokenism, regardless of any characteristic we could think of to draw a line. Mutuality is undeniably better for the collective. It's past time for the Christian church, conservative or progressive, to participate in dismantling each and every system of hierarchy.

THOUGHTS FROM STEPHEN

Striving towards mutuality is not all roses and sunshine. There is still deep-rooted patriarchy, misogyny, and misogynoir within me that needs to be uprooted and healed. In some ways, communication in our marriage is harder now. In the egalitarian framework, it requires me to humble myself to listen to Nicki and truly value her input. Then, we decide on something together, rather than me just taking her input but then ultimately making the decision I think is best. There is a lot of work to undo the many years of hierarchy that I lived in.

Being on this journey with Nicki has had joys and hardships. I have most enjoyed getting to be free from the restrictions of certain beliefs and the pressure to be the one who leads. This has allowed me to appreciate what other people have to offer and to celebrate people for being who they are. Specifically with Nicki, I've enjoyed feeling more like we are working together as a team instead of feeling like we are in opposition to one another. Instead, we can give space for each other to use our strengths and support one another in our weaknesses.

The part that has been hardest for me is the lack of steadiness. This journey has definitely thrown off my desire for inner peace and stability, so it's been hard to work through the tension and not have everything put together. With that said, I would still encourage anyone who is complementarian and starting to question gender roles to do so with an open heart. Research and examine other views for yourself to uncover different ways of understanding something that once seemed non-negotiable. Have conversations with women in various life circumstances. Hear about their experiences and listen with empathy. Don't live from a place of trying to maintain control and power at all costs. Follow the example of Jesus that is recorded in the Bible and empower others to flourish.

As a complementarian, the "fruit" was what's described in Genesis 3. Men think that they should rule over women. This is the fruit where no one wins. There is a power hold that men are seeking to maintain. Women are either rightfully pushing against this or think they have no right to offer their gifts in leading. Looking back, I realize that this is restrictive for everybody because it pits us against each other. To reiterate what Nicki has already stated, complementarianism sets up a false gender binary that excludes and erases so many people.

Now I am beholding good fruit that allows anyone to exercise their gifts, period. As egalitarians, we can offer our best selves to one another so we can live lives that benefit everything and everyone around us.

* * * * *

In August 2020, I, like many others, was struggling because of the COVID-19 pandemic. It had been a long, isolating five months, on top of the other major shifts in my life. For the previous four years or so, it was a cycle of emotional instability for me, often manifesting in anger. I had seen how much therapy helped Nicki. Reaching my wits' end, I finally recognized I needed help. I contacted the practice Nicki was going to and got connected to a therapist. She was not licensed in our state, so I had to wait for her to get her license to be able to provide me with virtual therapy services.

During that time waiting, I tried one-on-one Enneagram Coaching with Certified Enneagram Coach Milton Stewart. We had nine sessions where Milton really helped me grow in my awareness of emotions using an emotion wheel. When I first started, I could not label an emotion I was feeling and only thought of emotions in terms of some of the more well-known, "big" emotions. It was incredible how well he knew me and my motivations just by knowing my Enneagram type and subtype. I felt really seen, heard, and safe in my sessions with him.

By the time my coaching with Milton was nearing the end, the therapist I was in communication with received her license to practice in my state. So, I started therapy in January 2021 and continued for about a year. My biggest takeaway was getting to know my anger, learning why it was being activated and the good intentions it had, even though it sometimes caused harm.

In August 2022, I started a cohort of the 12-week Kaizen Complete Enneagram Program led by Milton. This time was such a catalyst for growth. I am currently doing group coaching with Milton where we meet twice a month and share what is going on and Milton provides personalized coaching in a group setting.

Through this process, I am growing in my understanding of how little I value myself, and how that leads to me surrounding myself with people who devalue me. I am realizing how easy it is for me to talk about boundaries but how hard it is for me to implement them. The group coaching is a space where I can show up authentically, be accepted for who I am, but with the purpose of healing where needed. This begins with disrupting my ego by breathing. My ego is so sneaky. It can easily fall into a pattern of doing something that could be good, but it is actually working against me to keep me in unhealthy habits. Enneagram Coaching has really helped me understand myself better and the motives behind what I do.

Honestly, I'm still working on how I handle conflict. I have grown in seeing that lack of conflict is not necessarily healthy. Working through conflict in a way that honors each party and moves us towards healing is healthy. This is what I want to strive for. I don't want my kids to think conflict is bad or that conflict is yelling. I want to help them engage in conflict, work through it, and come out stronger on the other side. Conflict also relates to boundaries. Previously, I didn't have boundaries or the language around boundaries. I lived as if my life was not my own and I needed to give it up in service to others and God. But once Nicki and I were together, this forced bumping into one another and often led to conflict.

With this, I am trying to figure out how much of my resistance to a new conversation is me trying to control Nicki, how much is about me wanting to not have my equilibrium and peace disrupted, and how much is about something that I just don't want for myself when it's something that could fit in this category of preference. If it's something I don't want and Nicki *does* want it, what does that decision-making process look like now?

It took this journey for me to view Nicki as equal. Now, I want to always give space for her to utilize her gifts without her feeling like she is doing something she isn't supposed to be doing. I don't feel like I have to bear the burden of leading our family alone. Instead, we can lead together in our different giftings. Putting into practice what I preach in this area isn't always easy, though.

It's been hard to give up my preferences. I can be stubborn, and I benefited the most from the former beliefs. Complementarian theology sets up a power dynamic. By that, I mean that with this theology men are the ones who lead and make the decisions, whether as a husband or a pastor or just as a man. To lead and be the one who makes the final decision is to have the power. The men who follow this teaching are not thinking, "How do I give up this power to benefit others?" Complementarianism also teaches that wives have to put their dreams on hold, or not have dreams and ambitions at all, in order to support and help their husbands in fulfilling their own quests.

In the past, I wouldn't have said there was hierarchy in our marriage, though I would have said I was the leader. This absolutely demonstrates that there *is* some level of hierarchy. If you have a leader, that means someone else is not the leader. For our relationship, I believe the hierarchy is leveling out, but I still feel the internal struggle against the hierarchical point of view.

* * * * *

I've had the privilege to serve as an assistant coach on Joshua's baseball teams for the past three seasons. I had wanted to coach baseball because I played baseball from the time I was three or four years old through the sixth grade. When I first started playing, I was hard on myself when I would strike out, as I shared earlier. When I struck out or got out, I would be sad, but I was not good with my emotions. I stifled them. One goal of mine is to help my children learn to connect with their emotions in healthy ways much sooner than I did so they don't have all the baggage to work through later on and can live a fuller, richer life.

As I write this, we just finished baseball practice an hour and a half ago. We have two more games and one practice left. Before the first season, I felt apprehensive about the time commitment, but it has been rewarding and life-giving. It is a highlight of my week. Joshua has progressed well during his short time playing. One thing I try to communicate to the players is that I am pleased with them and proud of them, not because of their performance but because of who they are. I believe this is what we are all seeking after, to be deeply loved and accepted for who we are. When we experience that, we can experience healing and live a confident and full life, doing good to others rather than hurting others.

One game recently, Joshua hit the ball and got out at first base. As he walked back to the bench, he was visibly disappointed. One of the coaches asked if he was okay. Stifling his sadness, he shook his head yes. I hadn't noticed this, but Nicki saw what transpired. That night, when we were putting him to bed, Nicki asked him about it when I walked in. Wanting to set my kids up for emotional health earlier than me, I talked with him about how he is not his emotions, but his emotions are part of him. It is good to feel the disappointment and sadness and not try to push it down because he needs those parts to live as his best self. So, to acknowledge the emotions, pay attention to them, and help them feel seen, heard, and valued.

The suppression of emotions that we culturally demand from boys made me think about when Nicki was reading *Jesus and John Wayne* by Kristin Du Mez. We were discussing it on a trip to Columbia to visit my family, mulling over the ways manhood within evangelical Christianity has vacillated between militancy and so-called "soft patriarchy." To the men who need war and who need to be detached from their emotions to give their manhood meaning and purpose, something's not right. In fact, something is gravely wrong. You need a new definition of manhood because your current understanding is toxic. Your current beliefs give evidence of your unhealth. This is what happens when we live from unhealthy places and don't heal and get better. We spread violence.

Just because something is a certain way doesn't mean it's how it should be. When it comes to the Bible we're reading, how much is instructive and worthy of emulation versus descriptive, or prescriptive versus descriptive? I would venture to say a whole lot of it is descriptive rather than prescriptive. We need to understand the cultural context in which these biblical texts were written to really understand what the writers were saying. We also need to ask ourselves if our beliefs are bringing freedom to others and giving space to use the gifts they have received or restricting others.

* * * * *

Working on this book has felt like an arduous task. A part of this is fearing the process, the work involved, being vulnerable in sharing my story, and not doing a good job. As I have worked on this book, I cringe at the beliefs I held, the way I lived out these beliefs, and the harm these beliefs and actions had on Nicki, me, and others. I can't go back and change the past, but I can do better. So, I will strive to do better. Better for myself, better for Nicki, better for my kids, better for fellow humanity, better for Mother Earth.

The morning after I wrote about our departure from Entrench, I felt terrible when my alarm went off at 5:30 a.m. My head hurt, my chest was tight, my stomach full, and I felt exhausted. My initial thoughts were that it was because I ate too many animal crackers and Cheez-Its too late while working on the book, or that it was because of the pollen I'd been around while working on the book at my favorite park in our city, or that I was up too late, or that life had been so busy the past few months. Then, it hit me; I just spent a lot of time reliving and processing those hurtful events, and that brought up a lot of underlying hurt in my body that hasn't healed. I remembered I felt this same way a few years ago after I processed my mother's dementia and reflected on my life with her. I cried intensely and felt like this the next day.

I hated the way I was feeling and just wanted to not feel like that. I said to Nicki, "Isn't writing supposed to be healing?" Then, it hit me. If this is what the writing is doing to me, it is actually helping me, even though it hurts now, and I want to experience the healing it offers. So, I will keep writing. It has invigorated me to try to build on this experience to help myself heal where needed, to work the hurt through me and get the toxins out of my body.

This book has forced me to come face to face with some things from my past, beliefs I held so firmly and of which I was so certain, that have caused such hurt and pain to others. While I wish I could go back and live those days differently, I recognize that it is a fool's errand to spend time obsessing over and, instead, to let it move me to live differently now and in the future. Nicki and I have worked a lot on ourselves but still have some recurring struggles. I believe we could really benefit from couple's therapy and continued work together to help us heal where needed and grow in even more mutuality.

* * * * *

Who benefits from egalitarianism? In the past I would have said women do. This shows that I saw egalitarianism as taking power men deserved and giving it to women to put women above men. Now that I've embraced egalitarianism, I understand that everyone benefits from this model. Mutuality ensures equality and flourishing for all people. I want to offer an invitation to complementarians. Lean into any defensiveness and discomfort you are feeling and work through it. Becoming egalitarian hasn't been easy, but it has been freeing.

Stephen and I are trying to get more levity back, like in our pre-dating days. We have built monthly lunch dates into our routines. Finding a baby-sitter we trust is tough, and we don't want to wear out the people we *do* trust. We devised a solution of going out when all the kids are in school. It's been such a bright spot each month to visit a different local restaurant from the list of places we've been wanting to try. This time together has allowed us to connect and converse without the kids interrupting us, as happens every time we try to talk at home.

Something else that has been really special is Stephen sending me videos after he gets to work on the mornings when I'm not awake before he leaves. If he didn't get to tell me good-bye, he records a quick, "I'm thinking of you, hope you have a great day, and I love you," message. Throughout 2022, I kept a journal of letters to give to Stephen as a gift in December. As a complementarian, the motivation for an act like this would've been to be a "good wife" who does things to build her husband up, even if it meant neglecting myself for his benefit. Not anymore. I filled a notebook of memories and notes for him because I wanted to. It's as simple as that.

In the past, Stephen prayed aloud before we went to bed. Now, we take deep breaths individually and together, syncing the rhythms of our bodies. When we first met, the thing that drew us to one another, and that we found most attractive about the other, was a love for Jesus. Jesus was the very foundation of our relationship. We even put that layer of white sand on the bottom of our unity container to demonstrate we were building a life together with Jesus as our bedrock. So, what happens when the very foundation you'd originally built everything upon is crumbling? That's what we're navigating now. I'm so grateful to be navigating it with someone like Stephen.

Outro

My heart was on fire. The number of people joining the movement to ban guns was climbing by the minute. Initially, Stephen was resistant when I told him I wanted to go to Denver on June 5, 2023 to participate in a sit-in with Here4TheKids to demand Governor Polis ban guns and implement a buyback program. Stephen didn't think it would ever happen, so what's the point of trying? He was also worried about what we would do with the kids if I flew out while he was working.

In the meantime, when a producer for a Race2Dinner documentary reached out to ask about me participating in an upcoming dinner, I told Stephen that if I was officially invited to participate, I would be saying yes. I would not be asking his permission. His feathers were visibly ruffled because he has been so used to me conforming. About two weeks later, I drove to Atlanta for the filming.

I was shaking slightly sitting around the table with six other white women as Regina Jackson and Saira Rao talked with us about acknowledging the power we have as white women. I felt connected to each of the women in that room as we used our imaginations to envision a world where there are no guns and where everyone is safe. Near the end of the dinner, Regina and Saira emphasized that the white women at the table have to get comfortable with opposing our husbands, fathers, brothers, uncles, and other men in our lives.

The next day, I thought about how I was raised by a white woman who was afraid of driving on the interstate. Her fear of the interstate, and many other fears, became mine. I felt empowered the first time I conquered the interstate on my own. Then, I married at the age of 20 and never had to travel alone. It became easier and more convenient to defer to Stephen. That isn't healthy for anyone.

As soon as Stephen and I got to talk about the dinner in Atlanta, I had the opportunity to oppose him. When I told him that I was going to Denver for the sit-in, he was irritated and rattled off reasons why I shouldn't go: safety, finances, and childcare. When I pointed out that his reaction was evidence of his whiteness because he wanted guaranteed safety and ease, he quickly responded that he knew his whiteness was showing up. As I declared that I wasn't asking his permission but informing him of my decision to go, he responded, "That's not mutuality."

My counter was, "Well, in a relationship with a foundation of patriarchy, I must make demands. It's your job to take responsibility for what you are feeling and address whatever emotions come up for you. We'll just have to figure out how to make it work." Even though Stephen was going to be "inconvenienced," I had to be in Denver.

I cannot wait on someone else to save me. No one else is coming to save me from the gun violence that is tied to anti-Blackness, which is tied to the toxic masculinity of white supremacy. I had to show up to save myself and my kids. Patriarchy doesn't exist for the benefit and protection of women. In my experience, each time the patriarchy could have stood up to defend women, it stayed seated, proving that it exists for the benefit of men and the protection of them and their reputations.

For 30+ years, I sat silently by, afraid of being labeled "high maintenance" or a "diva," while the men around me were praised for their "decisiveness" and "directness." No more. Meghan, Duchess of Sussex, interviewed Mariah Carey on her podcast *Archetypes* about being considered a diva, and I learned that the word "diva" derived from "goddess." As Black women gained access to this word, the meaning shifted.[86] Because of anti-Blackness, white women like myself have tried to distance ourselves from words like diva. These days, I am owning that I am a diva, a goddess. I am absolutely someone with high standards for how the men in my life need to treat me in order to maintain a relationship with me. It is more than okay to know what I want and to be clear and confident in that.

Earlier in this book, I referenced a well-known complementarian leader who has lamented that complementarianism, void of definition and reinforcement, is "*simply going to go away.*"[87] May it be so. This is something I can say yes and amen to. May complementarianism, patriarchy, "male headship," and all of this toxic hierarchy go always and forever away.

In our marriage, Stephen and I weren't trying to make complementarianism "go away." But it *is*. And I'm so glad it is. Where our flag was once firmly planted in the complementarian camp is now a healthier marriage. It's healthier because it's a partnership rooted in mutuality rather than a hierarchy that would default to Stephen's preferences. Checking off "egalitarian" didn't solve all of our problems. (Sidenote: anyone can be egalitarian on paper and still have unchecked misogyny, misogynoir, and toxic beliefs about gender.) Egalitarianism provided a better framework for Stephen and I to dismantle hierarchy, both individually and collectively.

Christian patriarchy was the framework of the first nine and a half years of our marriage. We are still addressing, dismantling, and redressing these misbeliefs. You've read some of our most vulnerable stories, and now you know all about how two overly-committed complementarians are becoming egalitarian.

Ahead

Once upon a time in the deep South, there was a girl who made herself small, hoping her invisibility would provide some protection. Bravely, she left the chaos of home behind and encountered different forms of chaos. More faces of the same patriarchal prism. She married young, and she married a steady man she knew would lead her well. Complementarianism provided the stability and predictability she was lacking, until she could create and sustain that stability and predictability for herself. When she did that, the patriarchal hierarchy of complementarian theology had to go.

Together, she and the steady man she married are cultivating a world where their kids don't have to grow up too fast. They think they're doing a "better" job than their parents, just as their parents would say they're doing a "better" job than the parents who came before them. As parents, these two hope that one day their own kids would say, "We're doing a 'better' job than our parents." That's kind of the whole point, isn't it? For one generation to make things better for the next.

Each of these complex, extraordinary characters hurled themselves over obstacles. They look back, as needed, to heal the here and now and to heal the future. They are examining the generational trauma baked into their origin stories so that they can process the pain and move it through their bodies. They are seeking to be emotionally healthy as individuals, so that they can be emotionally healthy in relationships with others, especially their children.

The girl who was little once upon a time is now a woman stepping into her power with other white women being led by Black, Indigenous, Women of Color (BIWOC). Because of BIWOC, she understands that the notion of making oneself small as a woman is a tool of the patriarchy. Of course, the patriarchy wants her to deny herself, put white men above herself, and think she doesn't have any power. Of course, the patriarchy wants to keep white women separated from each other and from women who are not white. Because the patriarchy knows that if we join forces, the system will collapse.

Who's ready for the demolition ahead?

Reflection/Discussion Guide

1. *Becoming Egalitarian* begins with an experience where Nicki is home with her kids while Stephen is at their church. Why do you think the book starts with this scene? How do the themes in this scene resurface throughout the book?

2. What misbeliefs about gender did you pick up in childhood that have shaped you?

3. Do you have any direct connection to complementarian theology? If so, how has it impacted you? If not, how might indirect exposure have impacted you?

4. How were Nicki and Stephen's identities tied to gender roles throughout their lives? How did their identities shift?

5. What is your relationship to codependency and enmeshment?

6. Which topic in Section 2 sparked the most memories for you? Take some time to journal or talk about those memories.

7. What religious messages were harmful for Nicki and Stephen? Have you internalized harmful religious messages? If so, how did this affect you?

8. Have you experienced spiritual abuse? What practices have helped you heal? How can you support and be a safe person for other people who have been spiritually abused?

9. The book subtitle is "Our Journey from Hierarchy toward Mutuality." What is the significance of this phrase?

10. What emotions do you think Nicki and Stephen were feeling in the conversation they had with the pastors before leaving Entrench Church? What emotions were you feeling?

11. What moments were turning points for Nicki and Stephen, individually and together? Could you relate to any of those turning points?

12. How have curiosity and compassion influenced Nicki and Stephen's spiritual journeys?

13. Each section begins with a quote about Eve. Which quote grabbed your attention the most? Why do you think that is?

14. Is there anything that Nicki and Stephen included in this book that you would like to know more about?

15. Which communities welcomed Nicki and Stephen throughout their lives? What purpose did each community serve? Which nurtured them successfully and how?

Acknowledgements

I would first and foremost like to thank Nicki. If it were not for you, I would still be holding onto the problematic theology of which I was so certain. Thank you for your patience and sticking with me through these years. You worked so hard to make this book happen. You truly are amazing and an inspiration!

Thank you also goes to:

Kim Marsh for helping us restructure our book and for your editing eye. Your tireless dedication to making this book the best it could be is appreciated.

Danielle Bolin for lending your superb artistic skills to design a fitting cover.

Our beta readers and launch team. Your support, insights, and feedback proved helpful and confirmed that this book is needed.

The Well Hawaii congregation for your support and encouragement in this book endeavor. We are grateful that you all are on this life journey with us and showing a better way.

All those who supported the Kickstarter to help make this book a reality.

Everyone who purchased this book. May you reap 30, 60, 100 times your investment.

Finally, a special thank you goes to Joshua, Emma Kate, and Levi. Without you, this book wouldn't have been written. The way you understand the world and love others is beautiful. We need more of your insights and compassion in this world.

-Stephen

My acknowledgements portion will be lengthier than Stephen's because we all know that I've got lots of words.

Thank you to our beta readers: Lauren, Toni, Heather, Christine, Kara, Brandy, Corrie, James, Megan, David, Chris, Bubba, John, and Lyda. You all signed up to provide us with feedback. Your insights via notes you emailed and/or our video call helped strengthen this book. The early support you all offered means so much.

Speaking of support of this story, thank you to everyone who contributed to the Kickstarter and/or preordered *Becoming Egalitarian*: Andi, Lauren, Paul, Megan, Tim, Brent, Colleen, Laura A., Laura V., Ruth, Corrie, Neva, Kari, Heather K., Mandy, Tabitha, EJ, Andrea, Alexis, Andrew, Marilyn, James, Marla, Susan, Toni, Katy, Anne, Erin, Miriam, Lina, Christine, Sarah, Bryan, Cynthia, Jessica, Gwen, Michelle, Danielle, Kamakoa, Alena, Lois, Clara, Lori, Lisa, Heather H., Edith, Cal, Nova, and Oneika. This book would still be sitting in my Google Docs if not for you all. Many of you are repeat Kickstarter supporters and/or members of the launch team, which is such an encouragement to this writer!

Special thanks to the following for hosting conversations about *Becoming Egalitarian*: Julia Postema and Jeremiah Gibson of the *Sexvangelicals* podcast, JoBeth Roberts of *JoBeth on the Journey*, and James Prescott of the *Poema Podcast*. Thank you also to Open Book members for the community and joy during writing circles and The Well Hawaii for surrounding us from afar as we've worked on this book.

In preparing for publishing, thank you to my editor, writing coach, and very dear friend Kim Marsh, founder of The Open Book Company. You've worked your magic once again! I feel so much more confident releasing this book because of you. Will you keep bringing books into the world with me?

Thank you to Danielle Bolin, my friend and graphic design genius. I don't know how you do it, but you nail it every time! You brought my vision to life for the cover and created something I love. I said it before and will say it again: I want to work with you forever and always.

To my "dissident daughter" friends, you keep me going, and you keep me grounded. It is one of the greatest gifts in this life to know you all and be known by you.

To my kids, y'all are the best. On our neighborhood walks, I love giving you difficult math problems to solve (Emma Kate), holding your hand when you aren't showing me how fast you can run (Levi), and listening to you talk about the kind of car you want when you grow up (Joshua).

To Stephen, I'm so freaking proud of you! Writing and launching a book with you has been such a sweet endeavor. Your self-reflective, introspective nature is aspirational. Let's keep evolving together, Steady Steve.

Finally, to our readers, thank you for picking up this book and holding space for us. May your commitment to curiosity be deep and your healing ever deeper. If you keep reading, I'll keep writing!

-Nicki

Notes

1. Rachel Held Evans. "Week of Mutuality: How It Will Work, Definition of Terms." Rachel Held Evans, 2 Sept. 2012, rachelheldevans.com/blog/mutuality-definition-terms.

2. "How the Enneagram System Works." The Enneagram Institute, www.enneagraminstitute.com/how-the-enneagram-system-works.

3. Throughout this book, we refer to our Enneagram numbers via the names that Certified Enneagram Coach Milton Stewart uses.

4. Rachel Held Evans. "It's Not Complementarianism; It's Patriarchy." Rachel Held Evans, 1 Sept. 2012, rachelheldevans.com/blog/complementarians-patriarchy.

5. Washington, Harriet A. *Medical Apartheid the Dark History of Medical Experimentation on Black Americans from Colonial Times to the Present.* Paw Prints, 2010, pp. 65-66.

6. "When Moya Bailey first coined the term *misogynoir*, she defined it as the ways anti-Black and misogynistic representation shape broader ideas about Black women, particularly in visual culture and digital spaces." Bailey, Moya. *Misogynoir Transformed: Black Women's Digital Resistance.* New York University Press, 2022.

7. Washington, Harriet A. *Medical Apartheid the Dark History of Medical Experimentation on Black Americans from Colonial Times to the Present.* Paw Prints, 2010, pp. 65-66.

8. Febos, Melissa. *Body Work: The Radical Power of Personal Narrative.* Baker & Taylor, 2022, p. 12.

9. "False Reporting - National Sexual Violence Resource Center." National Sexual Violence Resource Center, 2012, www.nsvrc.org/sites/default/files/Publications_NSVRC_Overview_False-Reporting.pdf.

10. Perry, Imani. *South to America: A Journey below the Mason-Dixon to Understand the Soul of a Nation.* Ecco, an Imprint of HarperCollins Publishers, 2023, pp. 236-237.

11. Kobes, Du Mez Kristin. *Jesus and John Wayne: How White Evangelicals Corrupted a Faith and Fractured a Nation.* Liveright Publishing Corporation, a Division of W.W. Norton et Company, 2021, p. 10.
12. Kobes, Du Mez Kristin. *Jesus and John Wayne: How White Evangelicals Corrupted a Faith and Fractured a Nation.* Liveright Publishing Corporation, a Division of W.W. Norton et Company, 2021, pp. 32, 55-56.
13. Kobes, Du Mez Kristin. *Jesus and John Wayne: How White Evangelicals Corrupted a Faith and Fractured a Nation.* Liveright Publishing Corporation, a Division of W.W. Norton et Company, 2021, p. 67.
14. Allison, Emily Joy. *#ChurchToo: How Purity Culture Upholds Abuse and How to Find Healing.* Broadleaf Books, 2021, p. 31.
15. Pappas, Nicki. "Broadening the Narrative: 37. Patriarchy Is Not God's Design with Meghan Tschanz (Bonus) on Apple Podcasts." *Apple Podcasts*, 16 Aug. 2021, podcasts.apple.com/us/podcast/37-patriarchy-is-not-gods-design-with-meghan-tschanz-bonus/id1523302765?i=1000532239591.
16. Pappas, Nicki. "Broadening the Narrative: 71. No Longer Silent with Miriam Delaney Heard (S5 E5) on Apple Podcasts." *Apple Podcasts*, 3 July 2023, podcasts.apple.com/us/podcast/71-no-longer-silent-with-miriam-delaney-heard-s5-e5/id1523302765?i=1000619218016.
17. Kegler, Emmy. *All Who Are Weary: Easing the Burden on the Walk with Mental Illness.* Broadleaf Books, an Imprint of 1517 Media, 2021.
18. Kobes, Du Mez Kristin. *Jesus and John Wayne: How White Evangelicals Corrupted a Faith and Fractured a Nation.* Liveright Publishing Corporation, a Division of W.W. Norton et Company, 2021, p. 108.
19. Kobes, Du Mez Kristin. *Jesus and John Wayne: How White Evangelicals Corrupted a Faith and Fractured a Nation.* Liveright Publishing Corporation, a Division of W.W. Norton et Company, 2021, p. 32.
20. Kobes, Du Mez Kristin. *Jesus and John Wayne: How White Evangelicals Corrupted a Faith and Fractured a Nation.* Liveright Publishing Corporation, a Division of W.W. Norton et Company, 2021, p. 16.
21. "Esther Perel." *Armchair Expert*, 29 June 2021, armchairexpertpod.com/pods/esther-perel.
22. Luehmann, Jo. "I Want Men to Defend Me, to Stand between Me and Other Men Being Abusive, to Stand in Solidarity with Me. I Want Men to Tear down the Patriarchy alongside Me by Not Tolerating Misogyny, Racism, or Any Abuse toward Me. I Can Defend Myself, and I Want to Not Have to." Twitter, 28 Mar. 2022, twitter.com/JoLuehmann/status/1508480083840753664.
23. Pappas, Nicki. "Broadening the Narrative: 39. #ChurchToo and

Domestic Violence with Emily Joy Allison (S3 E2) on Apple Podcasts." *Apple Podcasts*, 13 Sept. 2021, podcasts.apple.com/us/podcasts/39-churchtoo-and-domestic-violence-with-emily-joy/id1523302765?i=1000535260238.

24. I searched for the original tweet and couldn't find it. Sorry!

25. Heath, Heather Grace. *Lovingly Abused: A True Story of Overcoming Cults, Gaslighting, and Legal Educational Neglect.* Palmetto Publishing, 2021, p. 95.

26. Nagoski, Emily. *Come as You Are: The Surprising New Science That Will Transform Your Sex Life.* Simon and Schuster Paperbacks, 2022.

27. Strings, Sabrina. *Fearing the Black Body: The Racial Origins of Fat Phobia.* New York University Press, 2019.

28. "How Sperm Got All the Credit in the Fertilization Story." YouTube, 2 July 2021, youtu.be/fVKjzvDVGPs.

29. Butler, Josh. "Sex Won't Save You (but It Points to the One Who Will)." *The Gospel Coalition*, 1 Mar. 2023, web.archive.org/web/20230301170931/https://www.thegospelcoalition.org/article/sex-wont-save-you/.

30. Julia Postema and Jeremiah Gibson host the *Sexvangelicals* podcast and responded to the TGC article by Josh Butler. They are currently restructuring their podcast, so the episode was unavailable at the time of publication.

31. Graham, Ruth. "Popular Pastor Returns after Absence over an 'inappropriate' Online Relationship." *The New York Times*, 5 Dec. 2022, www.nytimes.com/2022/12/04/us/matt-chandler-village-church-dallas.html.

32. Folkenflik, David. "Tucker Carlson's War on M&M's." *NPR*, 23 Jan. 2023, www.npr.org/2023/01/23/1150844961/tucker-carlsons-war-on-m-ms.

33. Evans, Rachel Held. *A Year of Biblical Womanhood: How a Liberated Woman Found Herself Sitting on Her Roof, Covering Her Head, and Calling Her Husband "Master."* Thomas Nelson, 2012, p. 128.

34. I tried to find the original source for the quote, "If you can't say no, you aren't free to say yes." I was unfortunately unsuccessful.

35. Felbin, Sarah. "What Is Quiverfull, the Christian Religious Movement in "Our Father"?," *Women's Health*, 12 May 2022, www.womenshealthmag.com/life/a39980043/what-is-quiverfull-our-father/.

36. Wilkin, Jen. "Your Child Is Your Neighbor." *The Gospel Coalition*, 17 Sept. 2015, www.thegospelcoalition.org/article/your-child-is-your-neighbor/.

37. Evans, Rachel Held. *A Year of Biblical Womanhood: How a Liberated*

Woman Found Herself Sitting on Her Roof, Covering Her Head, and Calling Her Husband "Master." Thomas Nelson, 2012.

38. Rachel Held Evans. "It's Not Complementarianism; It's Patriarchy." Rachel Held Evans, 1 Sept. 2012, rachelheldevans.com/blog/complementarians-patriarchy.

39. Alsup, Wendy, and Hannah Anderson. "Toward a Better Reading: Reflections on the Permanent Changes to the Text of Genesis 3:16 in the ESV." Practical Theology for Women, 26 Sept. 2016, https://theologyforwomen.org/2016/09/towardbetter-reading-reflections-permanent-changes-text-genesis-316-esv.html.

40. Evans, Rachel Held. "Submission in Context: Christ and the Greco-Roman Household Codes." Rachel Held Evans, 2 Sept. 2012, https://rachelheldevans.com/blog/mutualityhousehold-codes.

41. Pappas, Nicki. "Broadening the Narrative: 71. No Longer Silent with Miriam Delaney Heard (S5 E5) on Apple Podcasts." Apple Podcasts, 3 July 2023, podcasts.apple.com/us/podcast/71-no-longer-silent-with-miriam-delaney-heard-s5-e5/id1523302765?i=1000619218016.

42. Febos, Melissa. *Girlhood.* Bloomsbury Publishing, 2022.

43. "Does the Bible Promote Misogyny? Pt 1 (Howard Brown) Judges 19:1-17;20-30;21:25 (9/9/18)." SoundCloud, 2018, https://soundcloud.com/christcentralchurch/does-the-biblepromote-misogyny-howard-brownjudges-191-1720-302125-9918.

44. "Does the Bible Promote Misogyny? Pt 2 (Howard Brown) Judges 19:1-17:20-30;21:25 (9/30/18)." SoundCloud, 2018, https://soundcloud.com/christcentralchurch/ccc-2018-09-30.

45. "Does the Bible Promote Misogyny? Pt 3 (Howard Brown) Judges 19:1-17:20-30;21:25 (10/14/18)." SoundCloud, 2018, https://soundcloud.com/christcentralchurch/ccc_2018-10-14.

46. Hill, Daniel. "The Biblical Confusion between the Words 'Justice' and 'Righteousness'." Daniel Hill's Blog, 12 Aug. 2014, https://danielgaryhill.wordpress.com/2014/08/12/the-biblical-confusion-between-the-words-justice-and-righteousness/.

47. Stevenson, Bryan. *Just Mercy: A Story of Justice and Redemption.* One World, 2019, p. 290.

48. Kobes, Du Mez Kristin. *Jesus and John Wayne: How White Evangelicals Corrupted a Faith and Fractured a Nation.* Liveright Publishing Corporation, a Division of W.W. Norton et Company, 2021.

49. King, Martin Luther. Letter from Birmingham Jail - Home

– CSU, Chico. https://www.csuchico.edu/iege/_assets/documents/susi-letter-from-birmingham-jail.pdf.

50. Lorde, Audre. *Sister Outsider Essays and Speeches*. Crossing Press, 2007.

51. Ritter, Tim, and Nate Hanson. "Gender Series." *Almost Heretical*, 2018, https://almostheretical.com/gender.

52. Preato, Dennis J. Junia, a Female Apostle: An Examination of the Historical Record, 26 April 2019, https://www.cbeinternational.org/resource/junia-female-apostle-examination-historical-record/.

53. Kobes, Du Mez Kristin. *Jesus and John Wayne: How White Evangelicals Corrupted a Faith and Fractured a Nation*. Liveright Publishing Corporation, a Division of W.W. Norton et Company, 2021.

54. Ritter, Tim, and Nate Hanson. "Gender: Authority over Her Own Damn Head (1 Corinthians 11:2-16)." *Almost Heretical*, 19 July 2018, almostheretical.com/episodes/authority-over-her-own-damn-head.

55. I couldn't find the original source for this information, but I read it at some point somewhere.

56. "Church Clarity: Ambiguity Is Harmful, Clarity Is Reasonable." Church Clarity, https://www.churchclarity.org/.

57. Bob and Helga. "An Egalitarian Review of Bible Translations." The Equality Workbook: Freedom in Christ from the Oppression of Patriarchy, 8 Aug. 2020, https://equalityworkbook.wordpress.com/2018/01/16/an-egalitarian-review-of-bibletranslations/.

58. Neuman, Scott. "Southern Baptist Leader Removed over Remarks on Rape, Abuse of Women." *NPR*, 23 May 2018, www.npr.org/sections/thetwo-way/2018/05/23/613604818/head-of-southern-baptist-seminary-removed-over-remarks-on-rape-abuse-of-women.

59. Baird, Julia, and Hayley Gleeson. "'Submit to Your Husbands': Women Told to Endure Domestic Violence in the Name of God." *ABC News*, 21 Oct. 2018, www.abc.net.au/news/2017-07-18/domestic-violence-church-submit-to-husbands/8652028.

60. Jankowski, P. J., Sandage, S. J., Cornell, M. W., Bissonette, C., Johnson, A. J., Crabtree, S. A., & Jensen, M. L. (2018). Religious beliefs and domestic violence myths. Psychology of Religion and Spirituality, 10(4), 386–397. https://doi.org/10.1037/rel0000154.

61. Piatt, Christian. "Mark Driscoll, Women as Penis Houses, and Crumbling Temples." *HuffPost*, 11 Nov. 2014, www.huffpost.com/entry/mark-driscoll-women-as-pe_b_5804964.

62. Evans, Rachel Held. *A Year of Biblical Womanhood: How a Liberated*

Woman Found Herself Sitting on Her Roof, Covering Her Head, and Calling Her Husband "Master." Thomas Nelson, 2012, p. 52.

63. Evans, Rachel Held. *A Year of Biblical Womanhood: How a Liberated Woman Found Herself Sitting on Her Roof, Covering Her Head, and Calling Her Husband "Master."* Thomas Nelson, 2012, p. 128.

64. Evans, Rachel Held. *A Year of Biblical Womanhood: How a Liberated Woman Found Herself Sitting on Her Roof, Covering Her Head, and Calling Her Husband "Master."* Thomas Nelson, 2012, pp.179-180.

65. Evans, Rachel Held. *A Year of Biblical Womanhood: How a Liberated Woman Found Herself Sitting on Her Roof, Covering Her Head, and Calling Her Husband "Master."* Thomas Nelson, 2012, pp.88-89.

66. Quient, Nicholas. "How I Submit to My Wife: Why a Feminist with a Hairy Chest Chose to Take His Beloved's Last Name." CBE International, 15 June 2022, www.cbeinternational.org/resource/how-i-submit-my-wife/.

67. Schulz, Marc and Robert Waldinger. "An 85-Year Harvard Study Found the No. 1 Thing That Makes Us Happy in Life: It Helps Us 'Live Longer.'" *CNBC*, 10 Feb. 2023, www.cnbc.com/2023/02/10/85-year-harvard-study-found-the-secret-to-a-long-happy-and-successful-life.html.

68. Taviano, Marla. *Unbelieve: Poems on the Journey to Becoming a Heretic.* Lake Drive Books, 2021, p. 296.

69. Pappas, Nicki. "Let's Put an End to the Rumors: Why I'm Not in Church." 6 Dec. 2019, http://broadeningthenarrative. blogspot.com/2019/12/lets-put-end-to-rumors-why-im-notin.html.

70. Westfall, Cynthia Long. *Paul and Gender: Reclaiming the Apostle's Vision for Men and Women in Christ.* Baker Academic, a Division of Baker Publishing Group, 2016.

71. Westfall, Cynthia Long. *Paul and Gender: Reclaiming the Apostle's Vision for Men and Women in Christ.* Baker Academic, a Division of Baker Publishing Group, 2016.

72. James, Carolyn Custis. *Half the Church.* Zondervan, 2015.

73. Westfall, Cynthia Long. *Paul and Gender: Reclaiming the Apostle's Vision for Men and Women in Christ.* Baker Academic, a Division of Baker Publishing Group, 2016.

74. Bessey, Sarah. *Jesus Feminist.* Howard Books, a Division of Simon & Schuster, Inc., 2013.

75. Strawn, Tina. "Unvaccinated Black Lives Matter Too." *Medium,* 6 Aug. 2021, medium.com/@tinastrawnlife/unvaccinated-black-lives-matter-too-6513b3d0943d.

76. Cleveland, Christena. *God Is a Black Woman*. HarperOne, an Imprint of HarperCollins Publishers, 2022.

77. Evans, Rachel Held. *Inspired: Slaying Giants, Walking on Water, and Loving the Bible Again*. Nelson Books, 2018.

78. Dupree-Dominguez, Molleen. "The Power of El Shaddai Is on Our Bible App." 29 Aug. 2019, molleendupreedominguez.com/2019/08/29/the-power-of-el-shaddai-is-on-our-bible-app/.

79. Cleveland, Christena. *God Is a Black Woman*. HarperOne, an Imprint of HarperCollins Publishers, 2022.

80. Kidd, Sue Monk. *The Dance of the Dissident Daughter*. HarperOne, 2016.

81. Andrea Miller created and hosted the course Liberating Eve & Freeing Ourselves. There are four sessions, and I highly recommend these workshops.

82. Lorde, Audre. "Uses of the Erotic: The Erotic as Power." 1978, www.centraleurasia.org/wp-content/uploads/2023/02/audre_lorde_cool-beans.pdf.

83. "Jamie Elizabeth Thompson: Pleasure with Power and Purpose." *The Time of the Feminine - A Global Sisterhood Podcast*, 21 Apr. 2022, open.spotify.com/episode/5DR39PB9dkMQAnD1BnJ8NV?si=N2JRyI5vS-bCtTDGYblH6lQ&context=spotify%3Ashow%3A2WaLUFo8C-GZhAe2s2O4Qj9.

84. Leola. "Pleasure Priestess, Holy Whore, & Sacred Prostitute, Episode 79." *Talk Tantra to Me with Leola*, 24 June 2022, www.talk-tantratome.com/podcast/episode/79c88ecb/pleasure-priestess-ho-ly-whore-and-sacred-prostitute-episode-79.

85. Strawn, Tina. *Are We Free Yet ?: The Black Queer Guide to Divorcing America*. Row House Publishing, 2023.

86. Meghan, Duchess of Sussex. "The Duality of Diva with Mariah Carey." *Archetypes with Megan*, 30 Aug. 2022, open.spotify.com/epi-sode/6S3Y5mKB9nJAk6wvZdbVo8?si=bUbW6CI5QOSc_Q43cilK-Mw.

87. Rachel Held Evans. "It's Not Complementarianism; It's Patriarchy." Rachel Held Evans, 1 Sept. 2012, rachelheldevans.com/blog/comple-mentarians-patriarchy.

Thank you for reading *Becoming Egalitarian:
Our Journey from Hierarchy toward Mutuality*.
If you enjoyed this book, please share an
online review on Amazon and Goodreads.

KEEP IN TOUCH WITH NICKI PAPPAS

Website: nickipappas.com
Podcast: *Broadening the Narrative*
Instagram: @broadeningthenarrative
TikTok: @broadeningthenarrative
Twitter: @broadnarrative
Facebook: facebook.com/groups/
broadeningthenarrative